IMAGES
of America

OLD BRIDGE

IMAGES
of America

OLD BRIDGE

Michael J. Launay

ARCADIA
PUBLISHING

ISBN 978-0-7385-0992-1

Published by Arcadia Publishing
Charleston, South Carolina

Printed in the United States of America

Library of Congress Catalog Card Number: 2002101527

For all general information contact Arcadia Publishing at:
Telephone 843-853-2070
Fax 843-853-0044
E-mail sales@arcadiapublishing.com
For customer service and orders:
Toll-Free 1-888-313-2665

Visit us on the Internet at www.arcadiapublishing.com

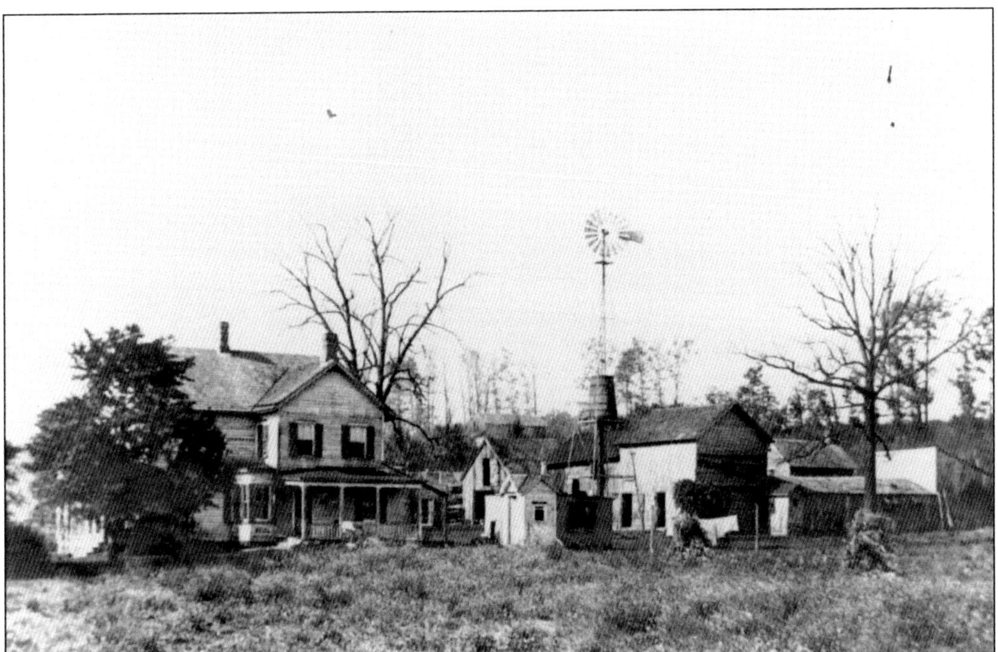

This photograph of Henry Odell Austin's farm offers a great view of a typical farm scene in the late 1800s. Austin purchased the farm in 1865 for $3,000. The precise location of this farm has never been determined.

Contents

Acknowledgments		6
Introduction		7
1.	Historic Homes and People	9
2.	Farming the Soil	33
3.	Business and Industry	49
4.	Faith and Education	75
5.	Fun and Relaxation	99
6.	All around the Town	115

ACKNOWLEDGMENTS

It would be impossible to thank each and every person who had a hand in preparing this book. I would, however, like to acknowledge a few who played an especially important role. I would like to thank the Madison Township Historical Society; its president, Pauline Drake; and all the officers and members for their support and assistance. I would also like to thank Rich Kujawinski, chairman of the Old Bridge Township Historic Preservation Commission, for making available his organization's files and photographs. I am also grateful to the Old Bridge Public Library and the Old Bridge Board of Education for their help. Cheesequake State Park also provided photographs and assistance for which I am most grateful. In addition, I would like to thank Carolyn Blahota, vice president of the historical society, and her husband, John Blahota, who shared their memories and photographs with me and assisted in the collection of others. Alvia Martin, curator of the Thomas Warne Historical Museum and Library, deserves a special acknowledgment, which I am happy to provide. Without her knowledge and assistance, this book could not have been written. I would also like to thank my son Michael John Launay for all his help rummaging through dusty files and photocopying documents and images. Last but not least, I need to offer my heartfelt thanks to my wife, June, for all her assistance working with the images and text, and especially for graciously accepting the loss of time and attention caused by the preparation of this book.

INTRODUCTION

Old Bridge Township was originally named Madison Township when it was incorporated on March 2, 1869. Prior to that, it was part of a much larger South Amboy Township. The first settlers in the area were the Native American tribe called the Lenni Lenape. Archaeological remains of their settlements have been found throughout the township, especially along Cheesequake Creek. The first European settlers began to arrive in the 1660s. Like much of New Jersey, the Old Bridge area was populated by a variety of nationalities and religions, including the English, Scottish, Irish, and French Huguenots.

The original settlers were mostly farmers, and Cheesequake Creek, which flows into the Raritan Bay, served as the center of trade. The discovery of fine clay deposits along the banks of the creek marked the beginning of the clay industry in Middlesex County and in New Jersey. The many creeks and streams within the township's borders powered the numerous mills that processed paper, cider, snuff, and black powder. Raritan Bay fulfilled the area's need for fish, clams, crabs, and oysters. Eventually, the two-and-a-quarter-mile coastline became a vacation spot for nearby urban dwellers.

The sheer size of the township, and the difficulty moving throughout it, led to the development of many hamlets and villages that are almost independent of each other. Some of these communities, such as Laurence Harbor, Old Bridge, and Cheesequake, are well known. Others, including Hebertsville, Browntown, and Morristown, are remembered by far fewer. Many of these villages developed their own schools and services.

Old Bridge Township remained predominately rural until the 1950s, when postwar prosperity and improved highway access spurred large-scale development. In 1976, the name of Madison Township was changed by referendum to Old Bridge Township. The reason for this was twofold. The first was an effort to gain a single postal designation and zip code for the township. The other was to avoid confusion with the Madison in Morris County. The effort failed in its first objective, and Old Bridge Township is still divided among various zip codes and names. The township is no longer confused with the municipality in Morris County, but it is now sometimes confused with the Historic Village of Old Bridge in neighboring East Brunswick.

Today, Old Bridge Township is mostly suburban, and single-family homes predominate. There are still, however, 4,500 acres of farmland and 8,500 acres of dedicated open space. The community is making a concerted effort to keep the remaining farmland free of development in an effort to fight suburban sprawl. Since the population has already grown to over 50,000, there is not much time.

To avoid confusion, whenever possible, I have referred to the township as Old Bridge throughout the book, even if the time frame is before the name change. When the reference is to the Old Bridge section of the township, or the Historic Village of Old Bridge, I have indicated it as such.

Of course, it is impossible to tell the full and rich history of the township in a book of this scope. Many people, places, and areas have been underrepresented and others overrepresented due to a lack of information, images, or space. Perhaps a future volume can do justice to those omitted.

One

Historic Homes and People

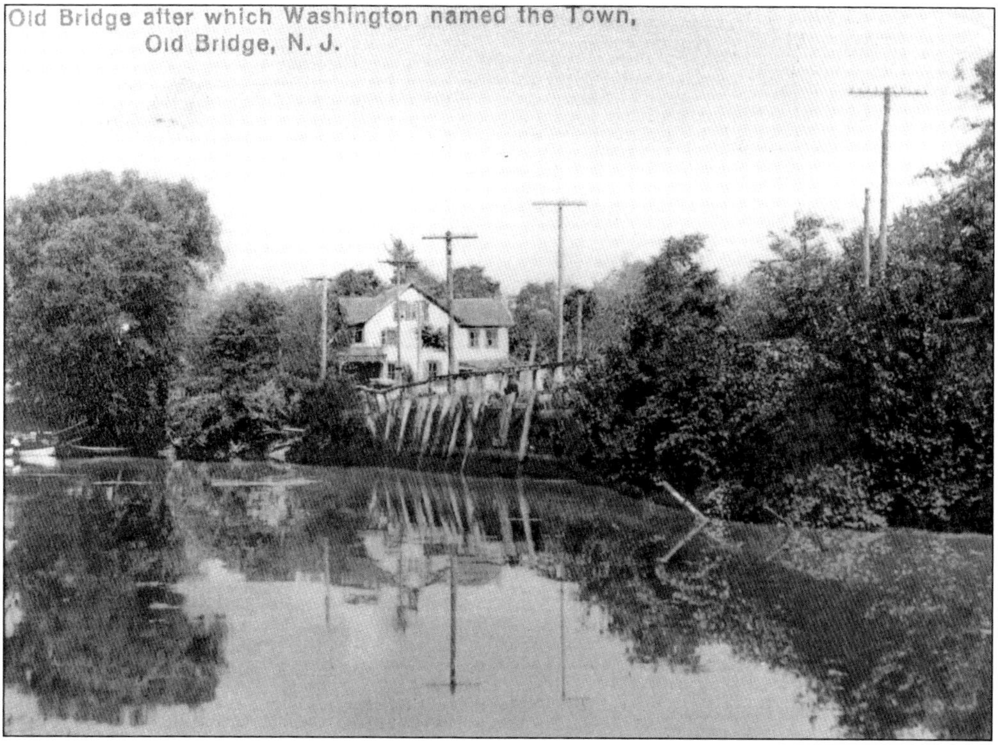

Tradition holds that the name Old Bridge was chosen by Gen. George Washington for the area during the Revolutionary War. Seen in this photograph is the "old bridge," which crossed the South River into East Brunswick.

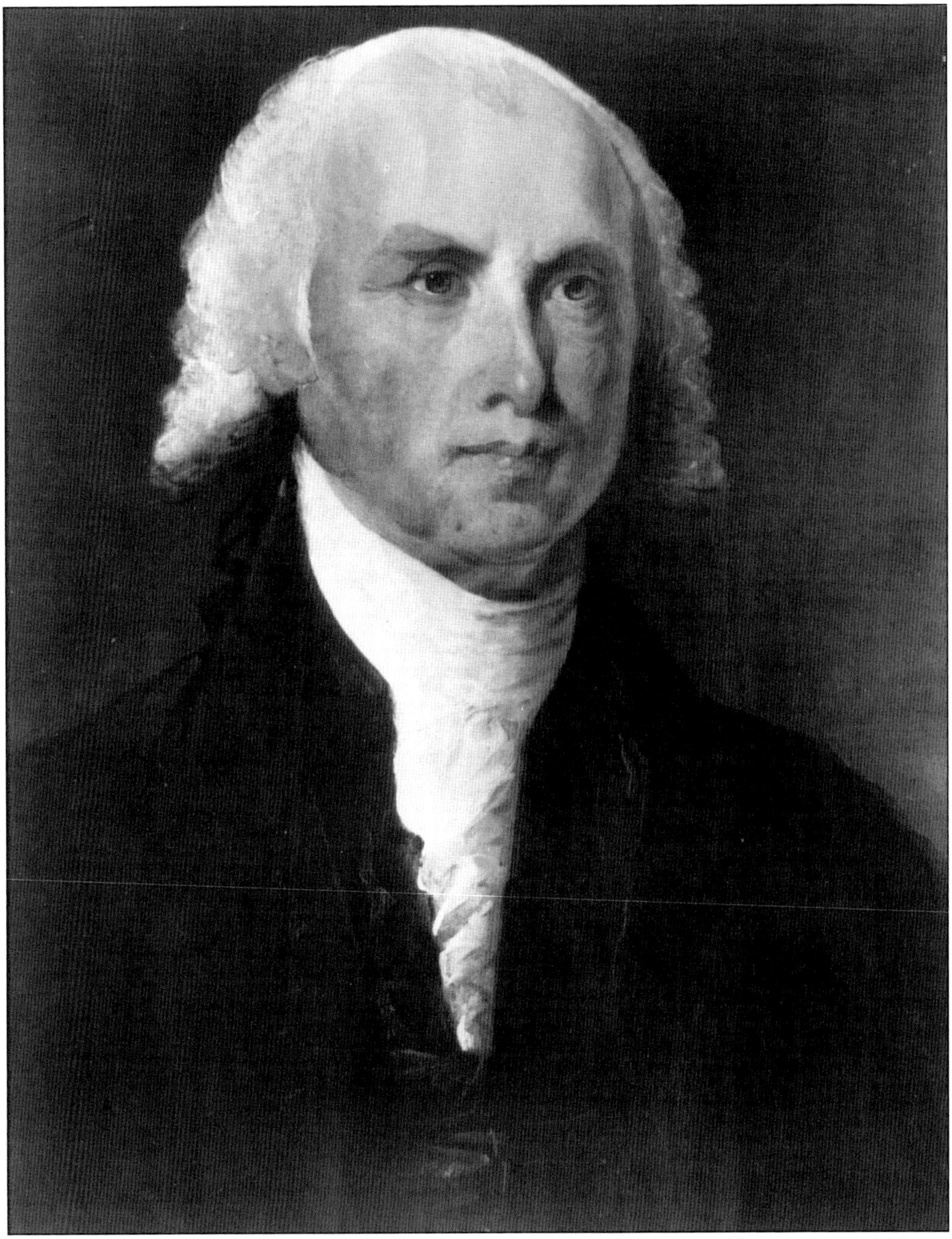

Old Bridge Township was known as Madison Township when it was founded in 1869. Its namesake was Pres. James Madison (1751–1836), who was no stranger to the area. Madison attended nearby Princeton University with Philip Freneau, who was later known as the poet of the American Revolution. The two became close friends, and Madison often visited Freneau's farm in adjacent Matawan Township. As a frequent visitor to the area, and a champion of farmers and small landowners, Madison was a fitting honoree.

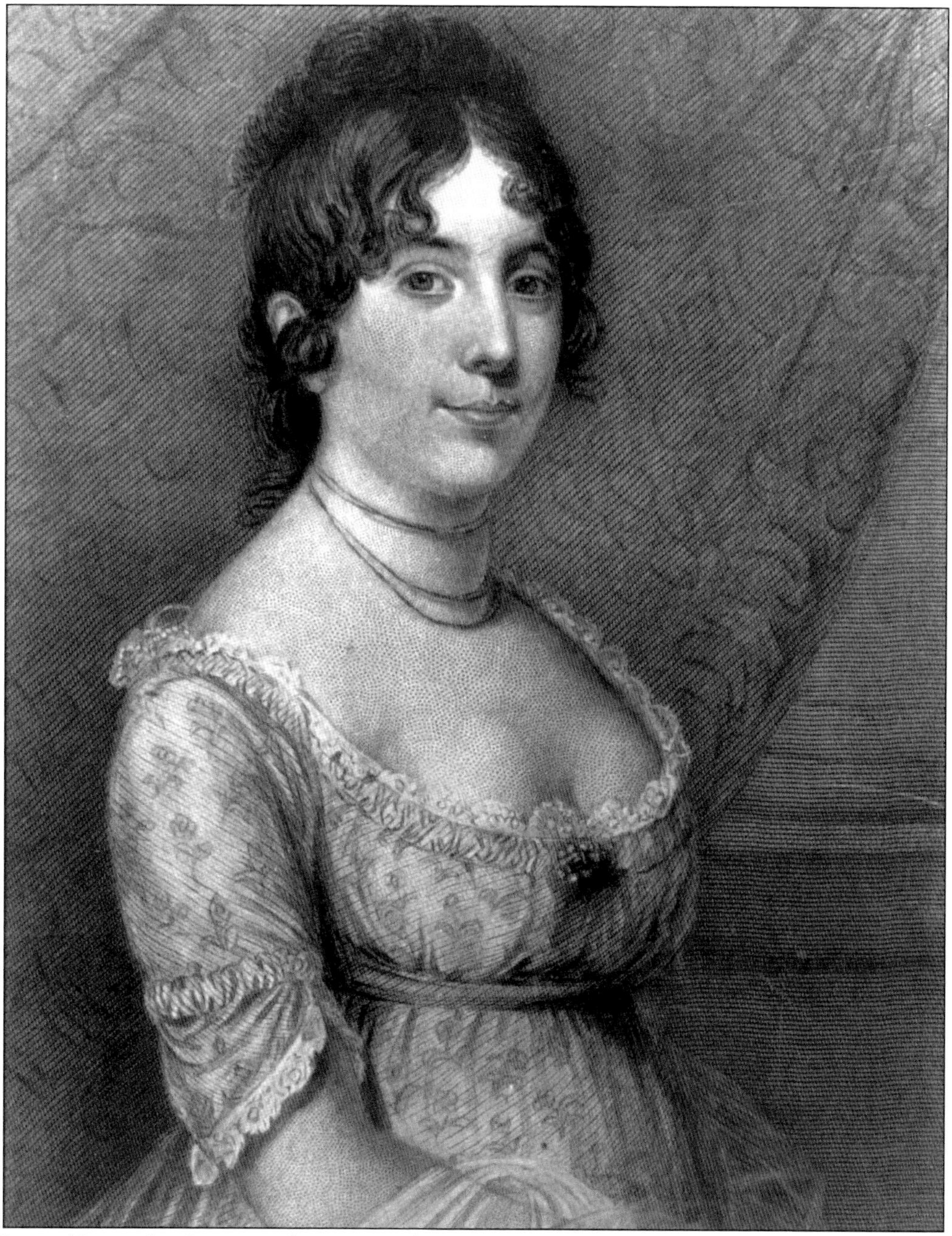

Legend has it that James Madison courted Mary Freneau, Philip Freneau's sister, during his stays at the family farm. Mary, however, married another. If the legend is true, there were no hard feelings, and Madison was invited to use the Freneau Homestead as a honeymoon retreat when he married Dolly Payne in 1794 at the age of 43. Although the couple was childless, their marriage was a happy one. In the 1970s, Madison Township was renamed Old Bridge Township.

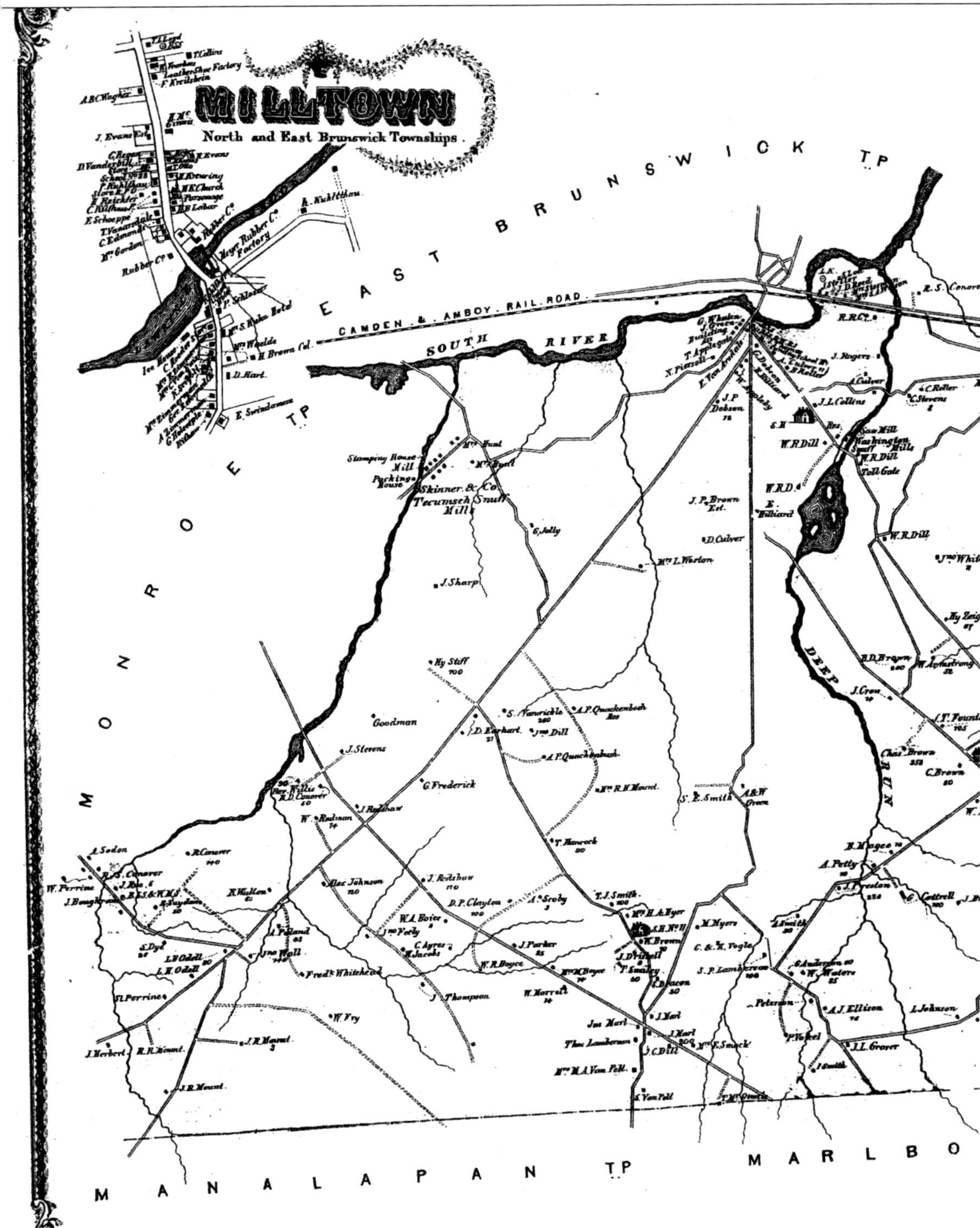

This map was printed only a few years after the formation of Madison Township. It shows the churches, schools, roads, and the Camden & Amboy Railroad line. It also shows most of the farms and homesteads in the township. Note the concentration of homes in certain areas,

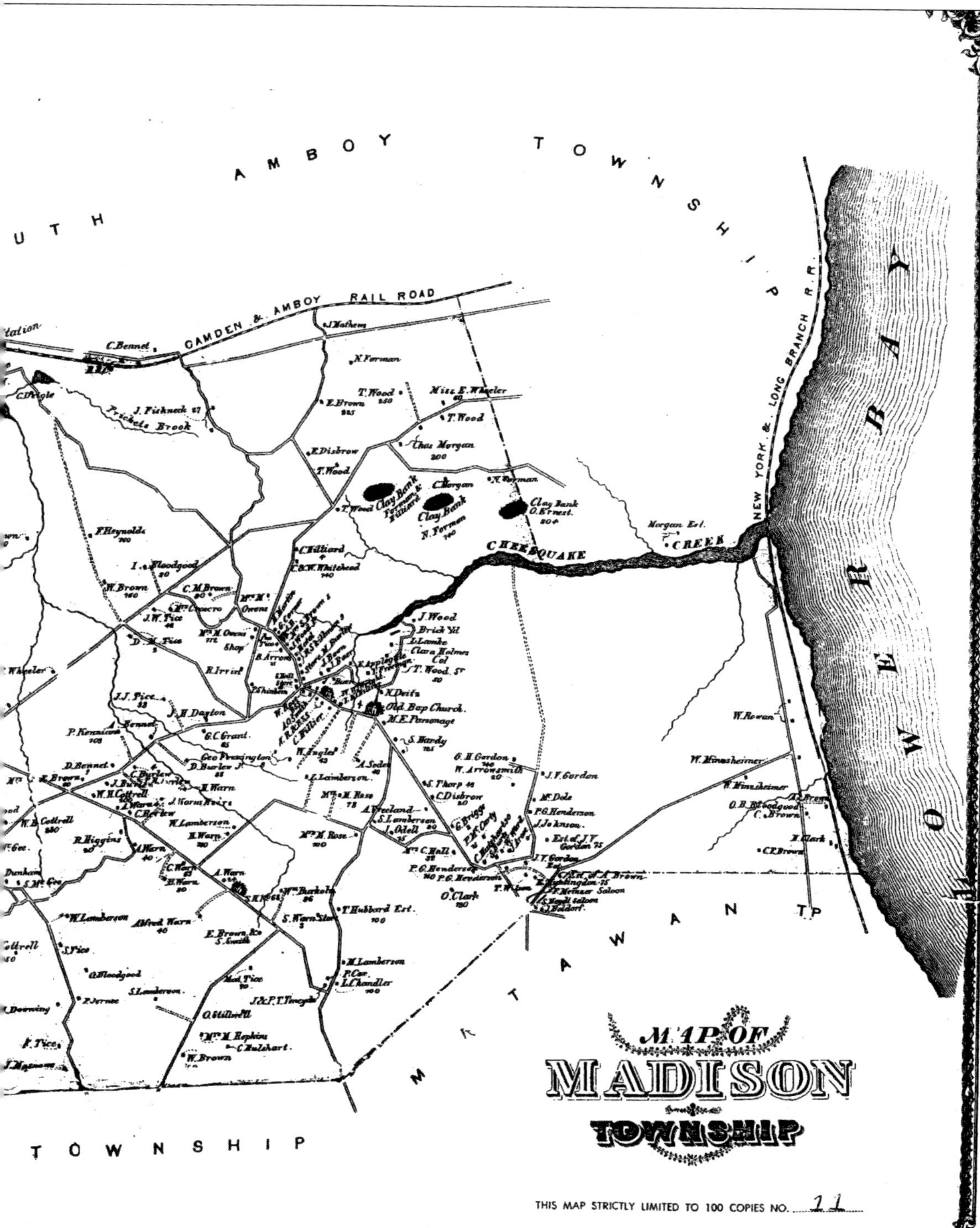

which were the first villages. The Raritan Bay is shown at the far left, with Cheesequake Creek flowing into it. The large stream in the middle is Deep Run, where many of the town's mills were located. The South River is seen at the top left.

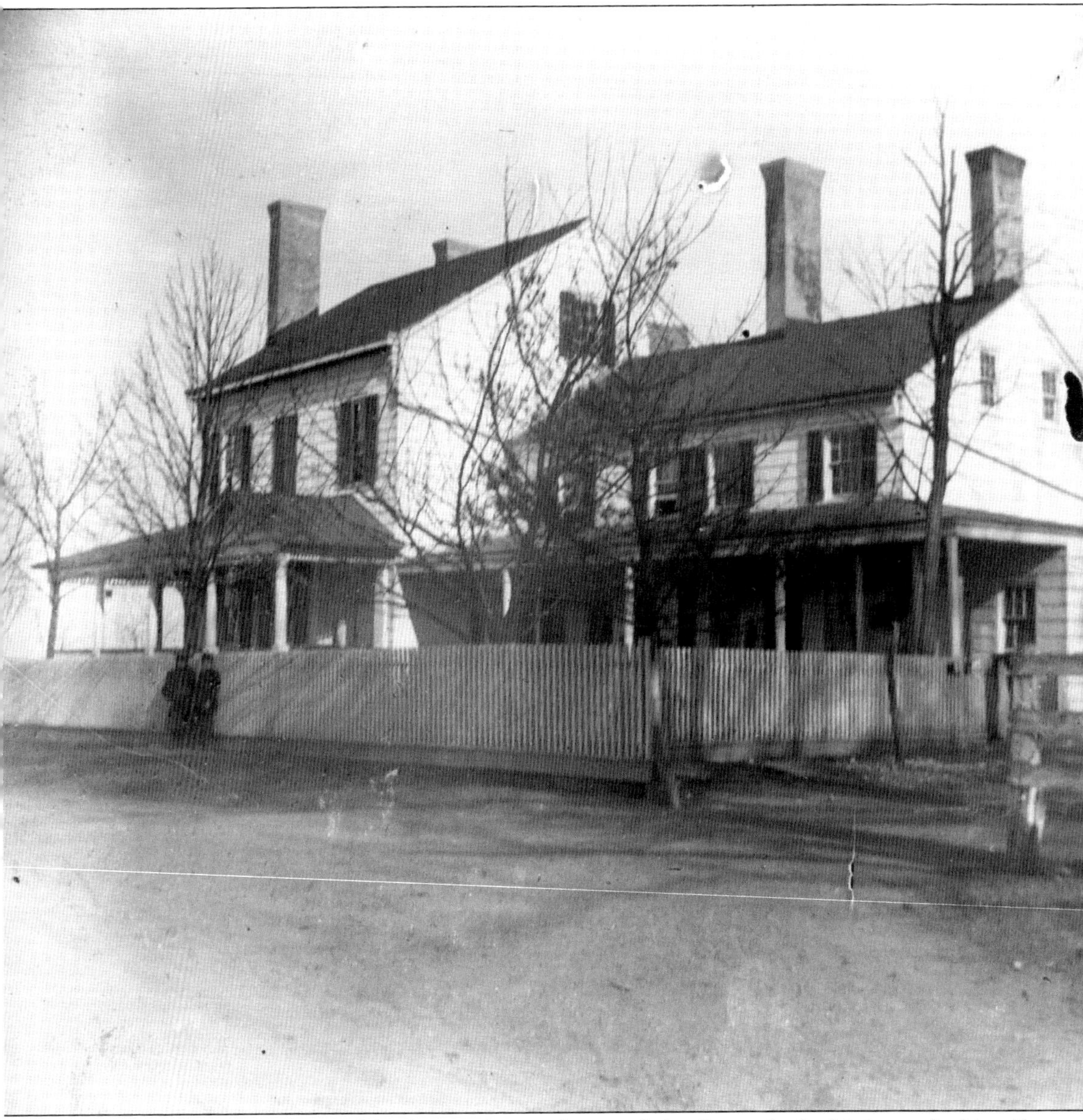

The Browns were some of the first settlers in the area. John Brown built this home for his wife, Susannah Reseau, in 1737. It was located on the north side of Route 516 and Bushnell Road. It was enlarged by the couple's descendants and was often referred to as the Bushnell House.

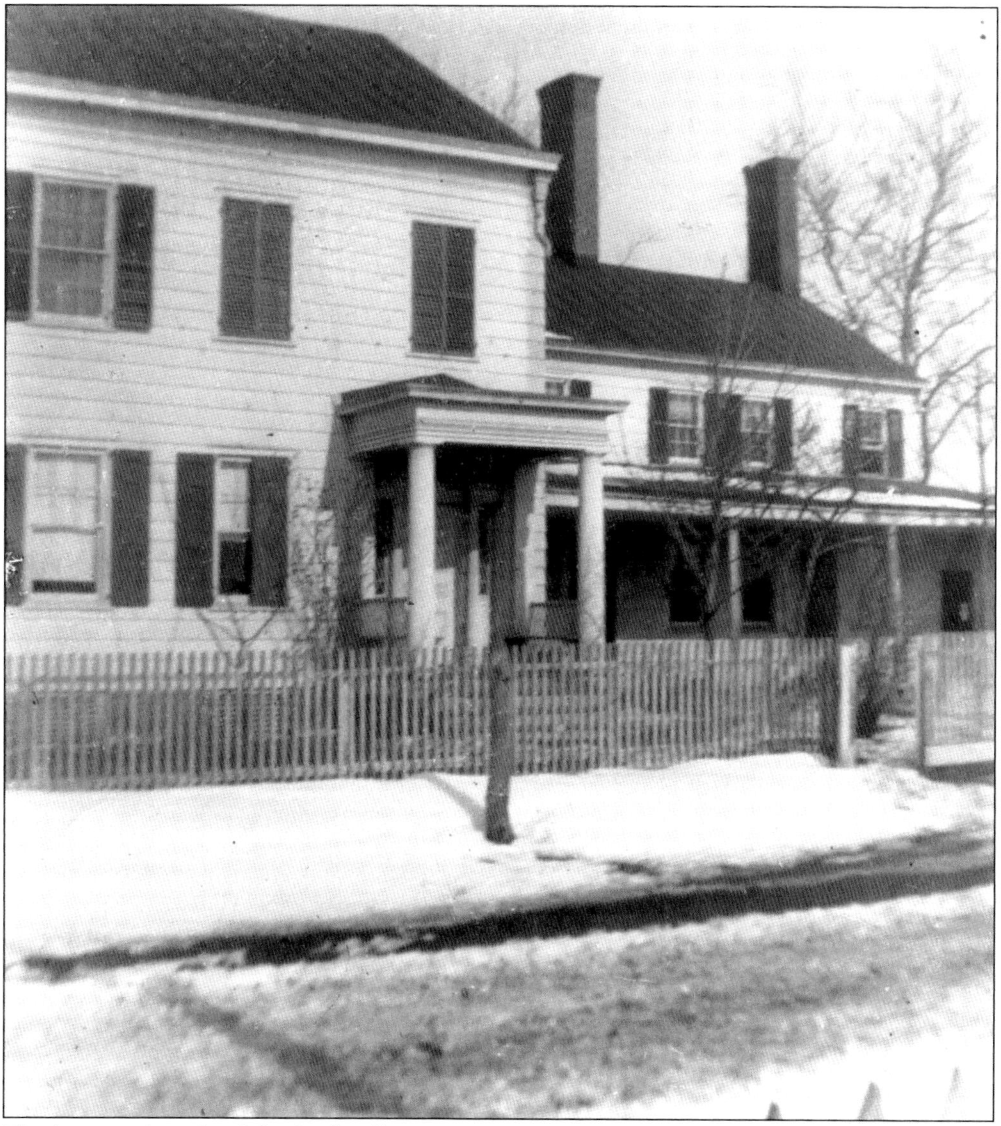

The lower right side of the Bushnell House was the original structure built by John Brown. In 1834, the house was expanded for the first time, using local timber and fieldstone to match the older portion. The house was abandoned in the early 1900s. After being heavily vandalized over the years, it was razed.

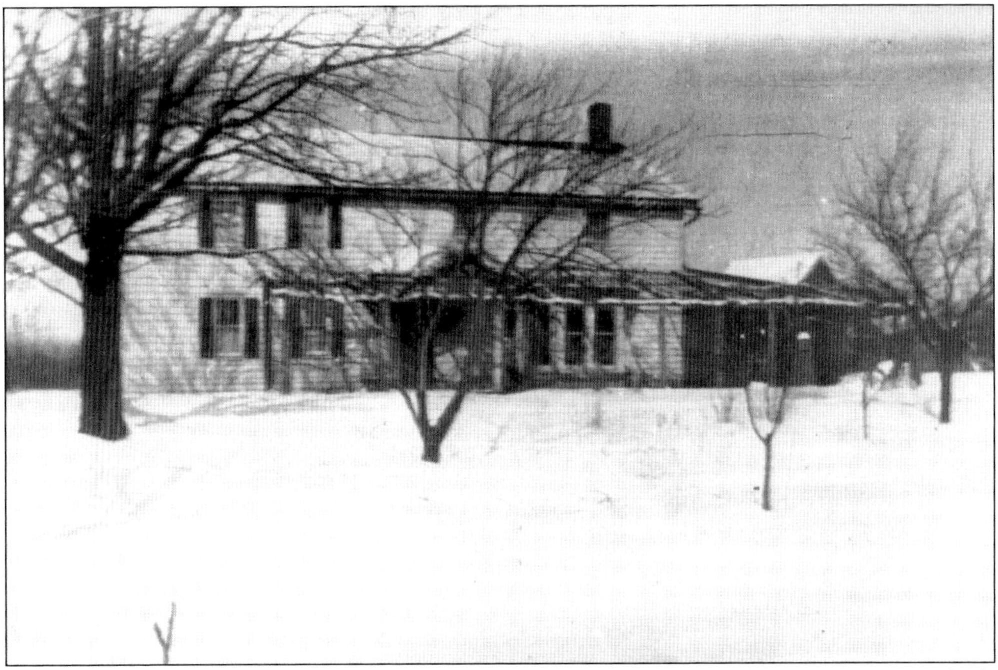

The D. Brown Homestead was located on Route 9 at the intersection of Route 516. It was built by descendants of John Brown, the builder of the Bushnell House. It later became known as the Jacob Gaub Farm. The Lutheran church now occupies the site.

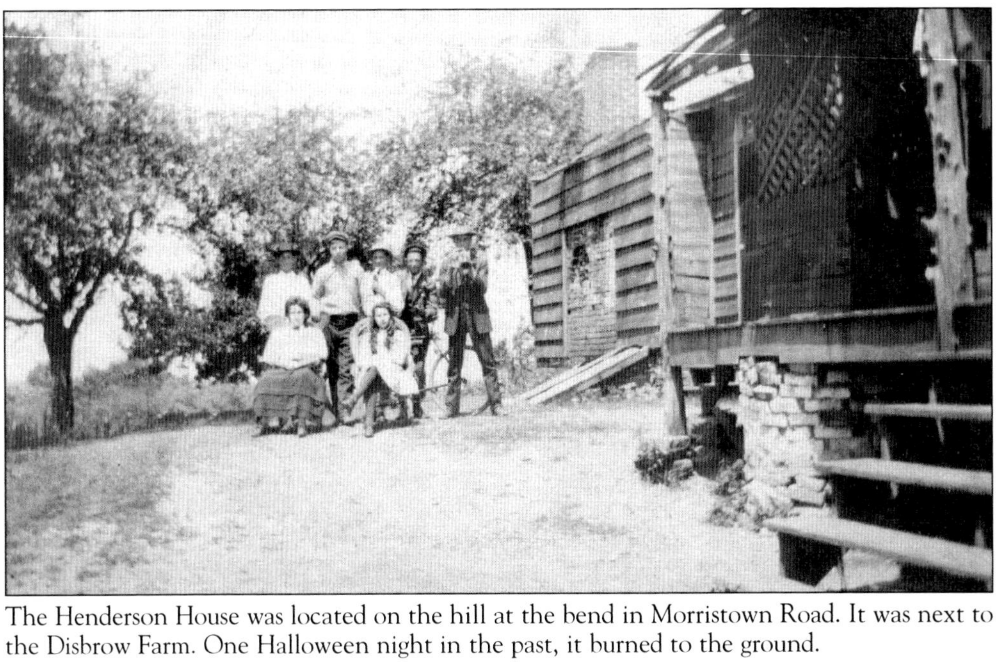

The Henderson House was located on the hill at the bend in Morristown Road. It was next to the Disbrow Farm. One Halloween night in the past, it burned to the ground.

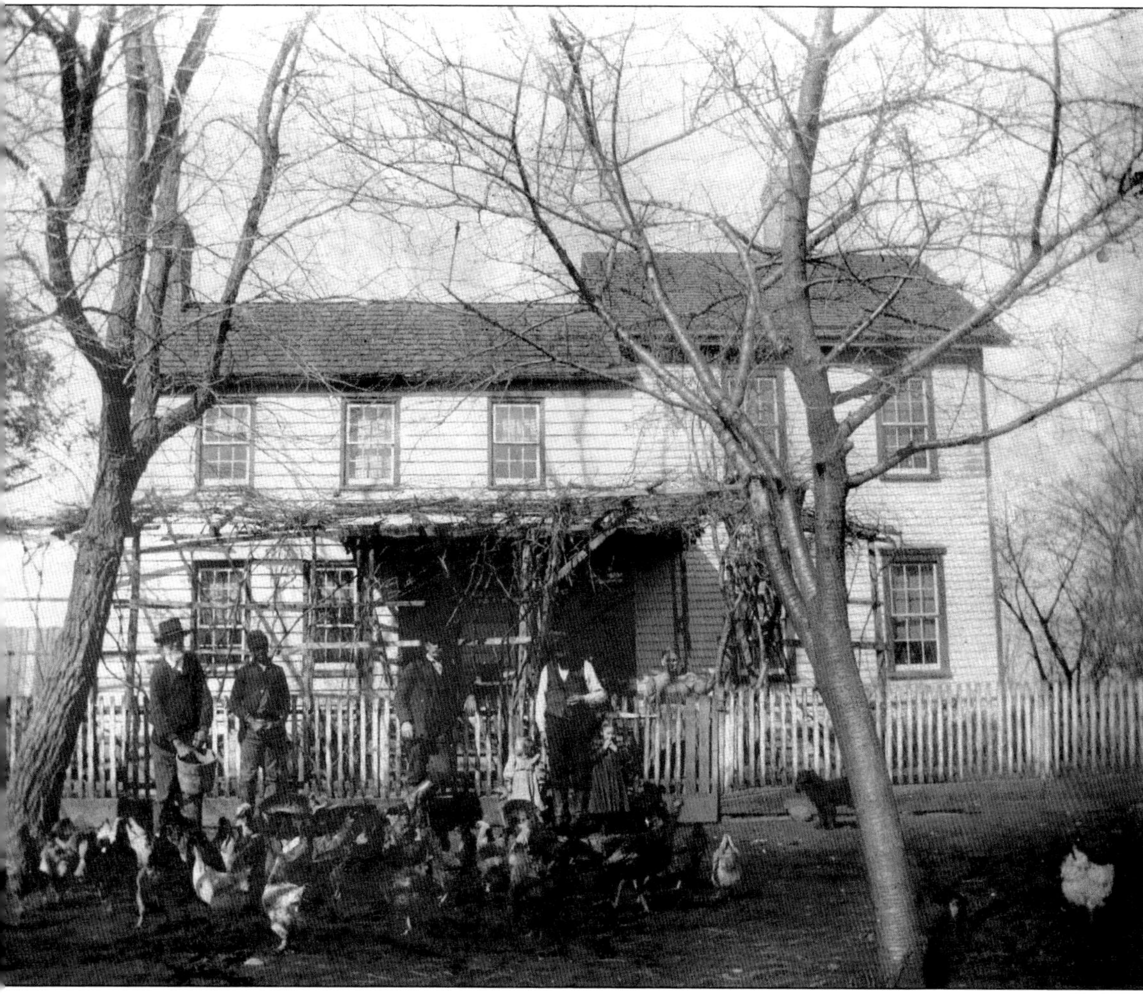

Formerly the Grant property, the Farrington House was fittingly located on Farrington Road in the Cheesequake area of the township. Were the chickens posing, or just did they just wander into the photograph?

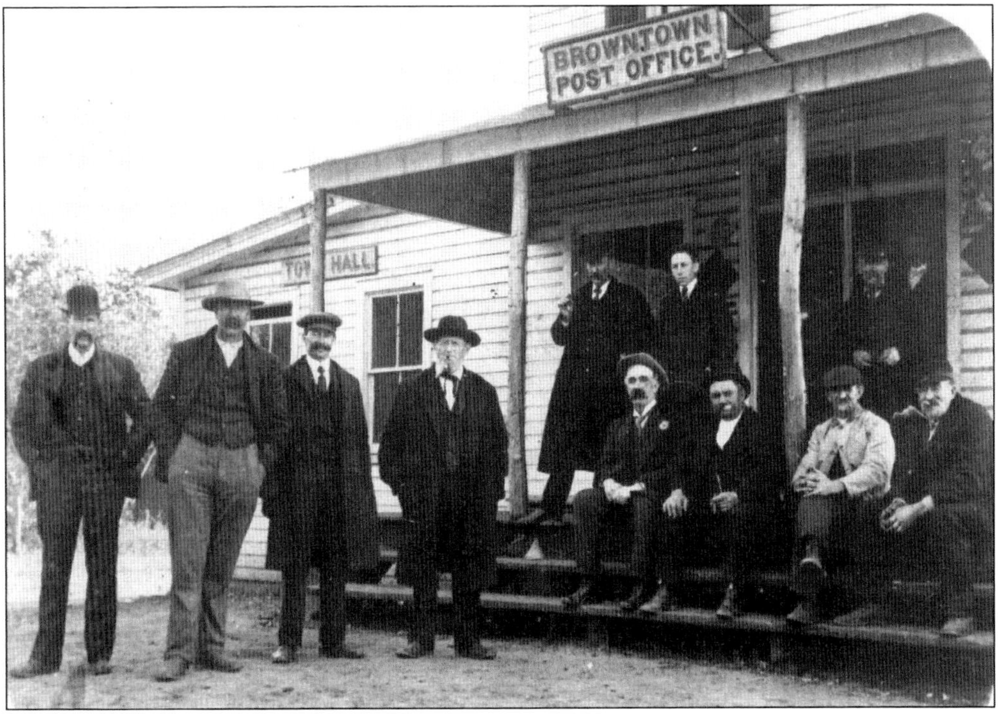

The Browntown post office and town hall building was located on Route 516 near Route 9. It was built in the early 1880s and became a post office in 1893. Pictured standing are, from left to right, William Crowley, Richard Burlew, William Ludi, Conrad Gaub, Asbury Fountain, John Uhl, George Struthers, and unidentified. Seated on the porch are, from left to right, Edward Zielgler, unidentified, Jacob Gaub, and unidentified.

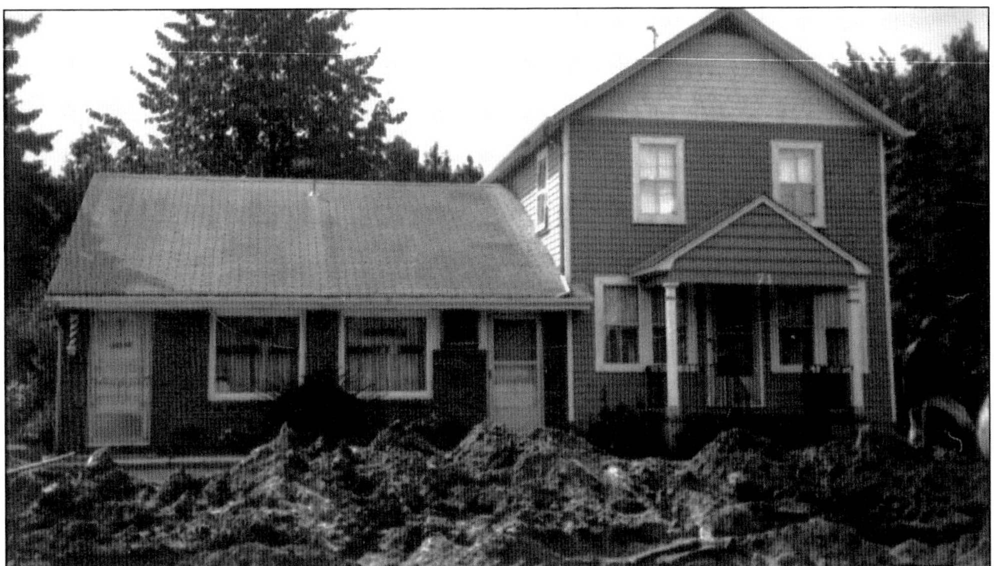

The Browntown post office closed in 1906, but the building continued to serve as a store through the 1950s. It survived into the 1960s as a private residence and now serves as an electronics store.

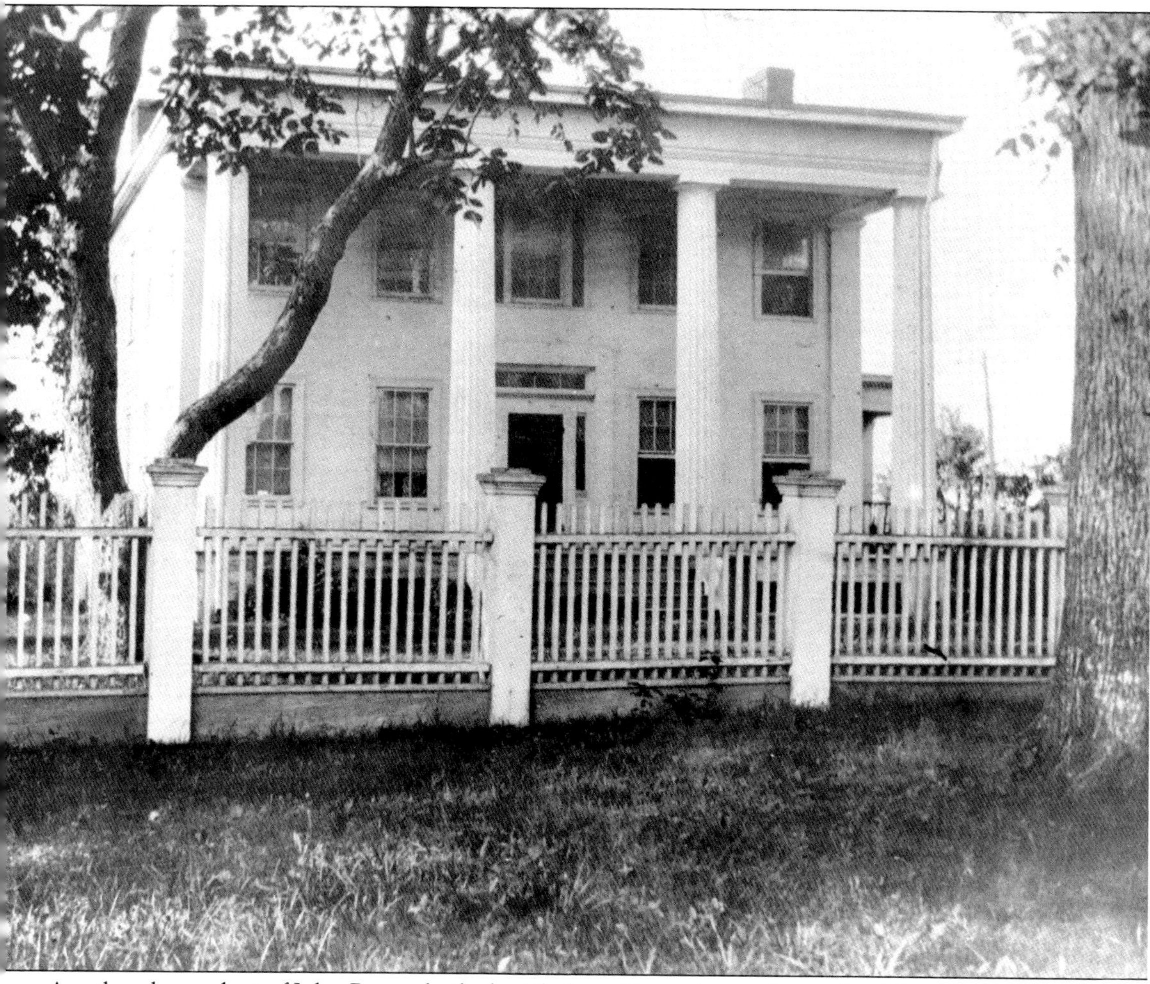

Another descendant of John Brown built the Clarkson Brown house, located on Throckmorton Lane. Clarkson Brown's daughter married James Fountain, and the home became known as the Fountain House. Fountain was the grandson of Rev. John Fountain, a well-known Methodist minister who lived and preached in the area.

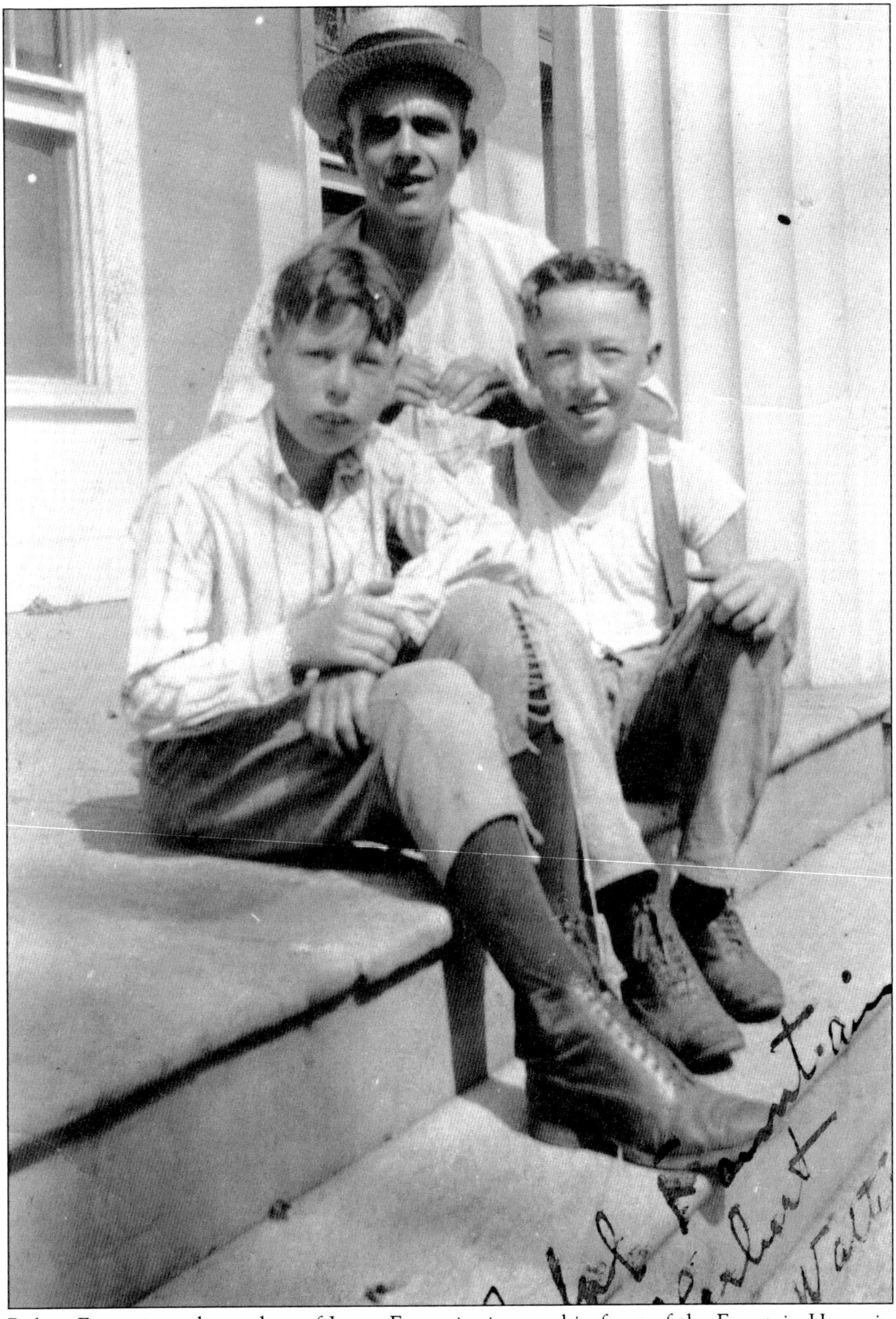

Robert Fountain, a descendant of James Fountain, is seated in front of the Fountain House in this 1919 photograph. With him are two children, Herbert and Walter Gaub, who lived on the farm across the street.

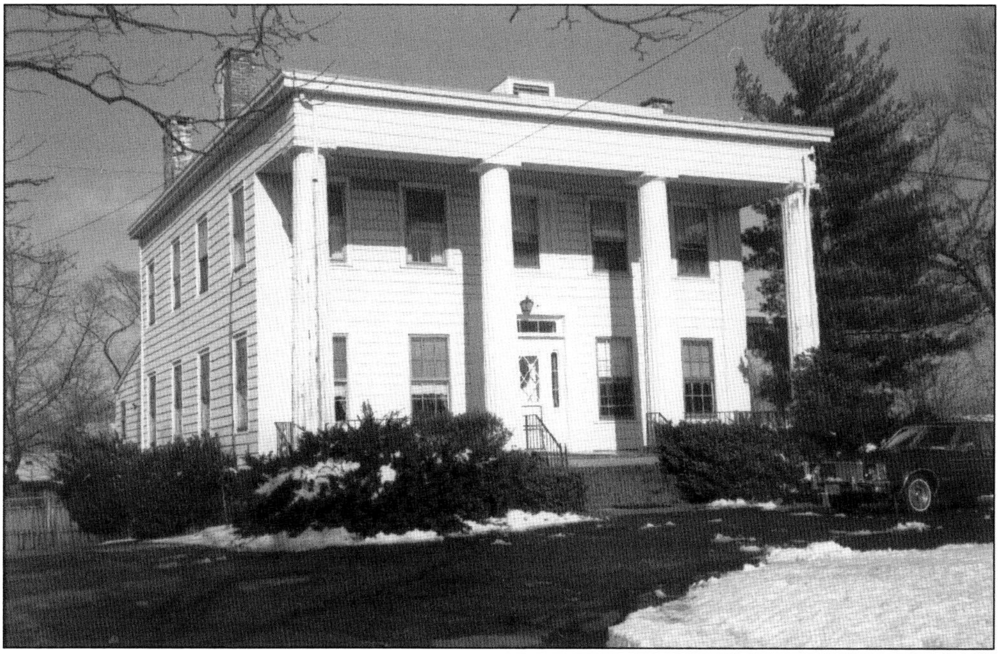

The Fountain House changed little over the years, as this more recent photograph shows. It is one of the few high-style Greek Revival homes in Middlesex County. Today, the house serves as the convent for St. Ambrose Church and School, which are located across the street.

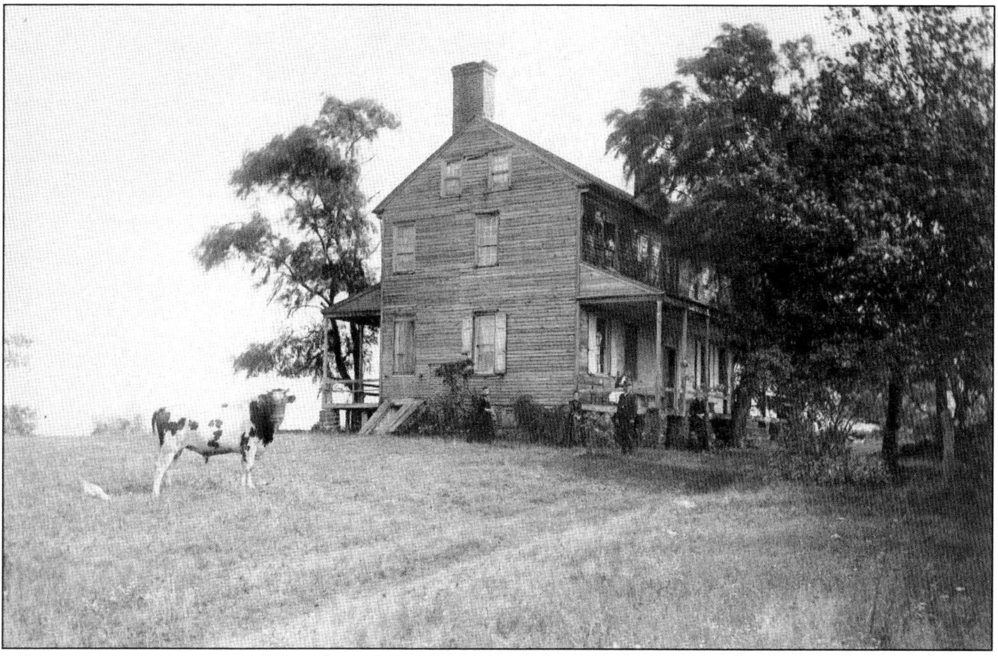

John Bowne was one of the first European settlers in New Jersey. He purchased land near the Lenni Lenape tribe in 1663. His brother, Capt. Andrew Bowne, owned 1,000 acres of land along the Raritan Bay between Whales Creek and Margaret's Creek. Their heirs built the Bowne Mansion, pictured here, on land owned by Andrew, where Laurence Harbor and Cliffwood Beach are today.

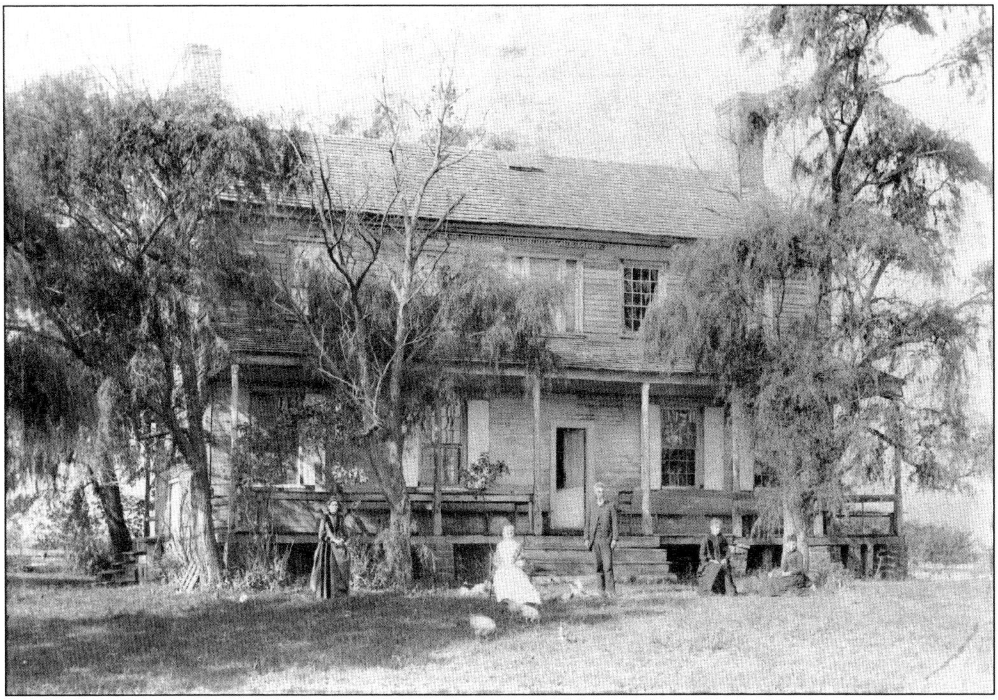

Here is a front view of the Bowne Mansion, probably in the late 1800s. Legend says that Margaret's Creek in Laurence Harbor was named for the Bownes' young daughter who drowned in the stream.

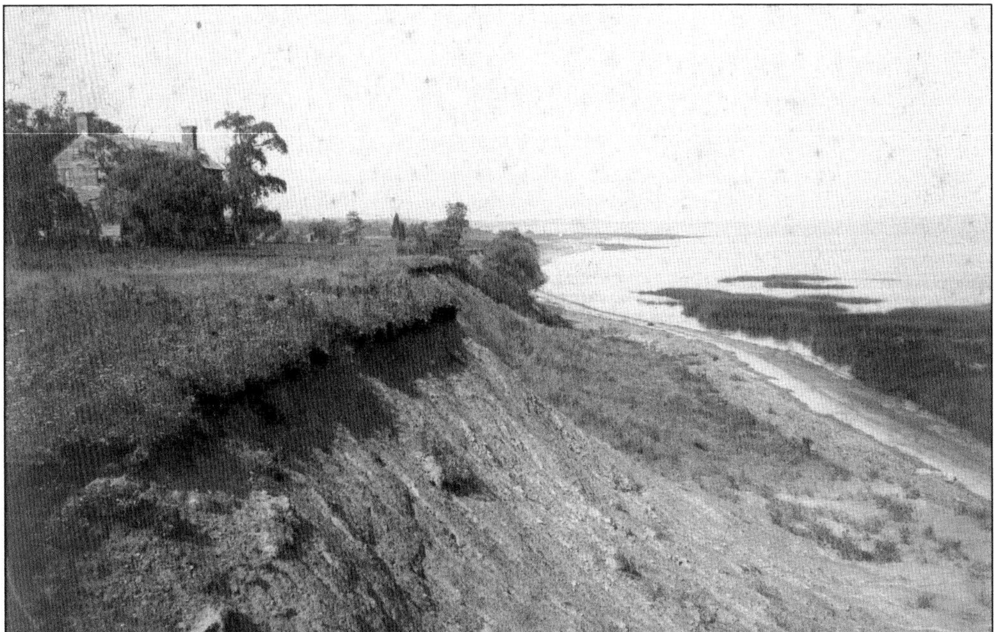

The Bowne Mansion stood on a bluff in Cliffwood Beach, overlooking the Raritan Bay. It was occupied by the Bownes until the mid-1800s, when the Brown family took possession. It was later purchased at auction by the Close family.

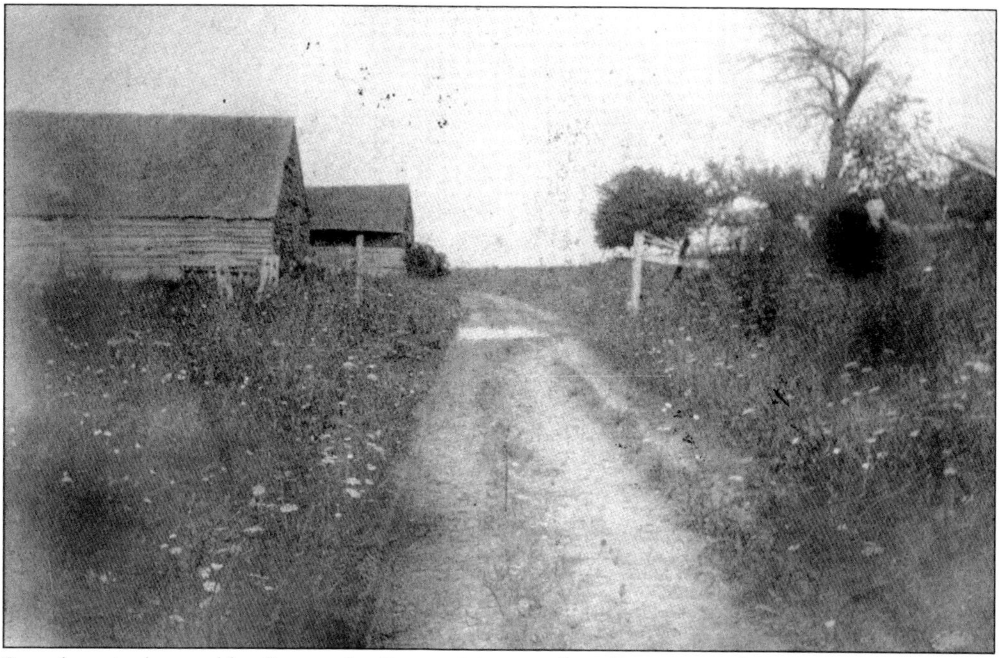

Seen here is the road leading to the Bowne Mansion from Route 35. The barn and smokehouse are shown on the left. In 1936, Gertrude Close Savage sold the property to the Knollcroft Development, the company that built the housing development occupying the site today.

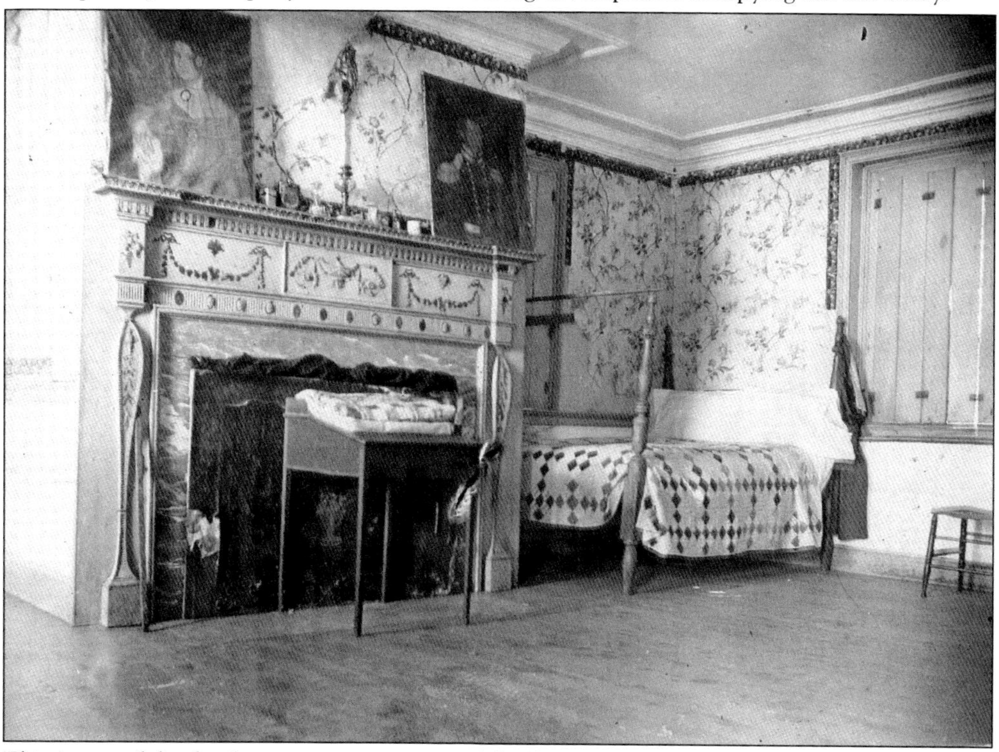

This is one of the few known interior views of the Bowne Mansion. It shows the Blue Room on the second floor. The Close family often used the room as a ballroom when they entertained.

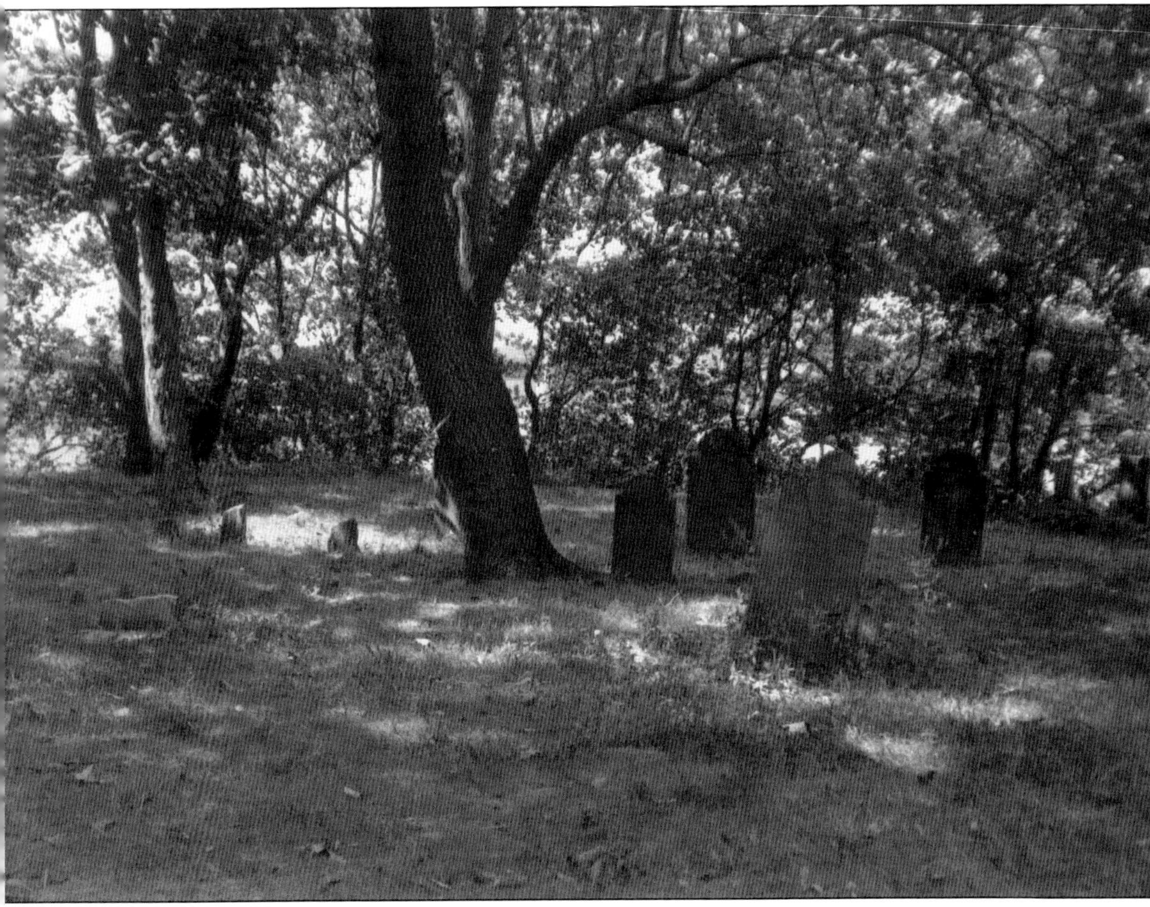

The Provost Cemetery occupies a bluff in Laurence Harbor that overlooks the Raritan Bay. Members of the Bowne family and the Provost family are buried here. The Provost Estate was in Laurence Harbor, adjacent to the Bowne property.

Built by John Tone c. 1740, the Tone House was located on 225 acres along today's Ferry Road. Tone was a member of the Light Horse Brigade of New Jersey during the Revolutionary War and was said to be a personal acquaintance of Gen. George Washington.

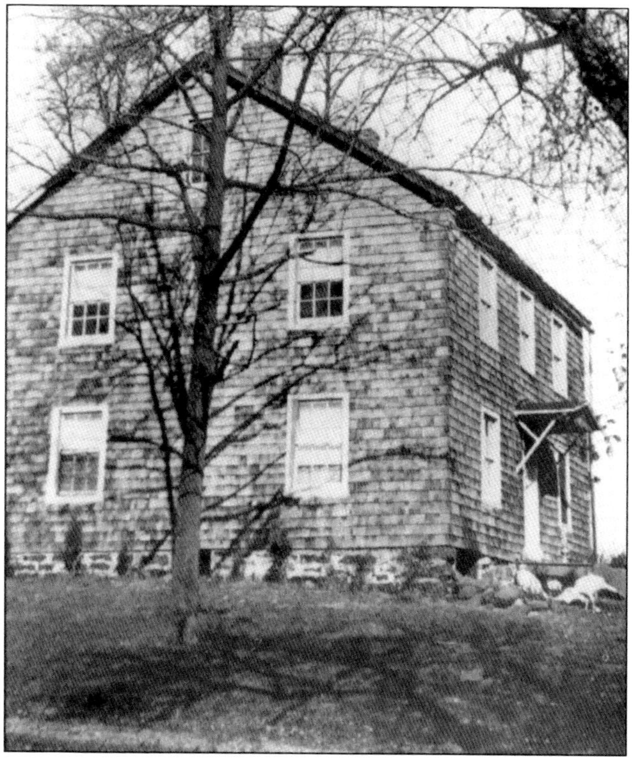

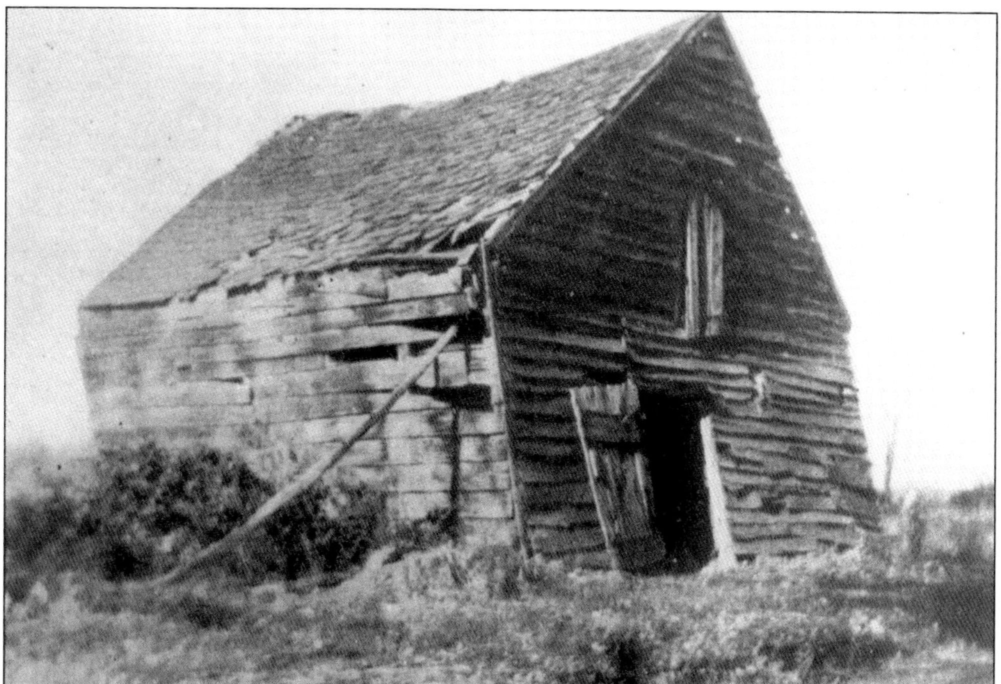

Opposite the Tone House stood the Old Coach House. Tone claimed it was well established that George Washington once slept there, but his assertion was never verified. The building collapsed in 1939.

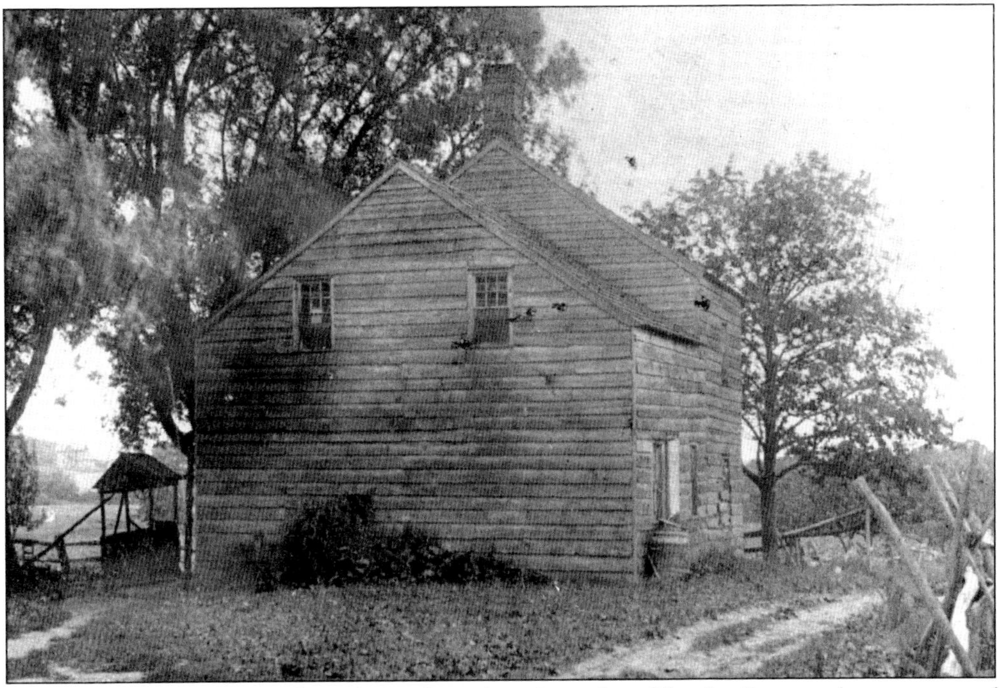

The Warne family was another of New Jersey's early settlers. The family owned many acres of land along Route 516, between Matawan and Browntown. This home was built by H. Warne on Partridge Road.

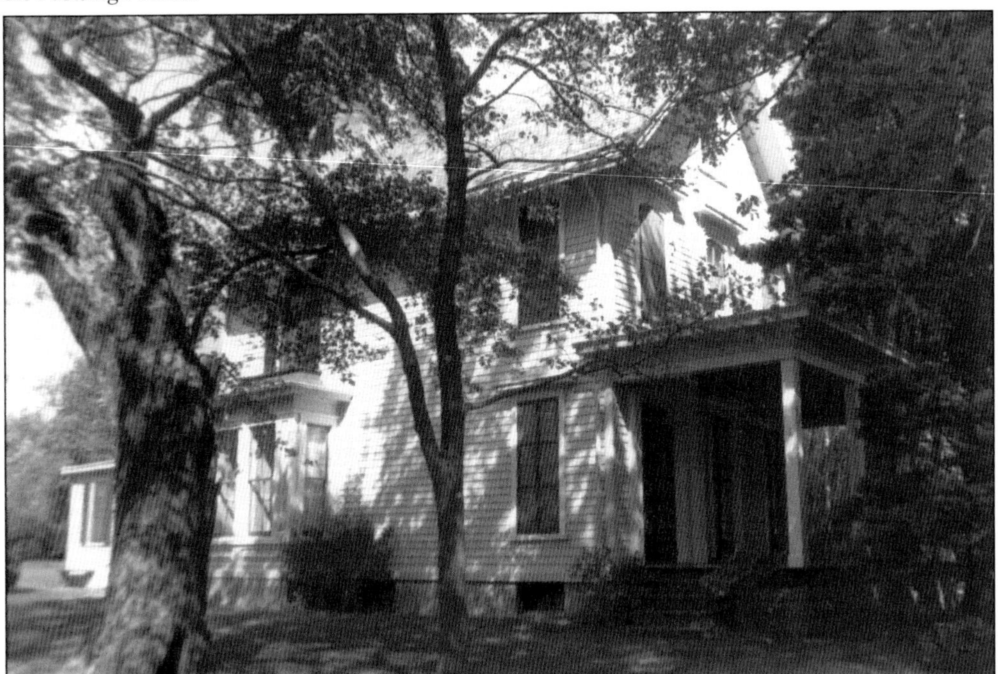

Abraham and Cornelia Warne raised their six children in this home. The home was built in 1825 and was located on Route 516 in the Cedar Ridge section of Old Bridge. Besides farming, Abraham also operated a mercantile business in New York City.

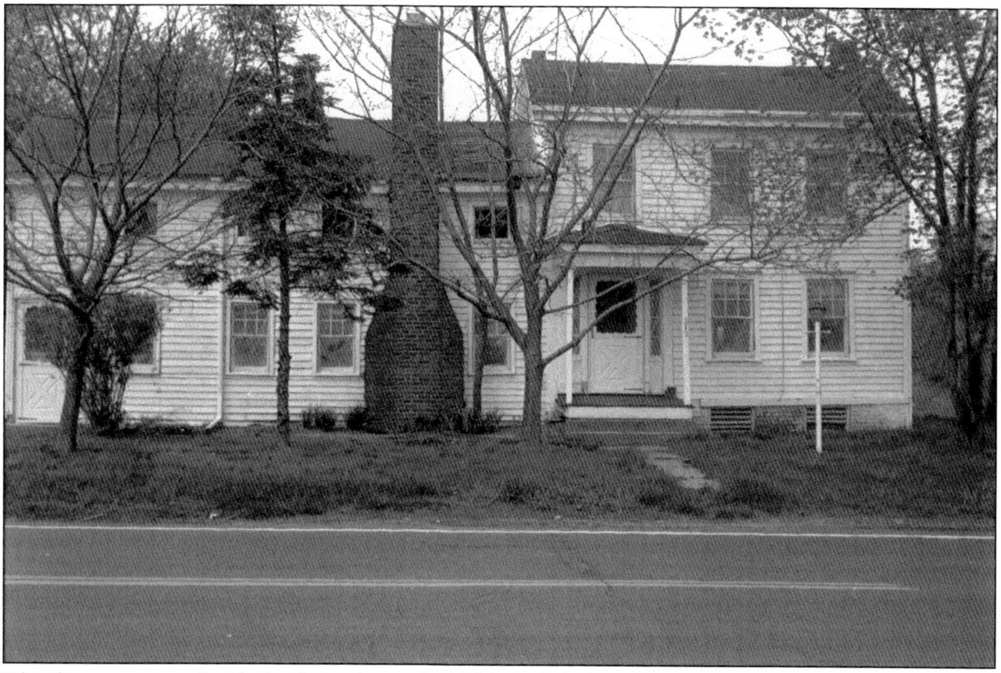

This house was probably built in the early 1800s by Mathias Tice. It is commonly known as the Warne Store because Stephen Warne occupied the house from 1862 until 1906. The house still stands at the intersection of Route 516 and Morganville Road, near the Matawan border.

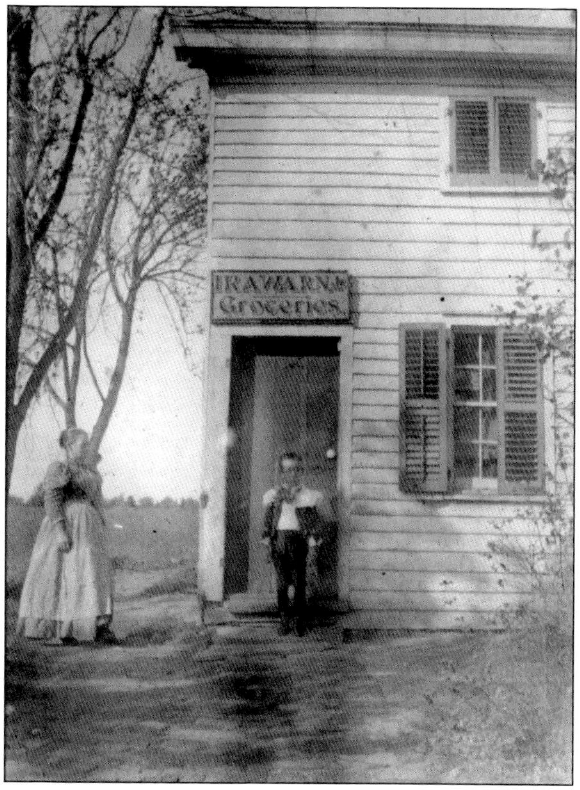

The house built by Mathias Tice also served as a store for a period of time in the late 1800s. The sign above the door reads, "Ira Warne, Jr. / Groceries."

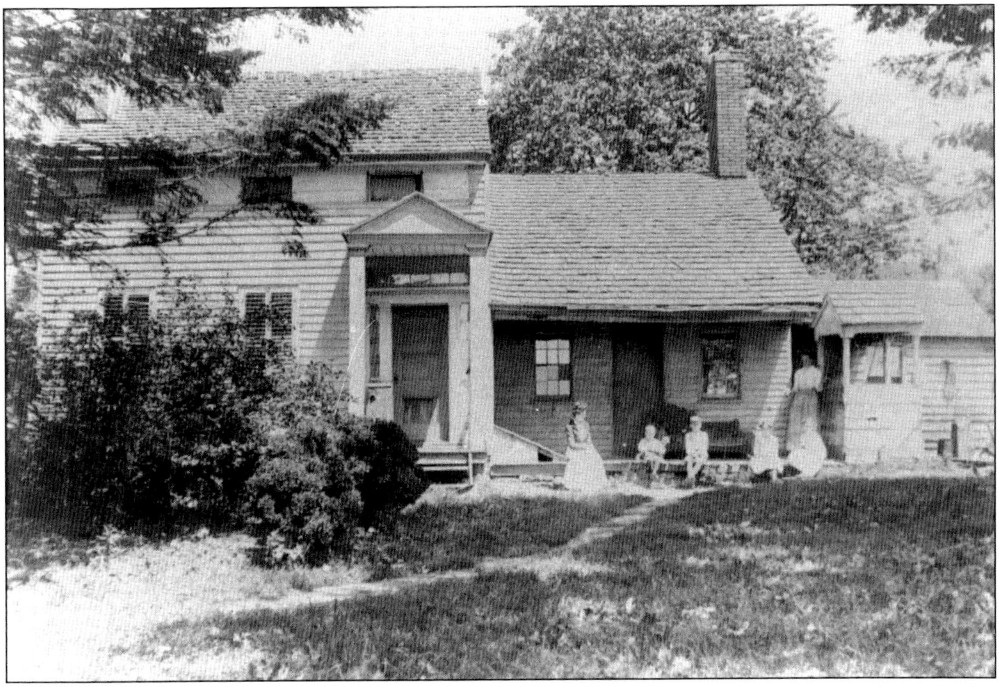

Joel Elias Quakenbush built his home in the 1800s on Texas Road. It was located across the road from the Serman Resort, which previously owned the land.

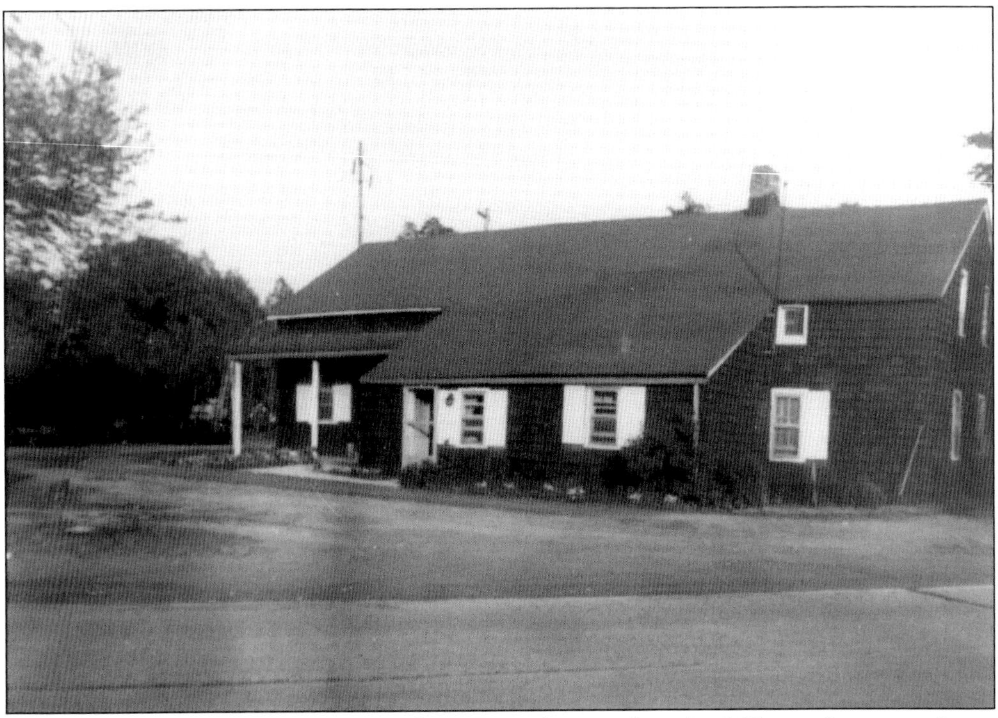

In 1864, a number of residents in Madison Township purchased a 265-acre farm in order to establish a home for the disadvantaged. The building still stands on Bordentown Road.

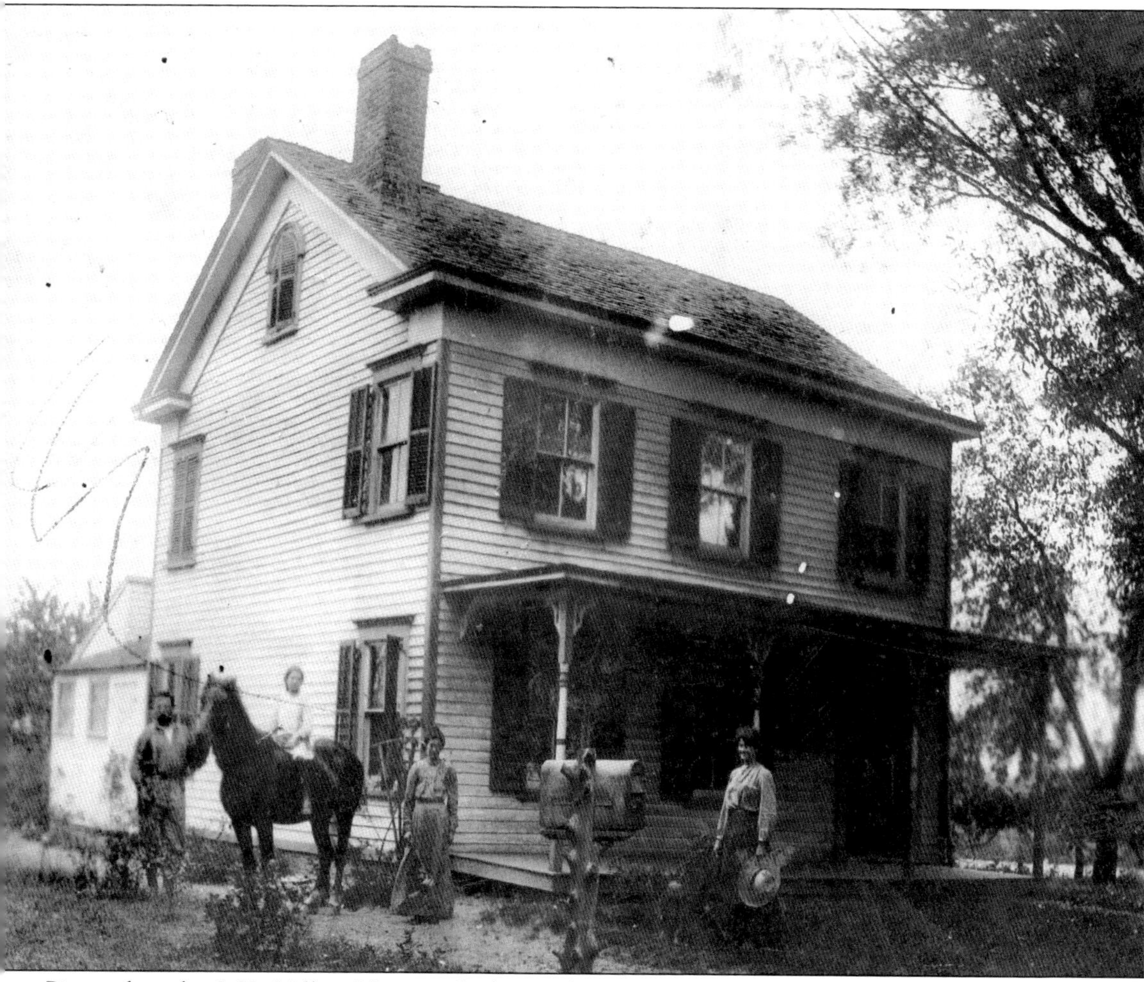

Pictured is the L.K. Hillier House, which was located in the Cheesequake section of the township. Originally, it was much larger and served as a hotel. A section of the house was torn down before this photograph was taken. Later, the home was owned by Jacob Loesch.

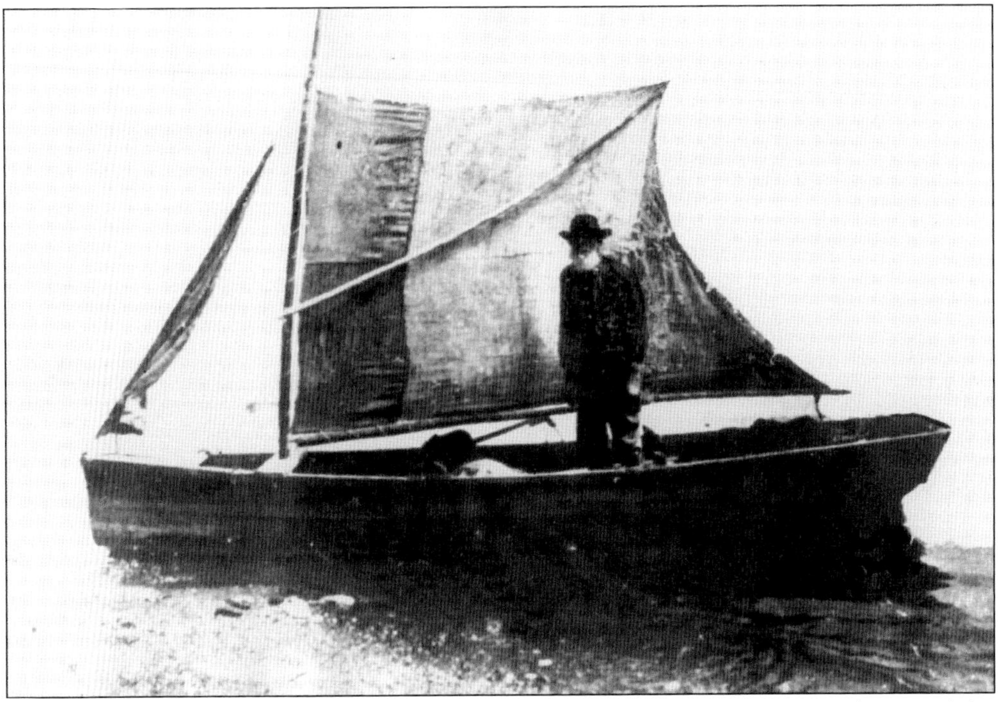

Burlew was another well-known name in the area. Abraham Burlew (1849–1915) enjoyed the water, much like many of his relatives and heirs, and often sailed in the Raritan Bay in his homemade boat with homemade sails.

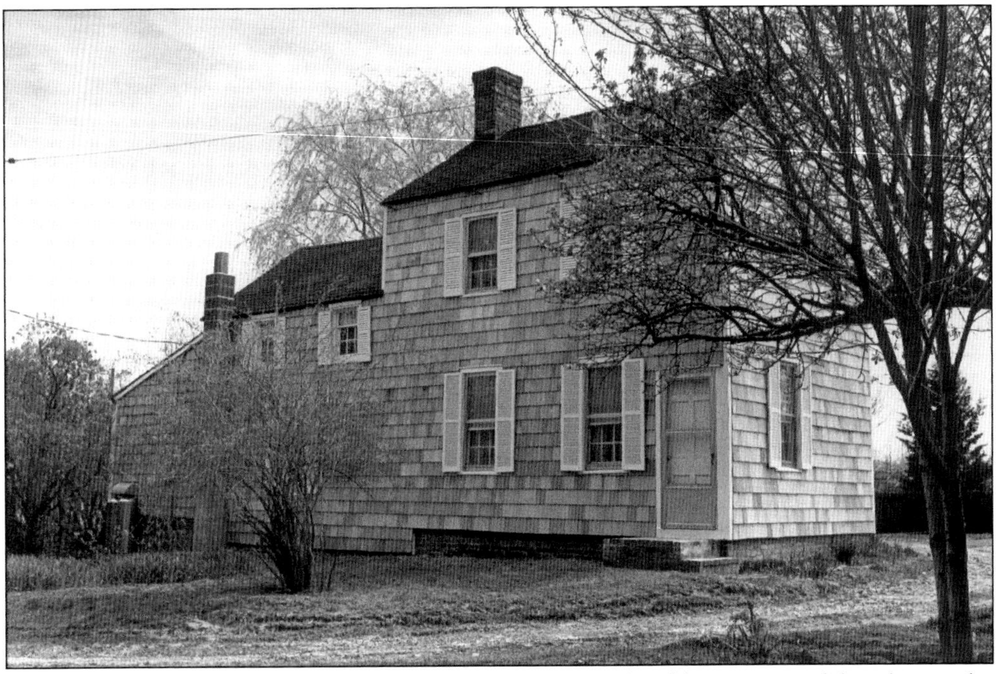

The Foreman family settled in the area in Colonial times. The oldest section of their home, the center, was built in the mid-1700s. It still stands on Morristown Road, overlooking exit 120 of the Garden State Parkway.

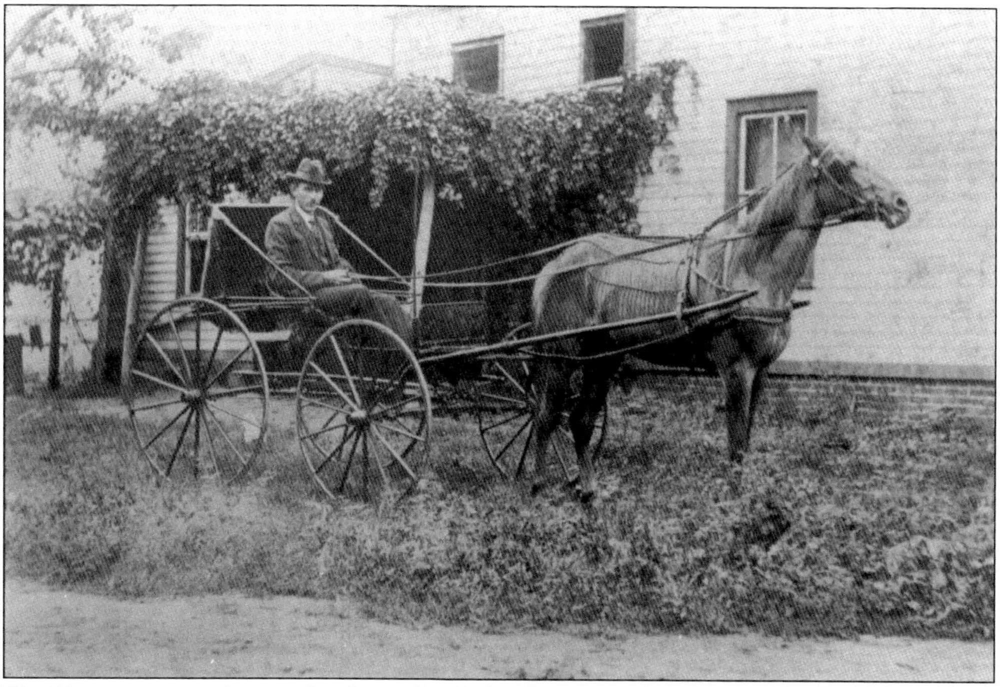

The Hausers were a farming family in the Cedar Grove section of town in the 1800s. Looking every bit the gentleman farmer, John Hauser poses in front of his house in his horse and buggy.

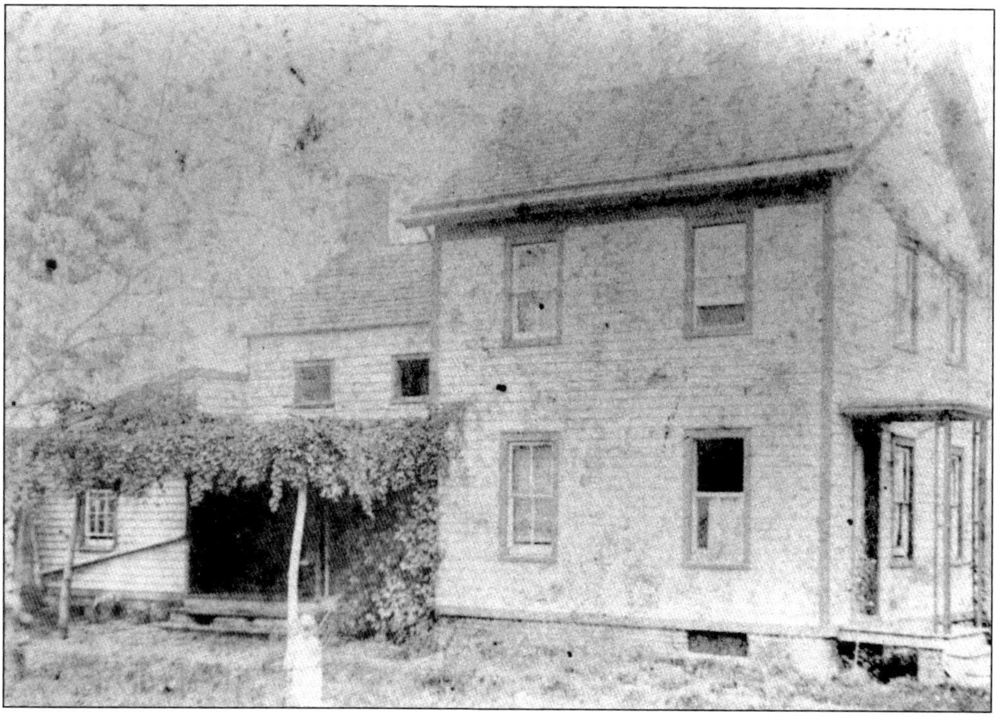

The Hauser homestead is pictured in the late 1880s with an unidentified child posing in front. The house was located off Route 516. It was demolished to make room for the Cedar Ridge High School, which is now the east campus of the Old Bridge High School.

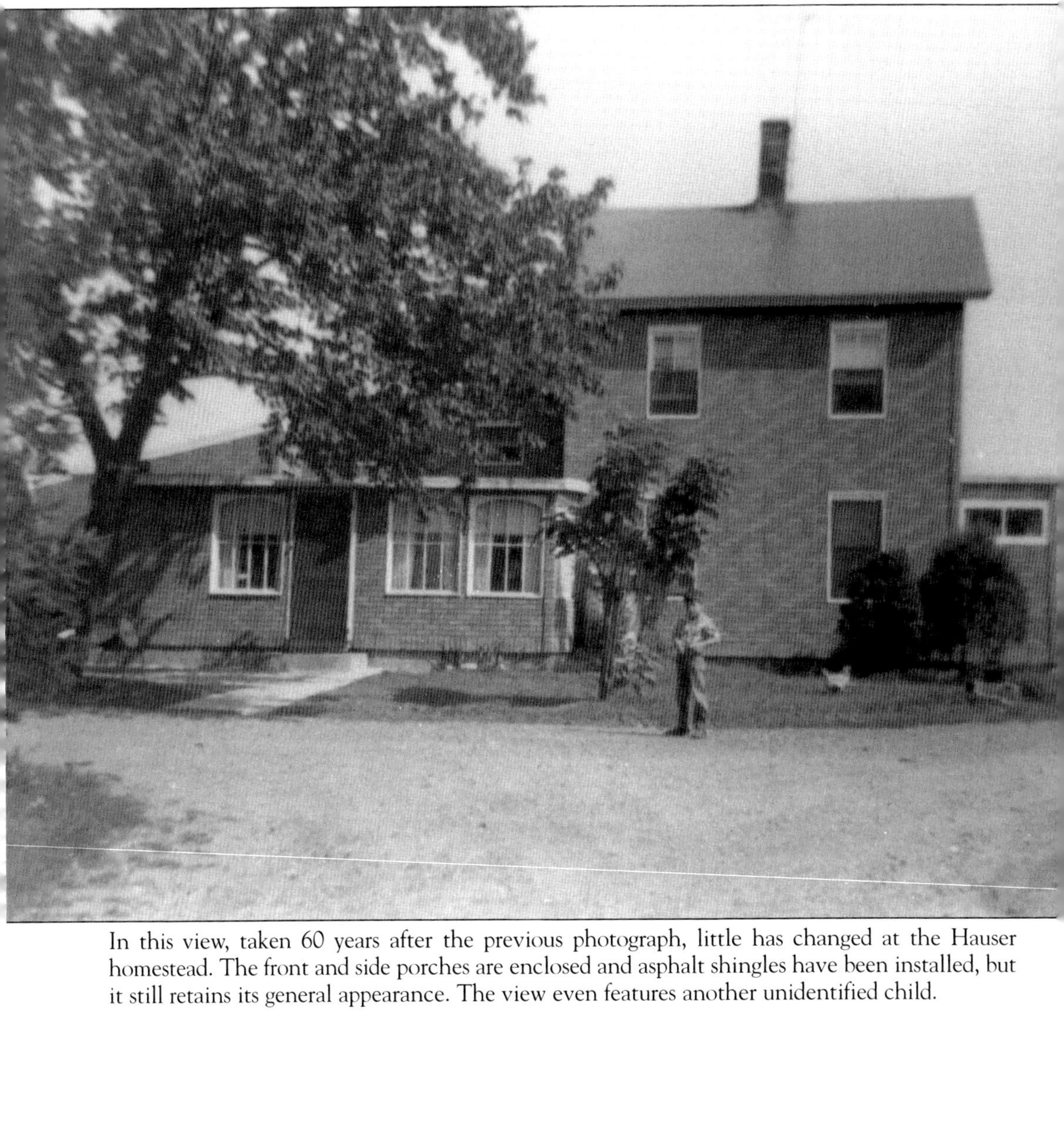

In this view, taken 60 years after the previous photograph, little has changed at the Hauser homestead. The front and side porches are enclosed and asphalt shingles have been installed, but it still retains its general appearance. The view even features another unidentified child.

Two

FARMING THE SOIL

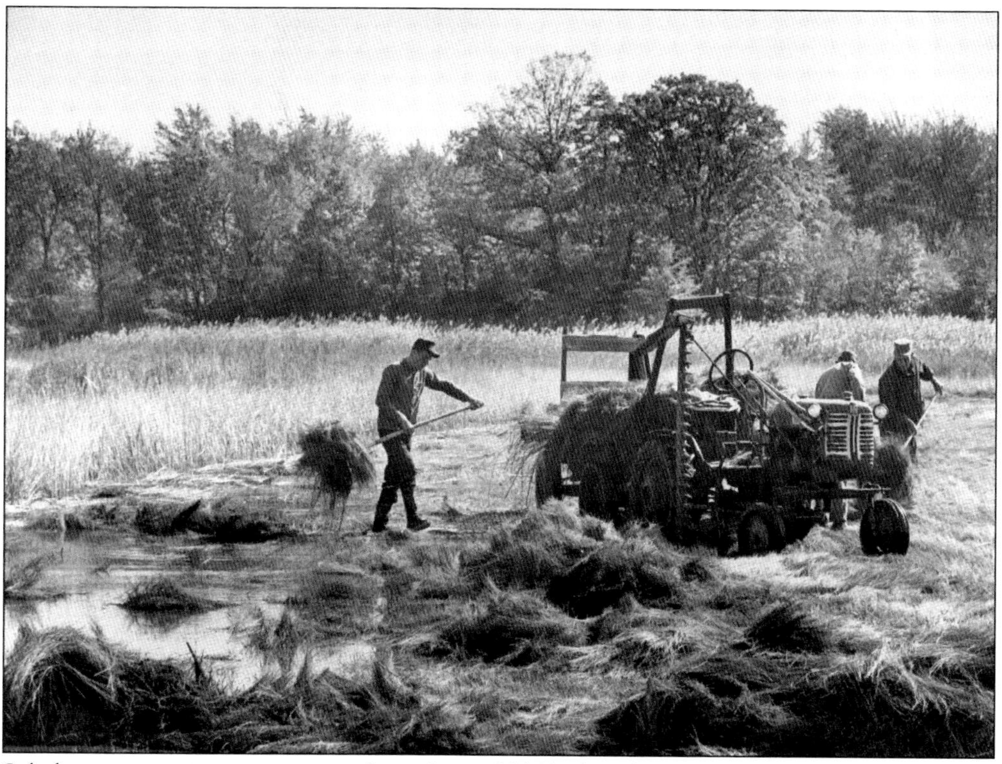

Salt hay was an important crop throughout Old Bridge's history. Harvesting the crop from the numerous marshes and swamps in the area was challenging, as farmers were forced to deal with the deep mud and pesky insects. The hay was used for fodder, packing material, and many other things.

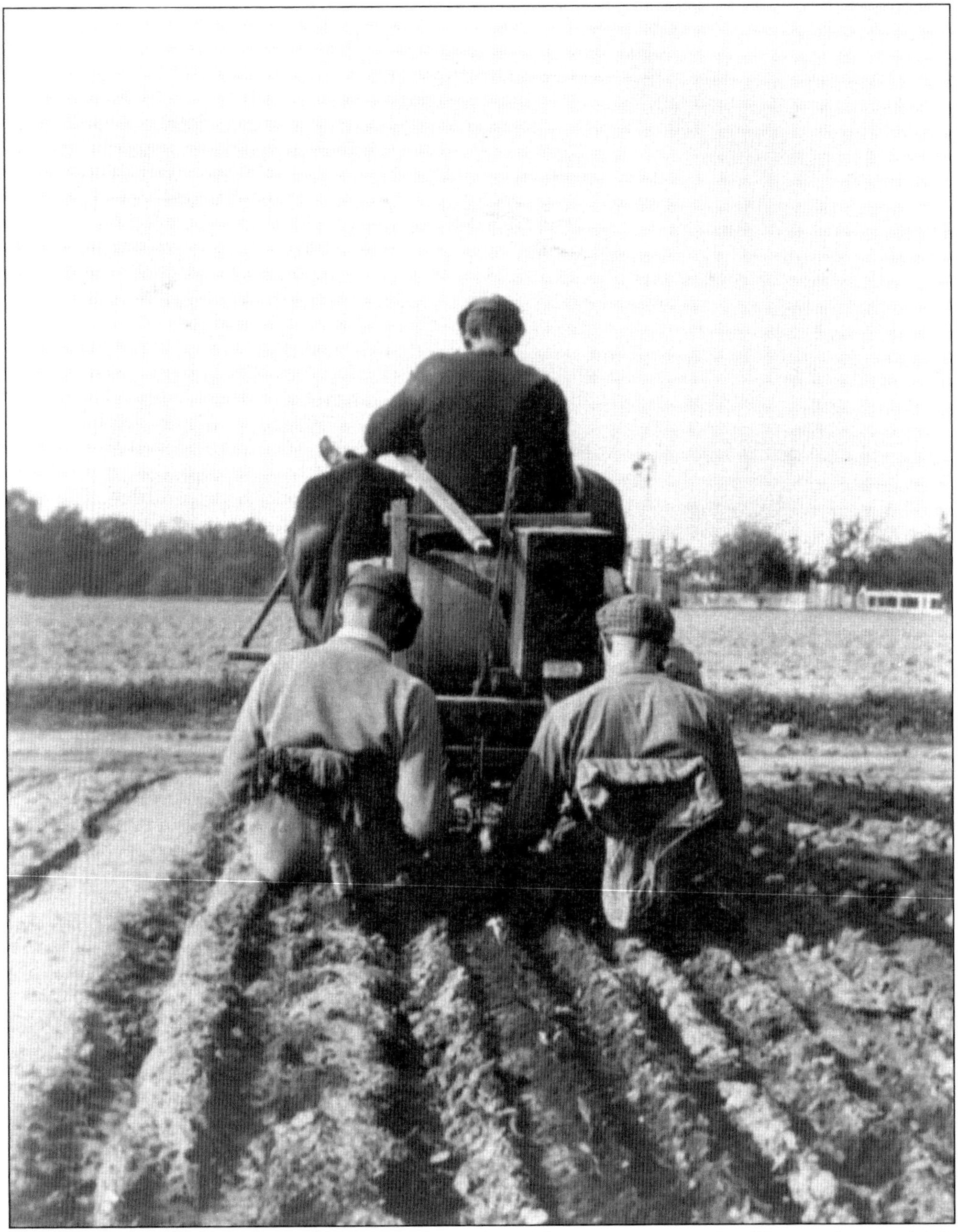

High-tech farming in the early 1900s required real horsepower on the Hauser farm, which was located off Route 516 in the Cedar Ridge area of the township. This horse-drawn planter, driven by John Hauser, breaks up the soil while Charles Hauser (left) and an unidentified helper plant two rows simultaneously.

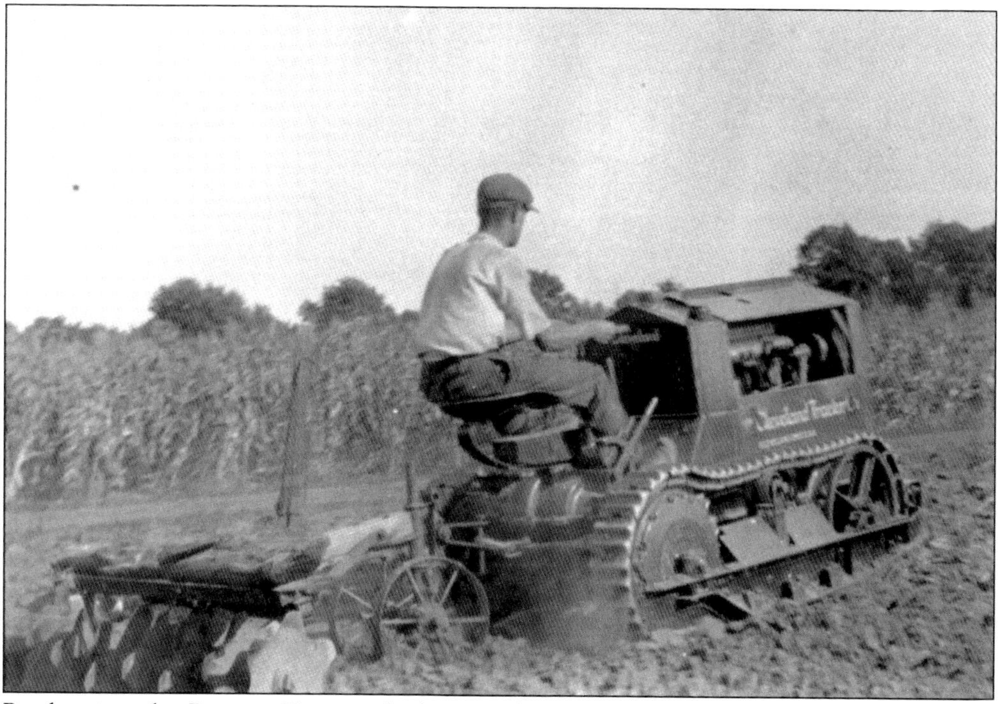

By the time the Roaring Twenties had come along, the Hausers had purchased one of the newfangled gasoline tractors. Clarence Hauser is the driver.

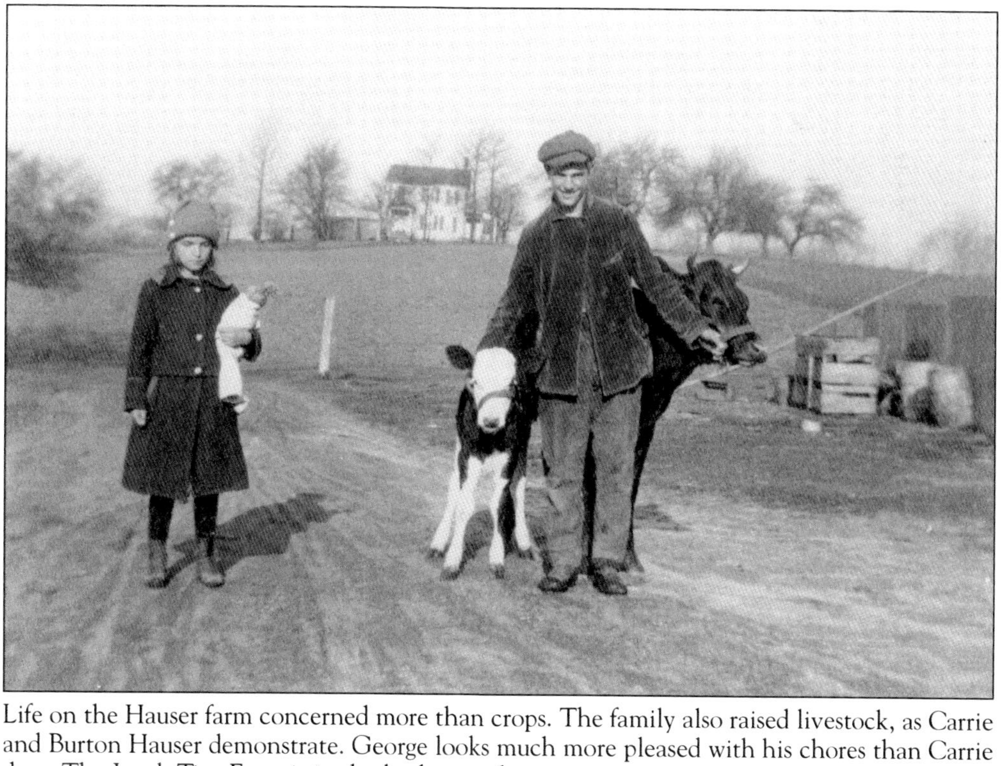

Life on the Hauser farm concerned more than crops. The family also raised livestock, as Carrie and Burton Hauser demonstrate. George looks much more pleased with his chores than Carrie does. The Jacob Tice Farm is in the background.

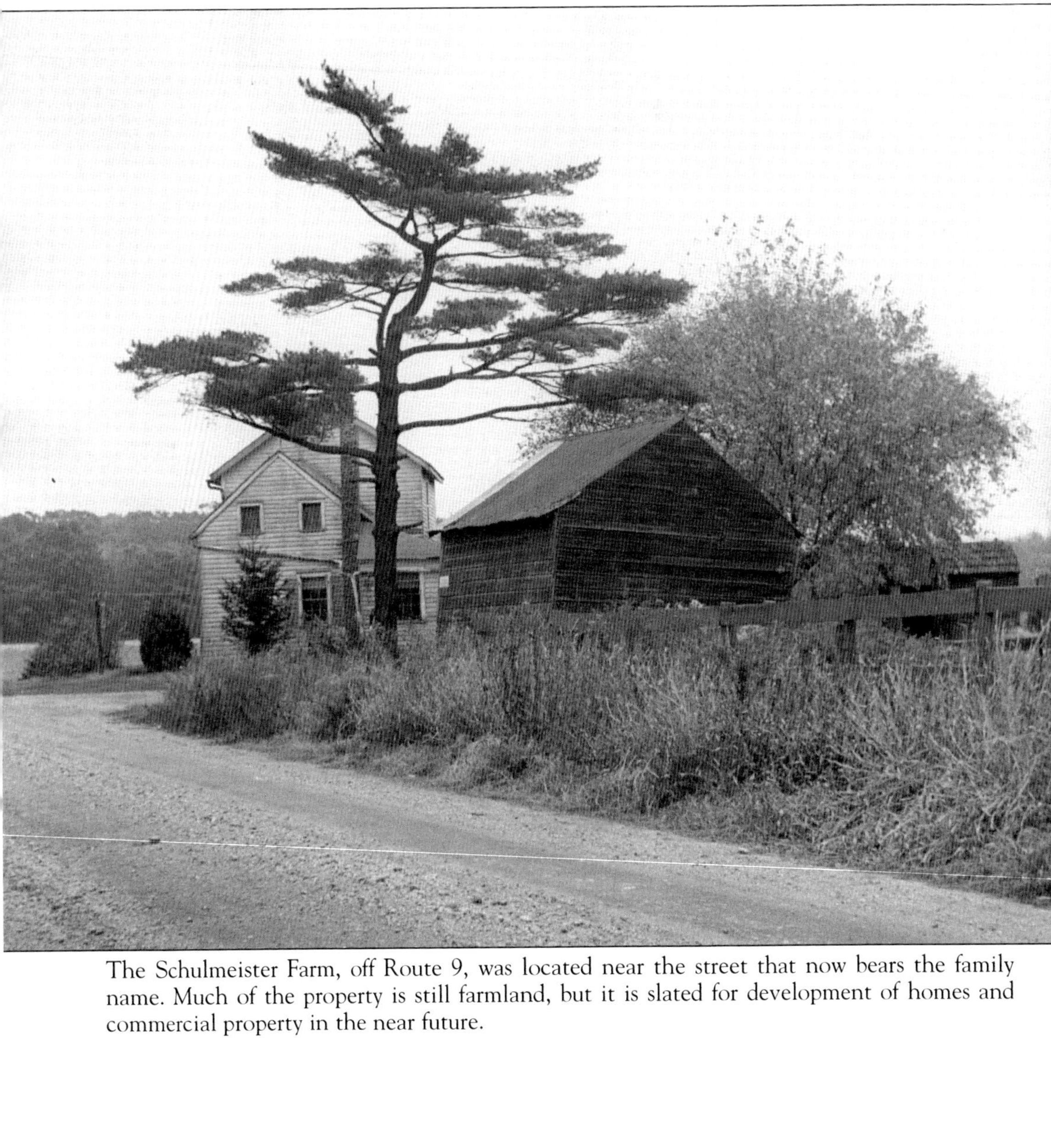

The Schulmeister Farm, off Route 9, was located near the street that now bears the family name. Much of the property is still farmland, but it is slated for development of homes and commercial property in the near future.

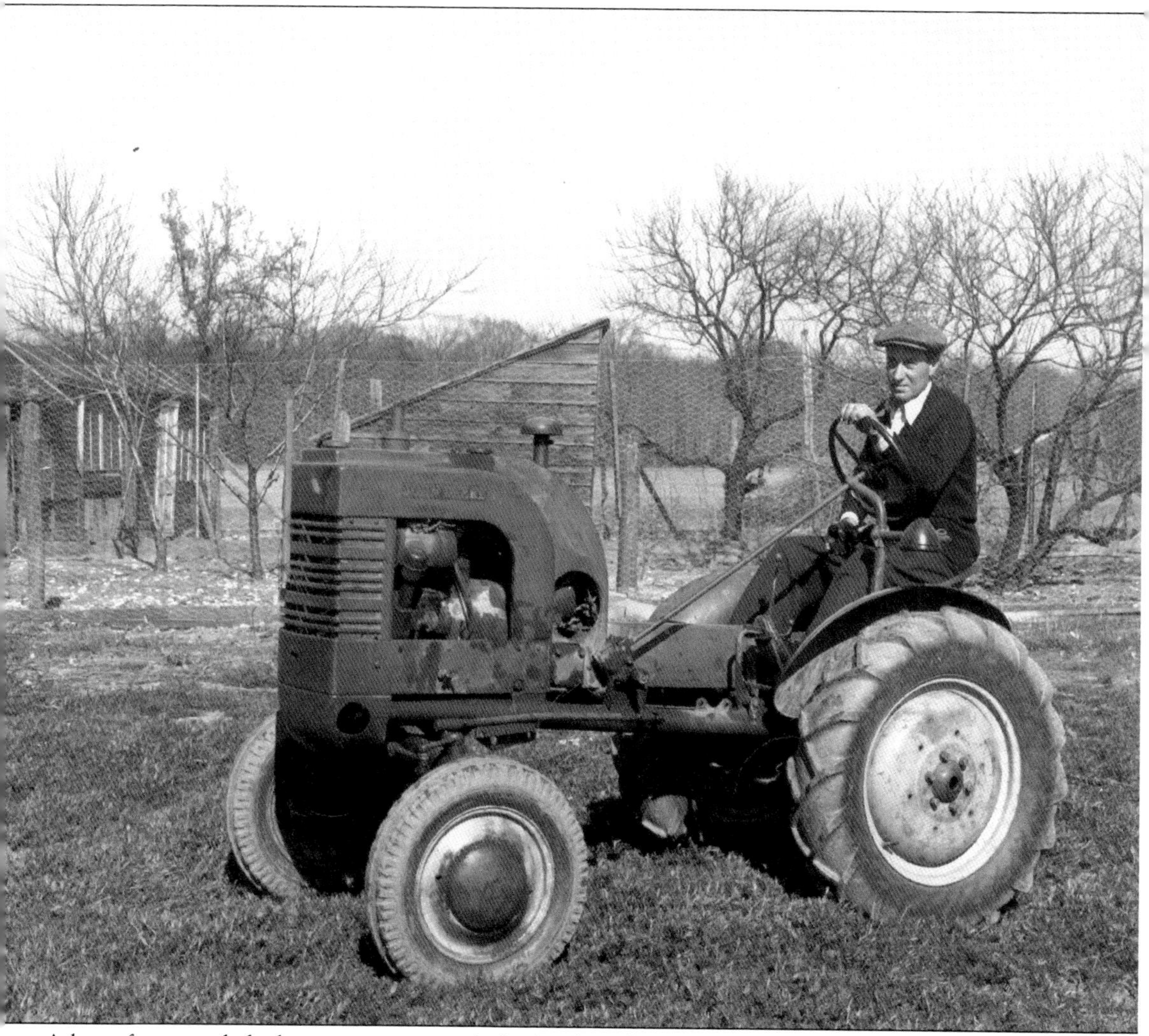

A large farm needed a large tractor to work the land. William Schulmeister shows off his tractor in this posed photograph.

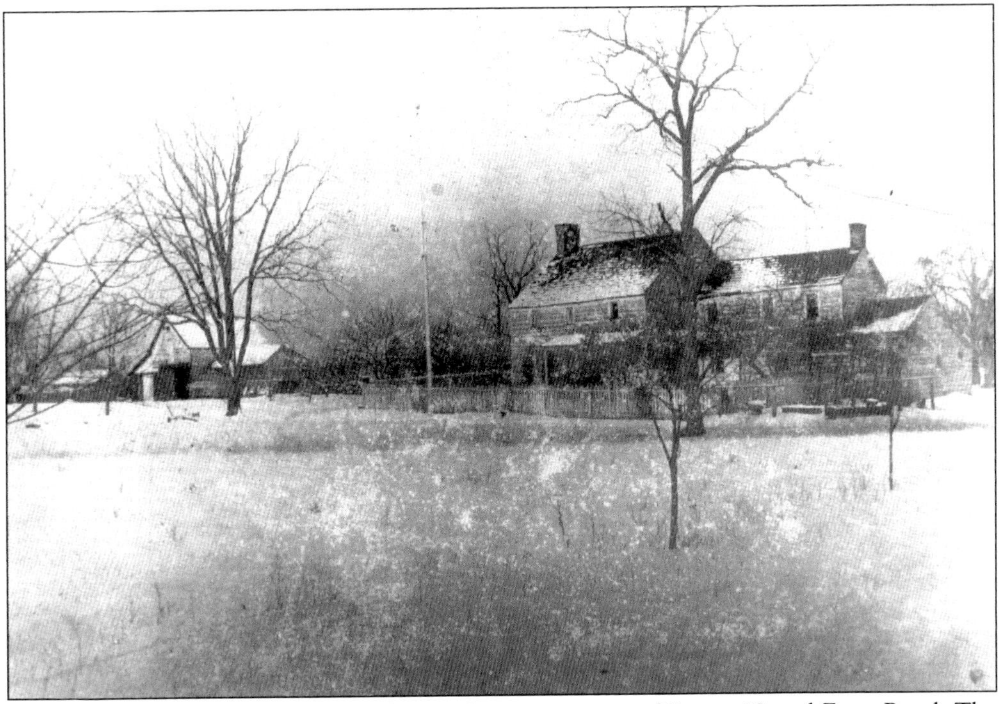

The Walter Green Farm was located near the intersection of Route 18 and Ferry Road. The Raritan Bay Medical Center occupies the site today.

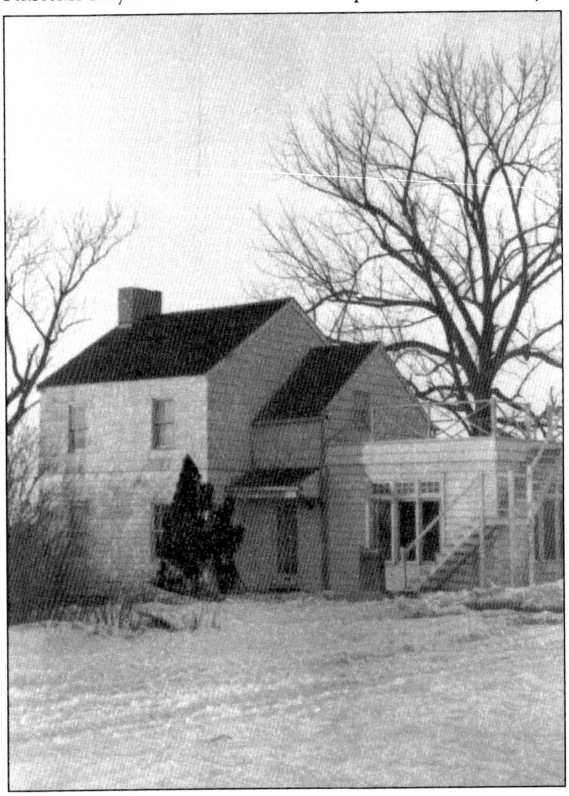

The Disbrow house still stands on Morristown Road near the street named for the farm, Disbrow Road. This photograph was taken in December 1949. Much of the area has changed, but the house is still recognizable.

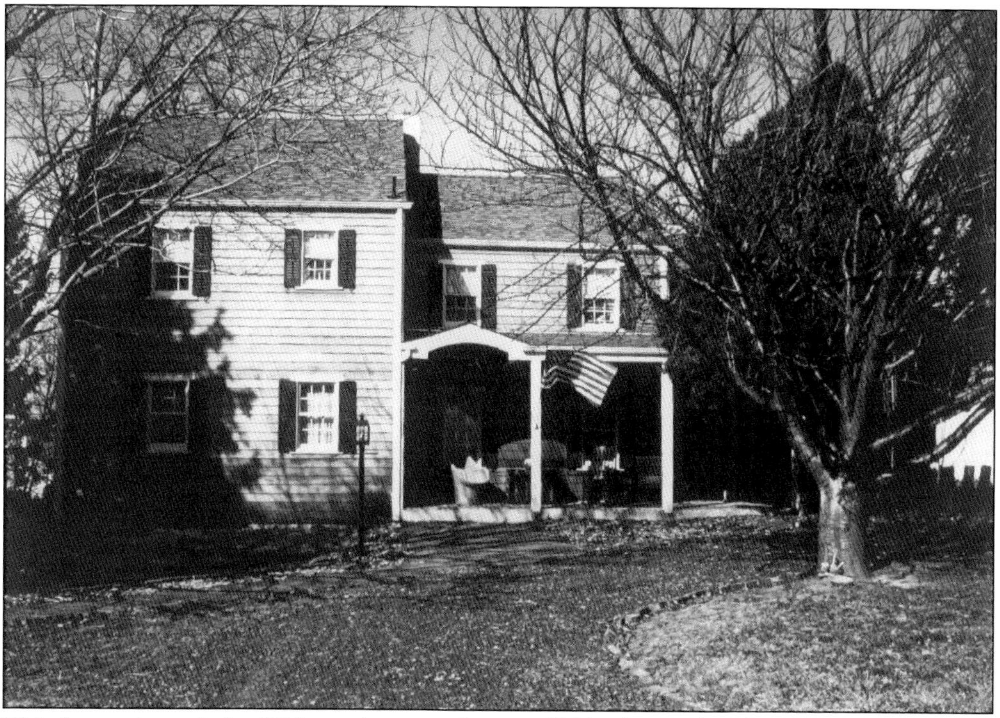

This later view of the Disbrow house, taken *c.* 1980, shows the changes over the years. Especially note the changes on the right side of the home.

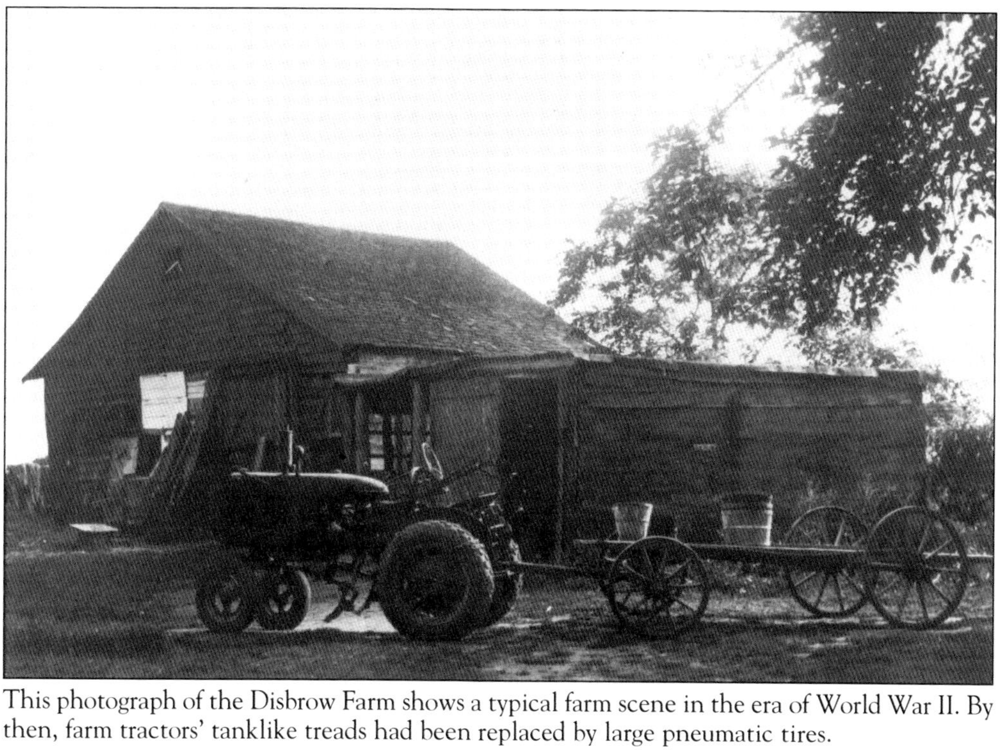

This photograph of the Disbrow Farm shows a typical farm scene in the era of World War II. By then, farm tractors' tanklike treads had been replaced by large pneumatic tires.

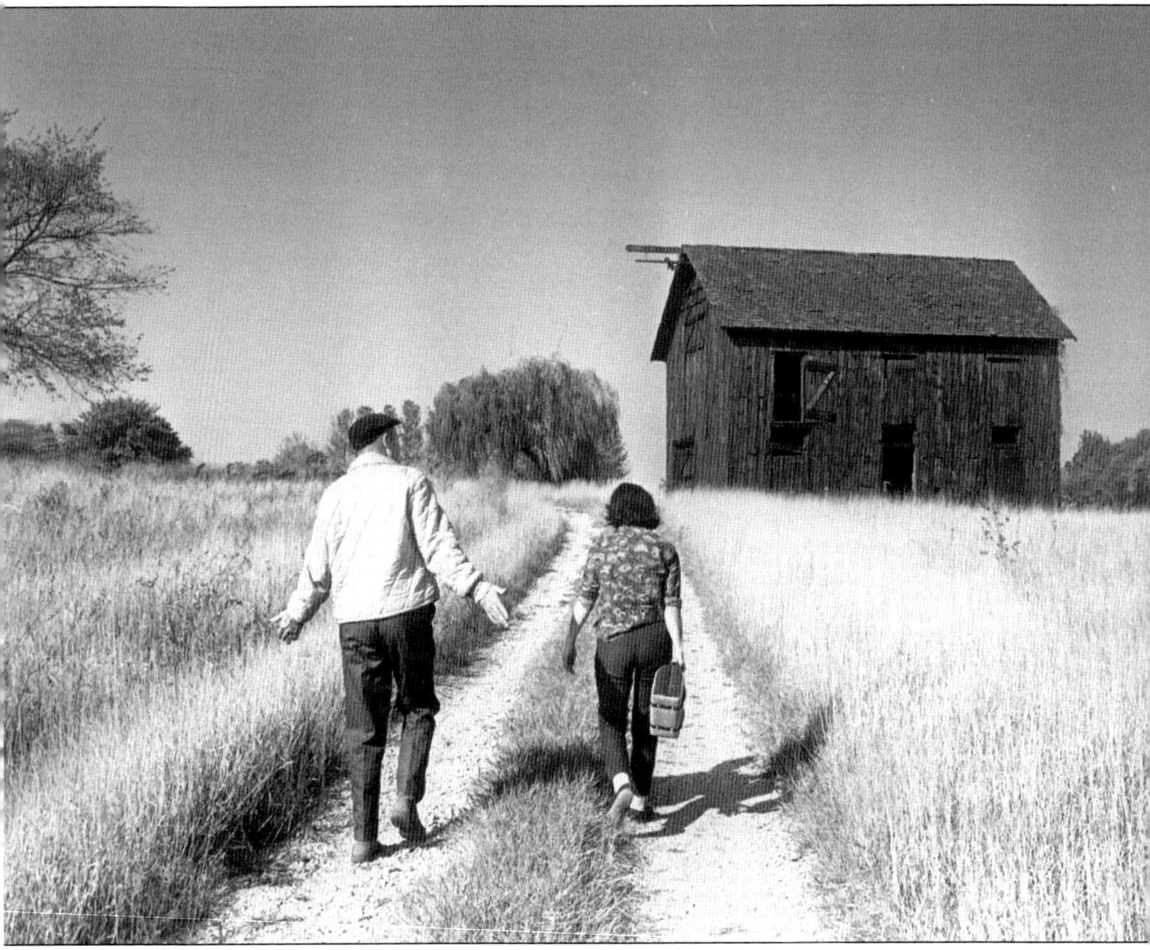

An unidentified couple appears to be arguing as they approach the barn at the Arrowsmith Farm. The Arrowsmith Farm was located on Route 34, west of Disbrow Road. If the barn appears to be on the verge of collapse, it was. It collapsed soon after this photograph was taken.

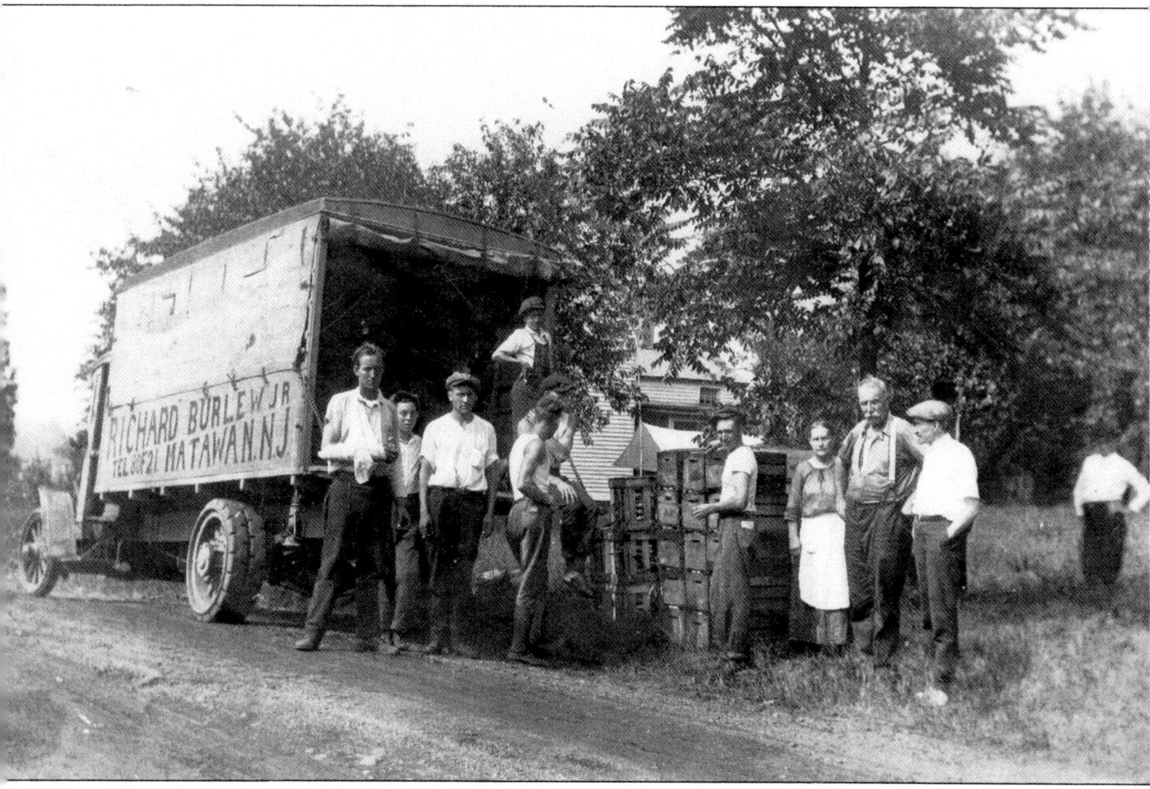

Richard Burlew transported produce by truck from many of the area farms to Perth Amboy and other nearby urban markets. This photograph was probably taken near Route 34 and Cottrell Road, where Cheesequake Farms is today.

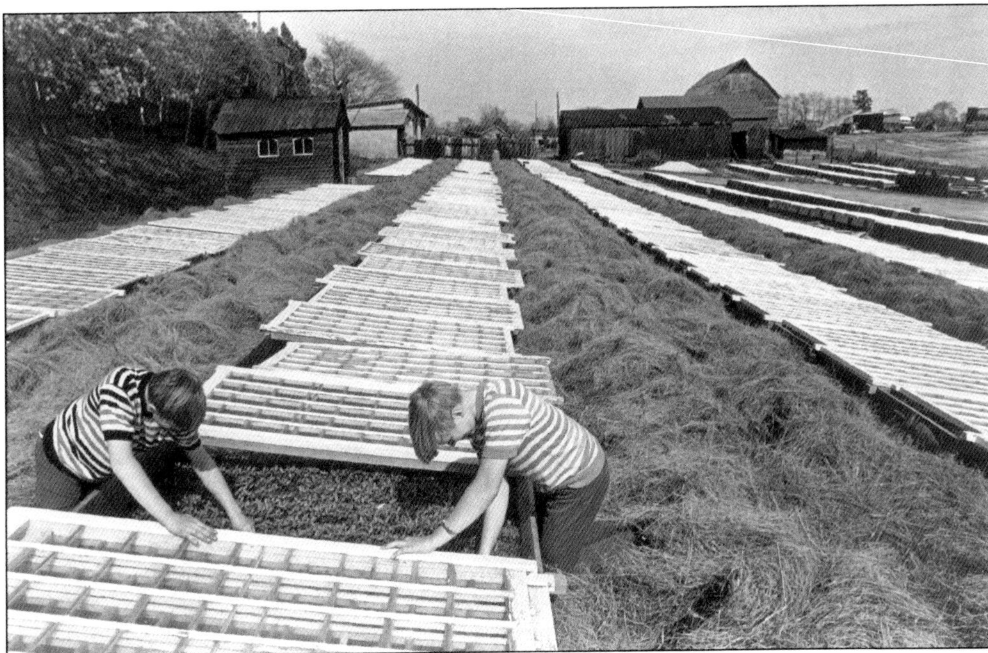

As in many farms throughout New Jersey, hotbeds were used to protect the seedlings in the spring. These young men are tending to one of the extensive beds on Farrington Farm.

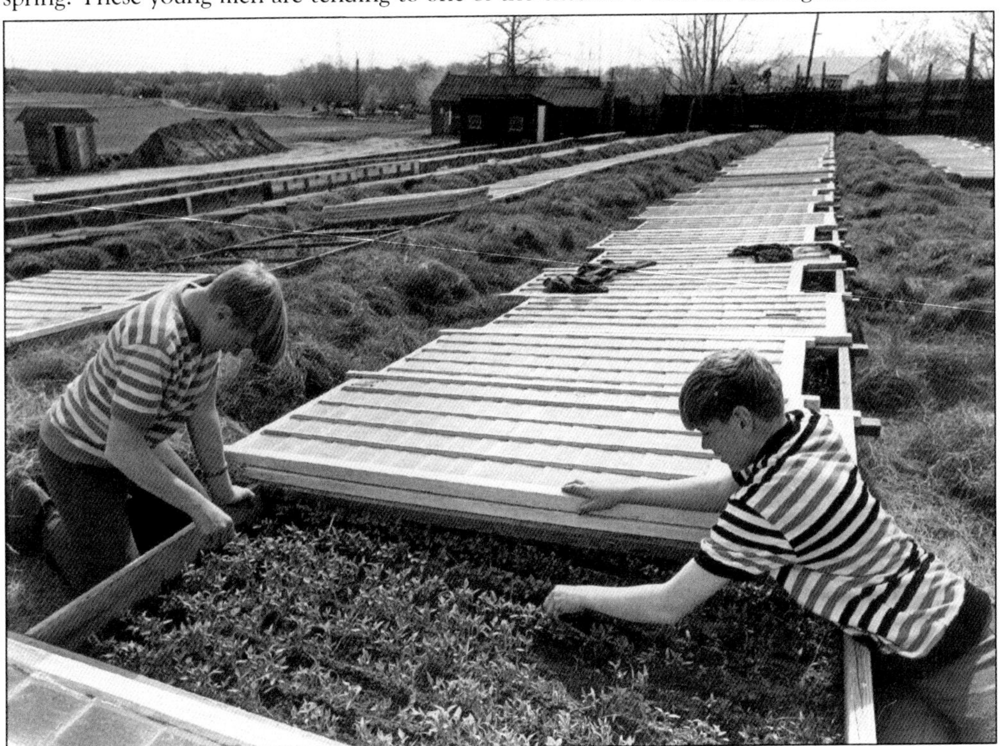

A close-up of the hotbeds on Farrington Farm shows the actual seedlings. When they were developed enough, the seedlings were transplanted and crop growing could begin. Why the matching shirts?

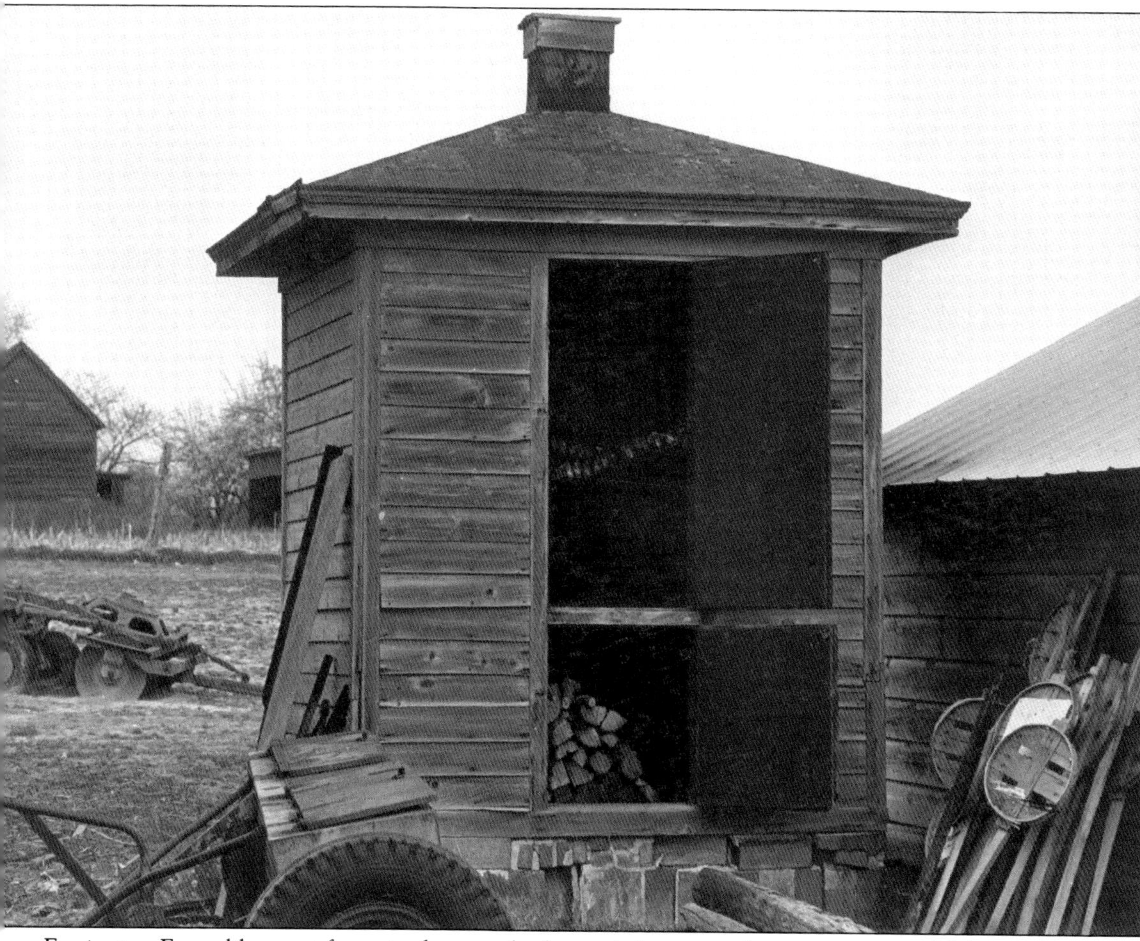

Farrington Farm, like most farms in the area, had a smokehouse used to cure meats and fish. The process helps preserve the meats and adds a smoky flavor. Smoking food is an art, not a science. Various woods heated at different temperatures are used to enhance the taste.

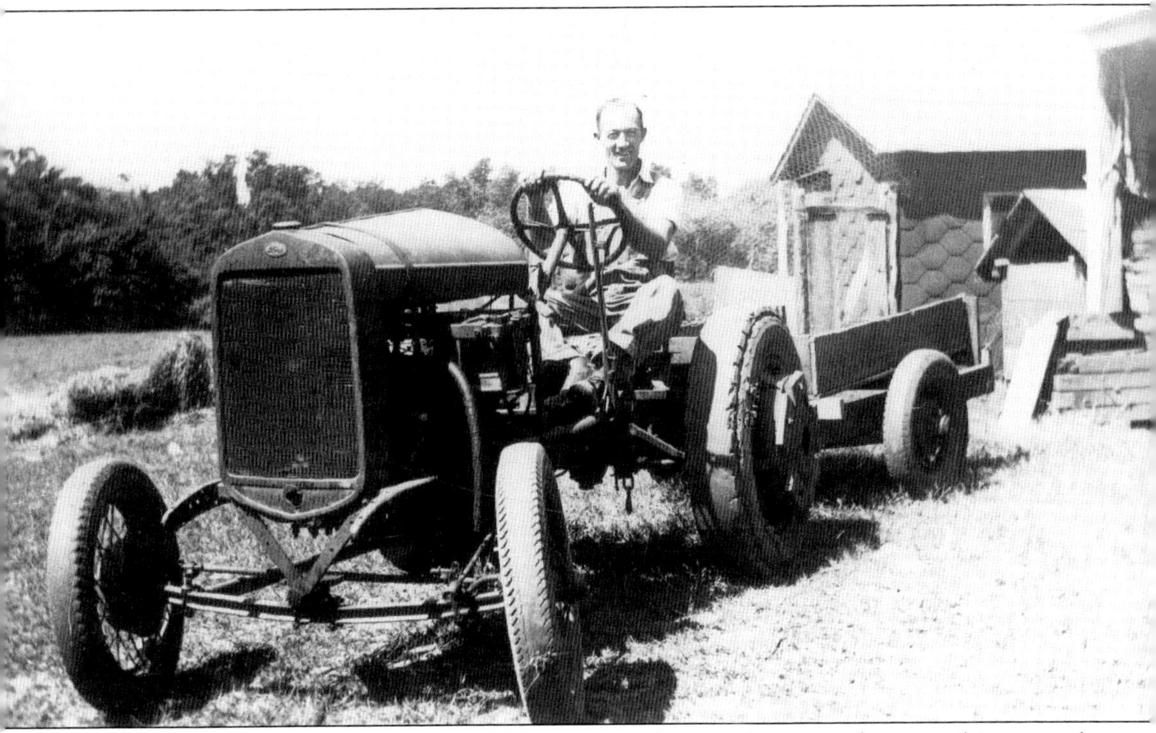

The Gaubs were a farming family that acquired many farms in the township over the years. Here, Walter Gaub (also pictured as a child on page 20) is seen riding his tractor in this 1928 photograph.

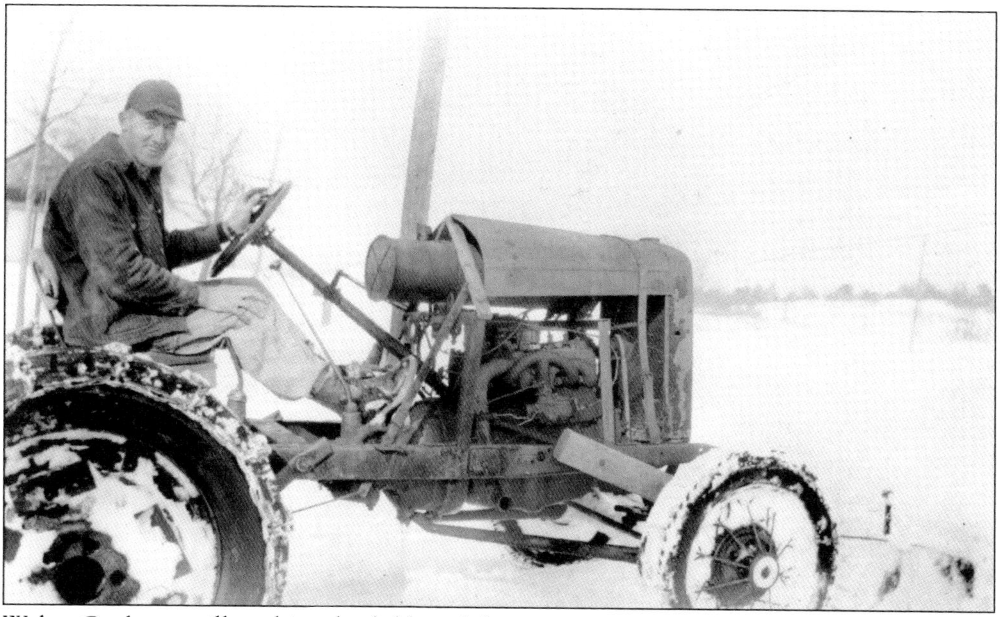

Walter Gaub was still working the fields with his tractor in 1948. This winter scene shows how farmers moved about their fields when ice and snow covered them. As on automobiles, chains were attached to the rear wheels of tractors to improve traction.

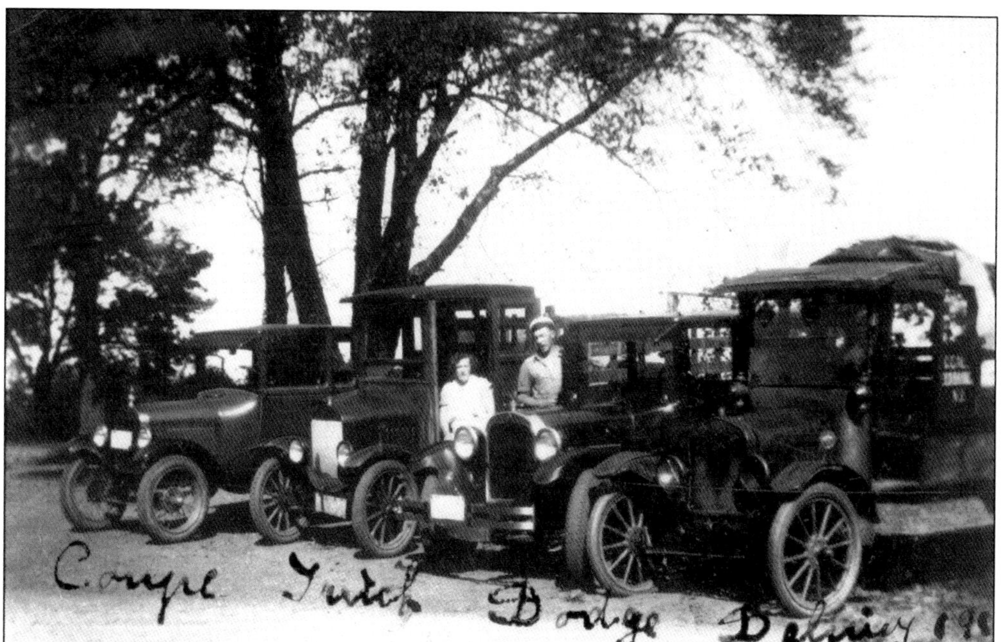

It would almost appear to be an antique automobile show on the Gaub Farm, except this photograph was taken in 1928, before the vehicles were antiques. The cars are identified as a coupe, a truck, a Dodge, and a delivery vehicle.

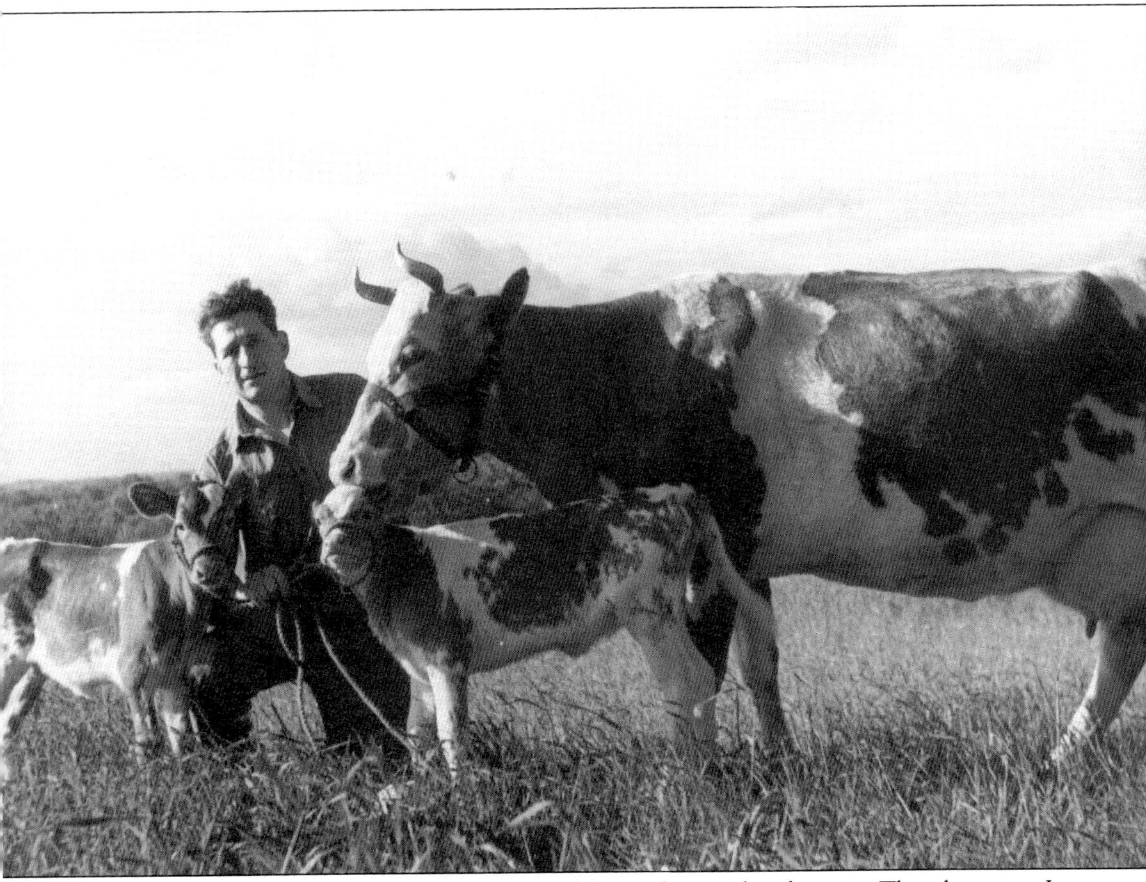

Otto Gaub looks over one of his cows and her calves at his farm on Throckmorton Lane. The farm was located across the street from the Fountain House, where St. Ambrose Church stands today.

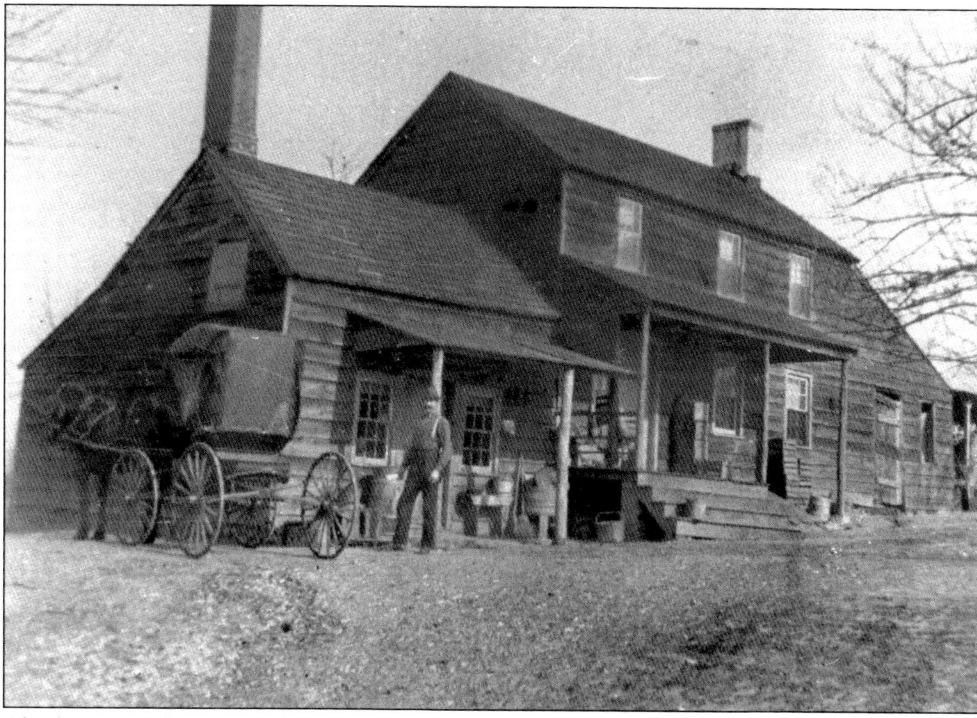

Charles Brown had a farm near the intersection of Schulmeister Road and Old Mill Road. Note the covered buggy to the left. Brown sold the farm to his nephew James Burlew. The house was located on the hill behind the Little League fields on Schulmeister Road.

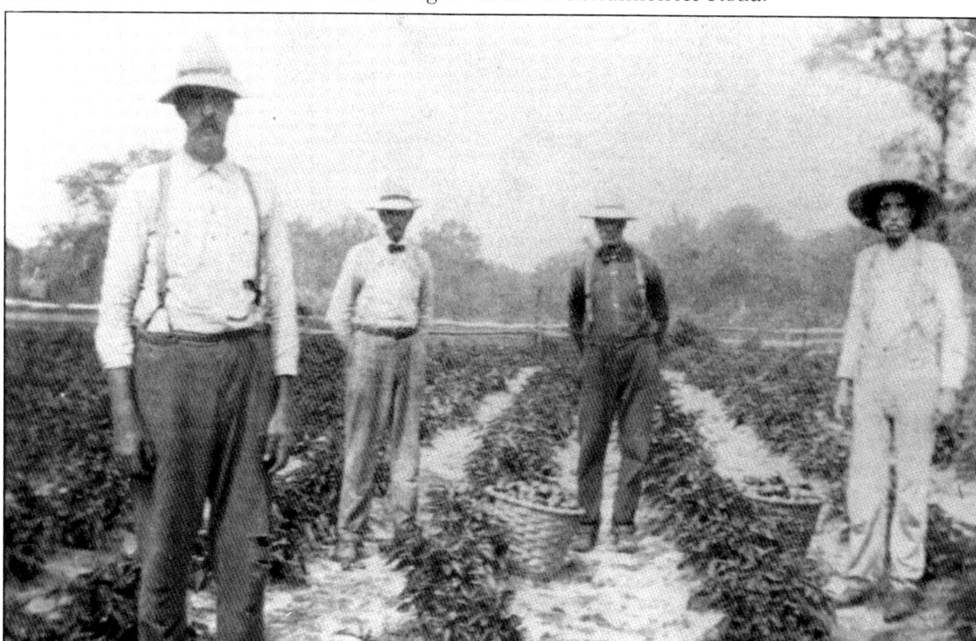

The Clayton Brothers Farm was located on 156 acres between Texas Road and Greystone Road. Elmer Clayton (left) and three others pause from the tedious and difficult job of picking tomatoes. None of them look too happy at their task.

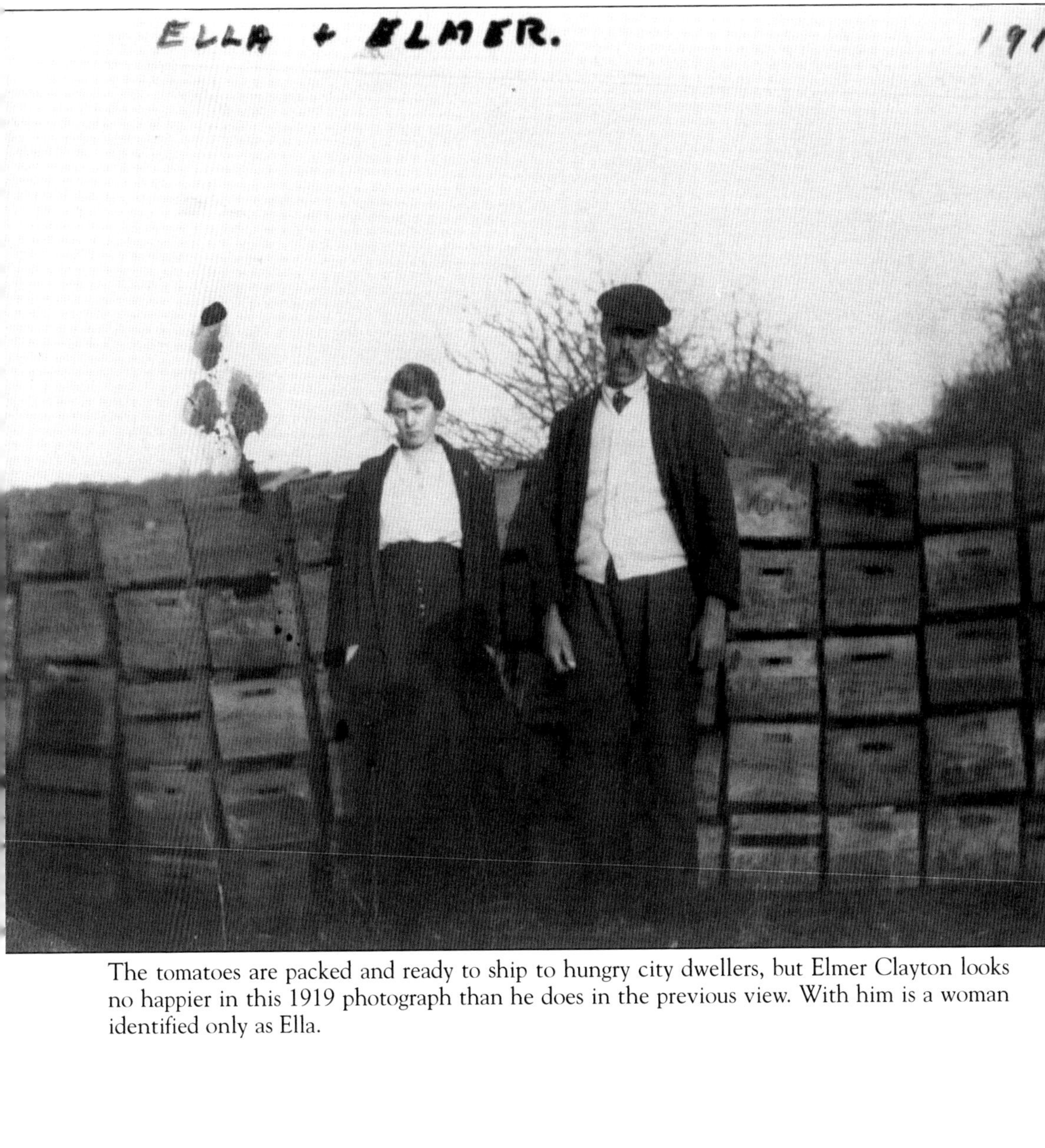

The tomatoes are packed and ready to ship to hungry city dwellers, but Elmer Clayton looks no happier in this 1919 photograph than he does in the previous view. With him is a woman identified only as Ella.

Three

BUSINESS AND INDUSTRY

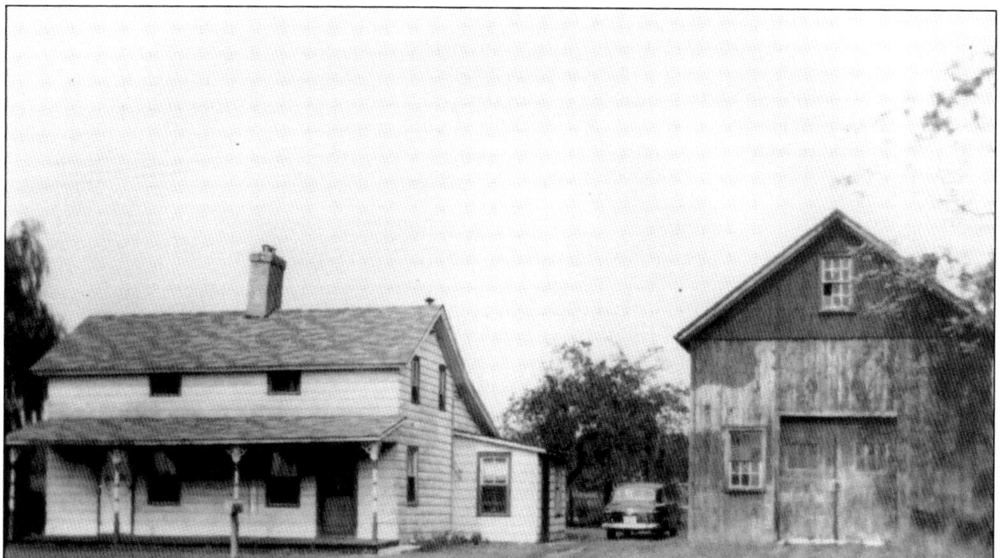

Blacksmiths were an absolute necessity for both farmers and tradesmen before the age of automobiles and tractors. Daniel Gaub operated a blacksmith shop on Route 34 near Cottrell Road. The shop has disappeared, but his home, shown on the left, still stands.

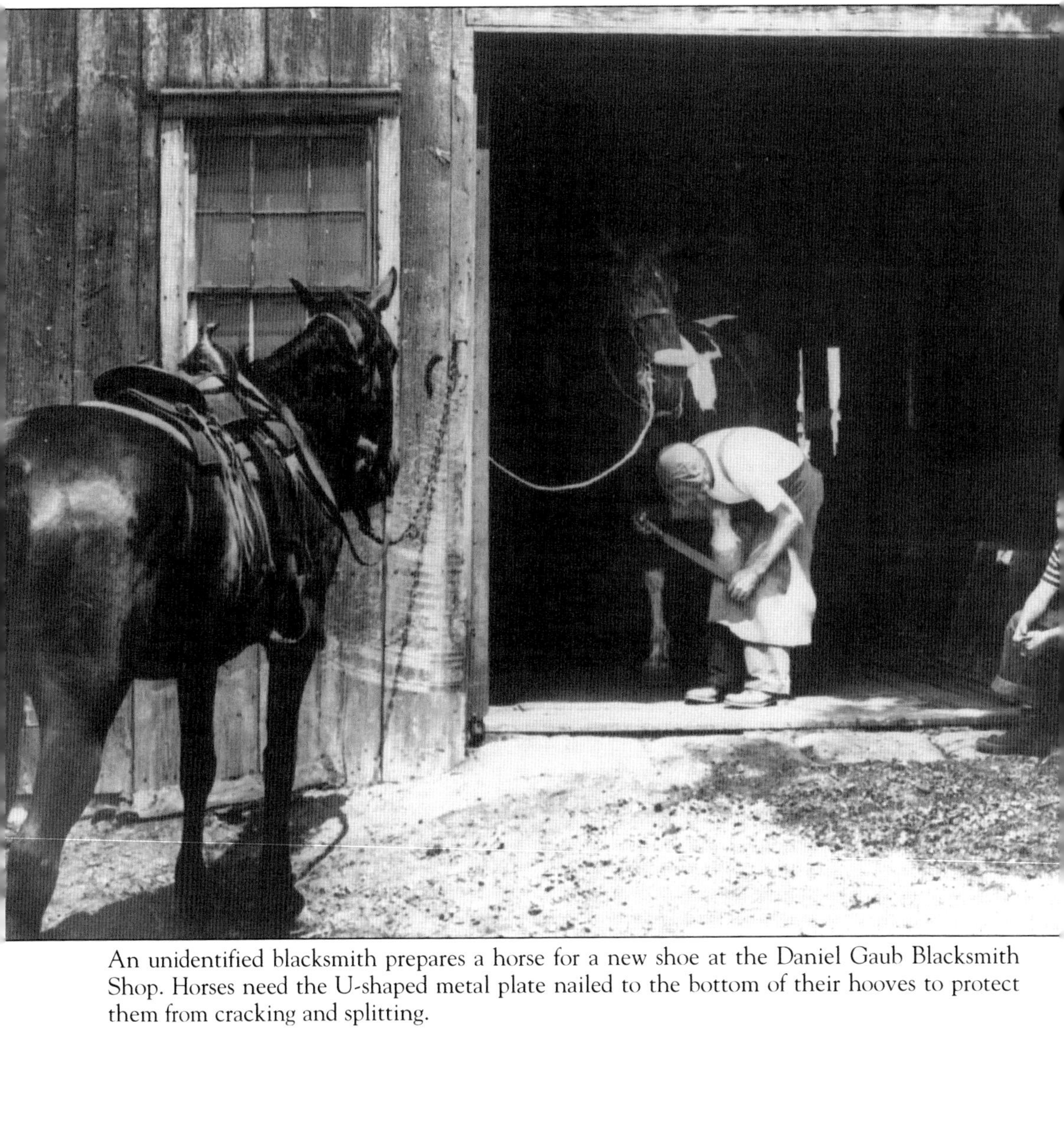

An unidentified blacksmith prepares a horse for a new shoe at the Daniel Gaub Blacksmith Shop. Horses need the U-shaped metal plate nailed to the bottom of their hooves to protect them from cracking and splitting.

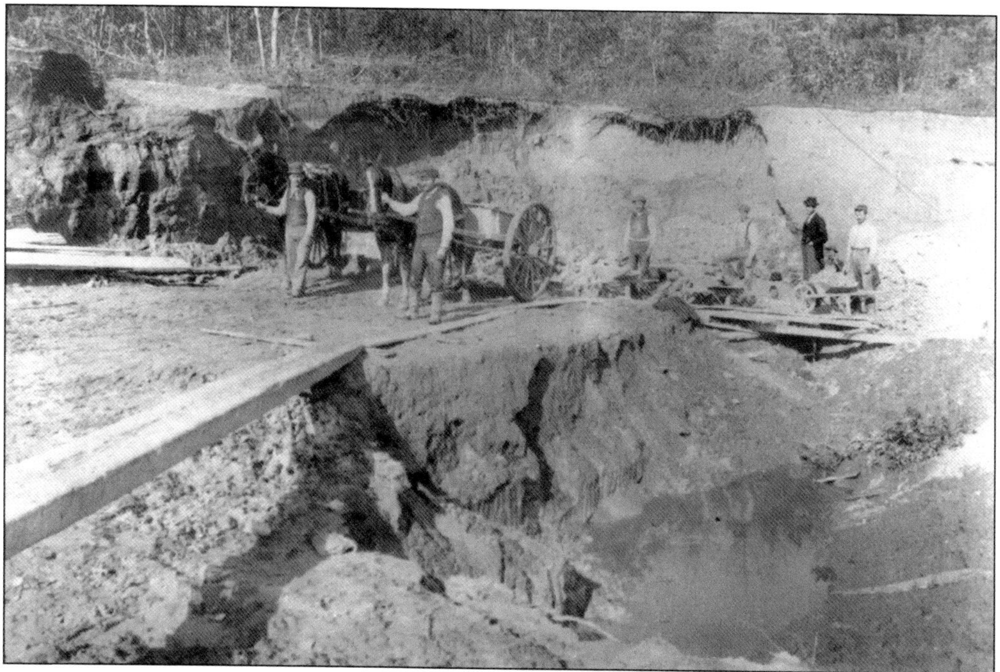

The clay soil in the area surrounding Old Bridge was used for pottery and bricks even before the arrival of the first European settlers. By the 1800s, clay was a major industry. Many of the small ponds in the area are actually the remains of pits dug to extract clay. The Perrine clay pit was located near Route 9 and Ernston Road.

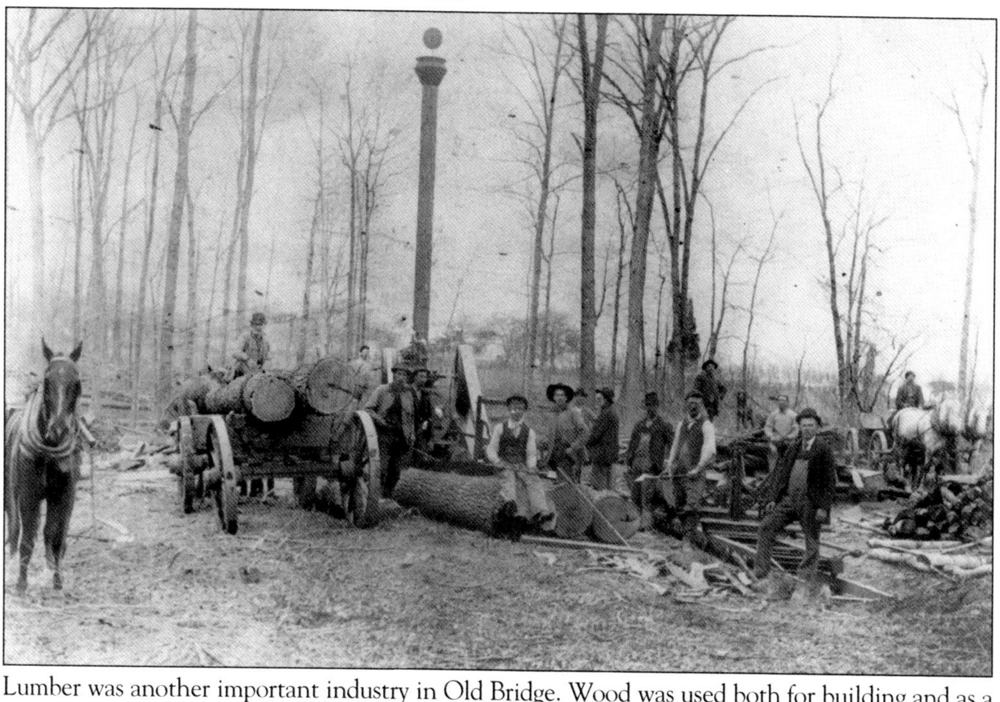

Lumber was another important industry in Old Bridge. Wood was used both for building and as a heat source. An unusual saw pit was located off Englishtown Road. The logs were lowered into the saw pit and fed into a steam-driven saw. Note the steam pipe in the center of the photograph.

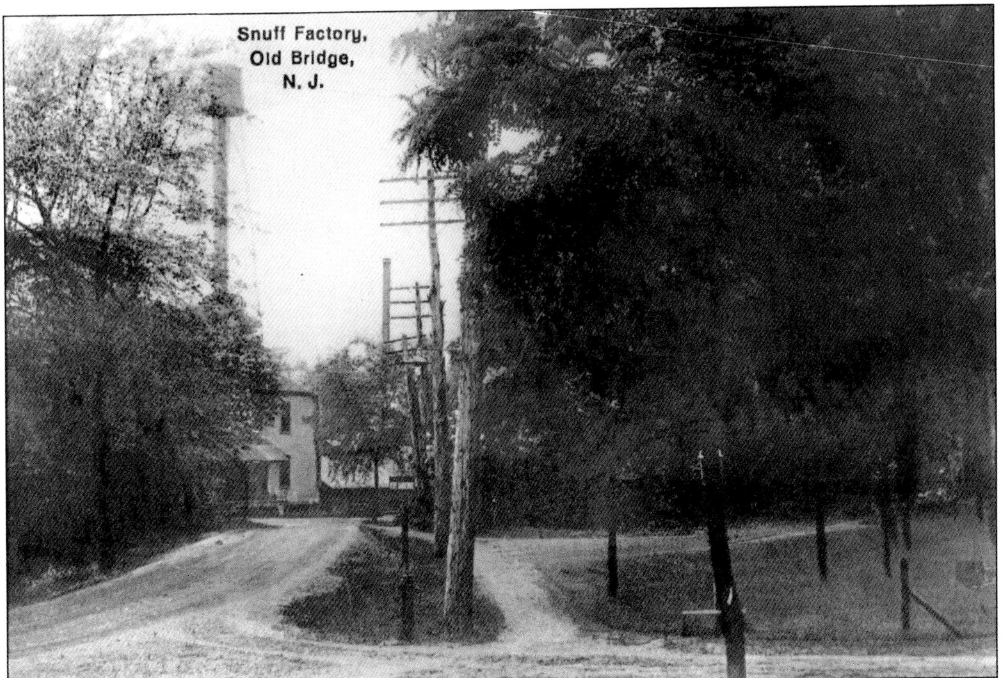

There were many snuff tobacco mills in the area, and at least two in Old Bridge. In fact, the nearby township of Helmetta was named for the Helmetta Tobacco Company, which produced snuff tobacco there until the 1990s. The Washington Snuff Mill, seen here, was later known as the Dill Snuff Mill.

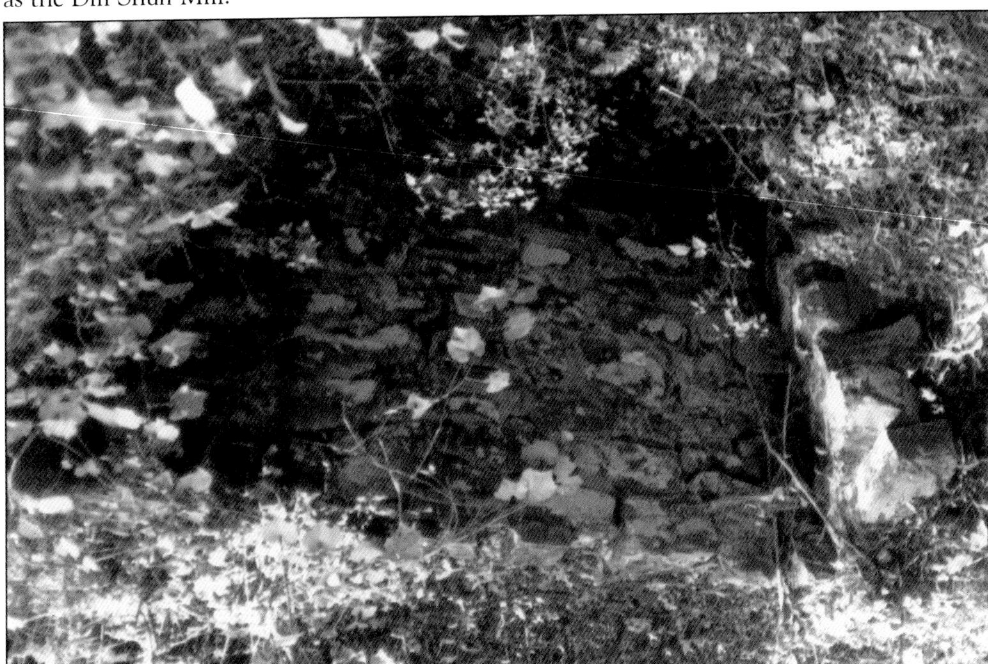

Time and the elements have reduced the Dill Snuff Mill to a few brick foundations and walls today. The mill was located off Route 516, along Deep Run, which it used for its power source.

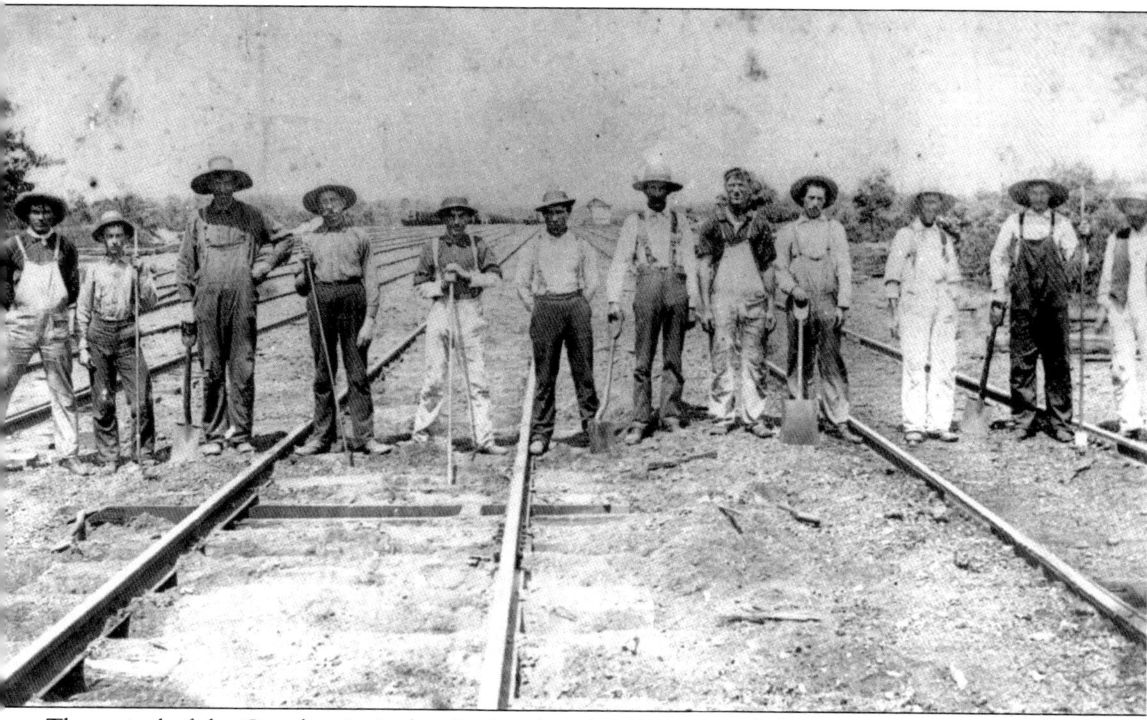

The arrival of the Camden & Amboy Railroad in the 1800s provided much needed work and cash for laborers in the Old Bridge area. The work was backbreaking, but the men were used to working hard, either on the farms or in the villages. The break the men took to pose for this photograph was probably well deserved.

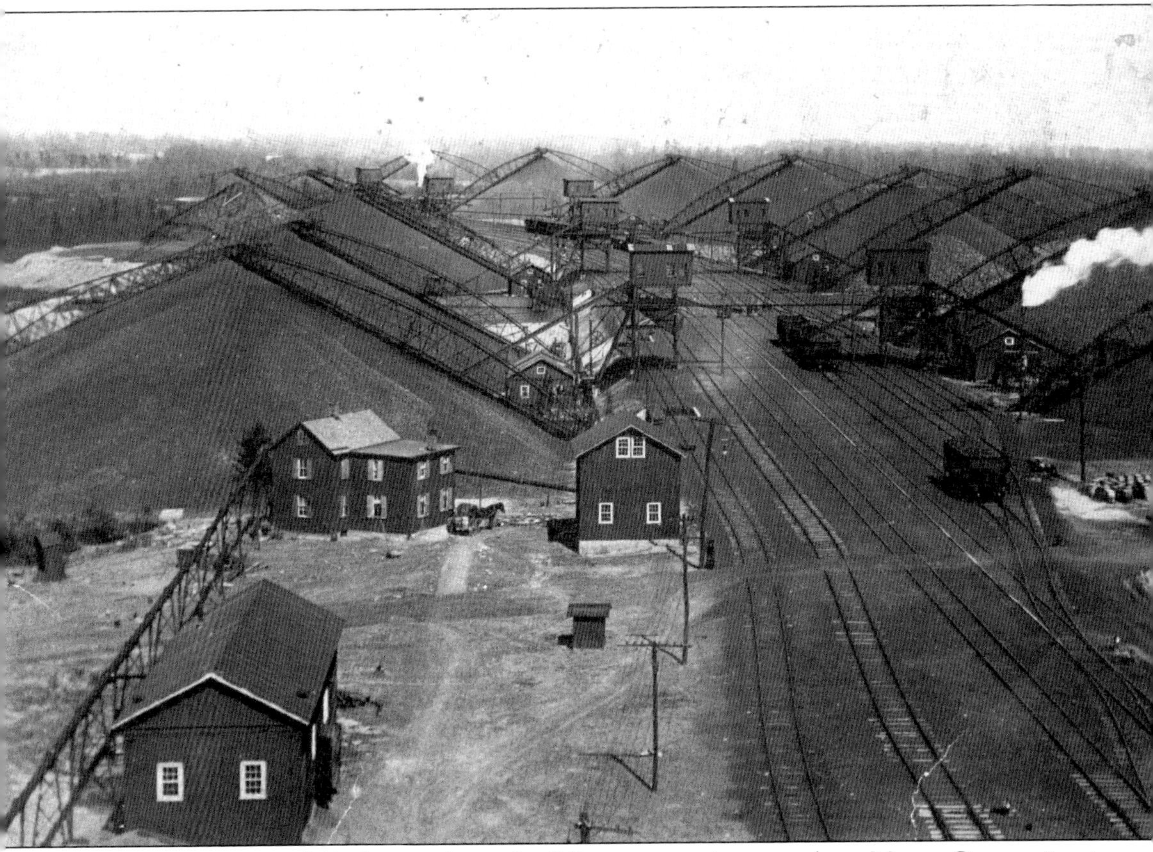

The Runyon Coal Yards were located off Browntown Avenue where Manzo Contracting is located today. Before trains ran on diesel fuel and electricity, coal yards were a necessary and dirty evil along the rail lines.

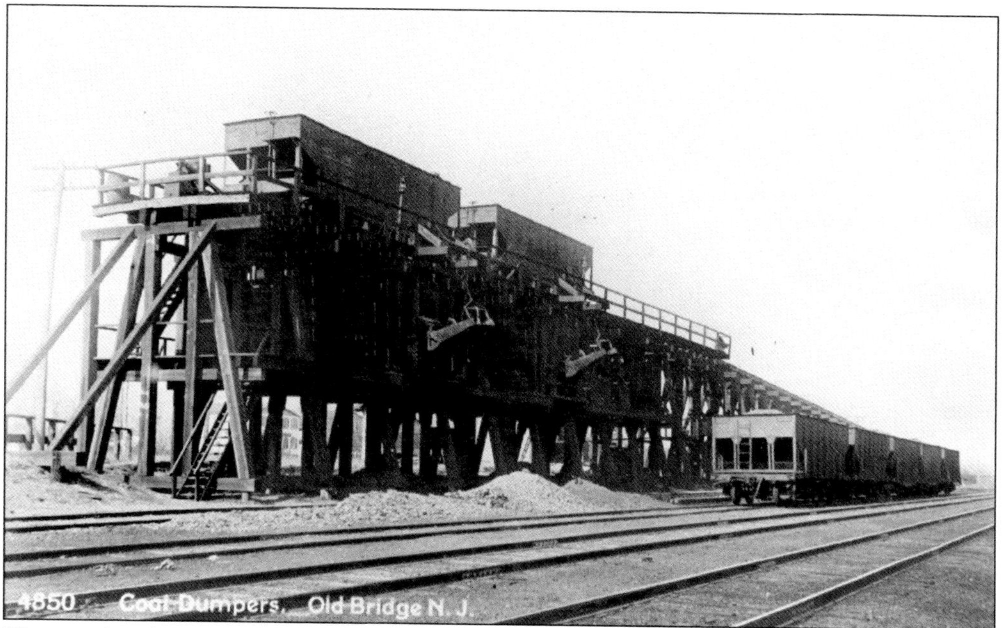

These railroad cars at the Runyon Coal Yard were used to transport the coal from the yard to the docks at South Amboy on the Raritan Bay. The coal was then loaded onto barges and shipped to New York City.

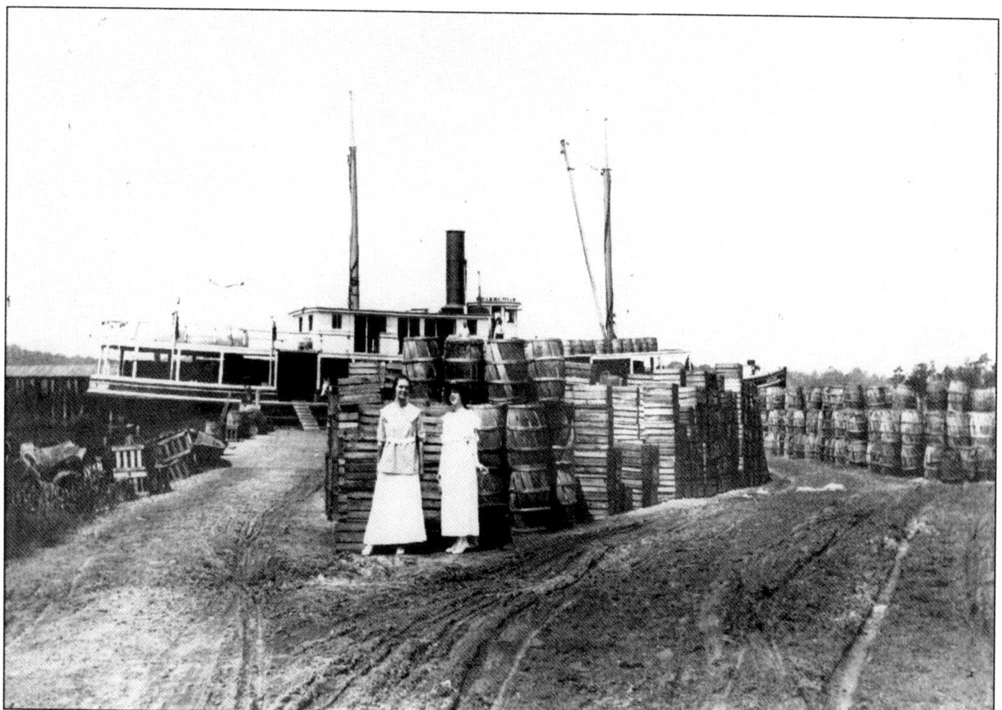

Another important means of transportation in Old Bridge was the steamship. Area farmers transported their goods to Steamboat Landing, located at the foot of Dock Road on the Cheesequake Creek. The goods were then shipped down the creek and across the Raritan Bay to New York City and other nearby ports.

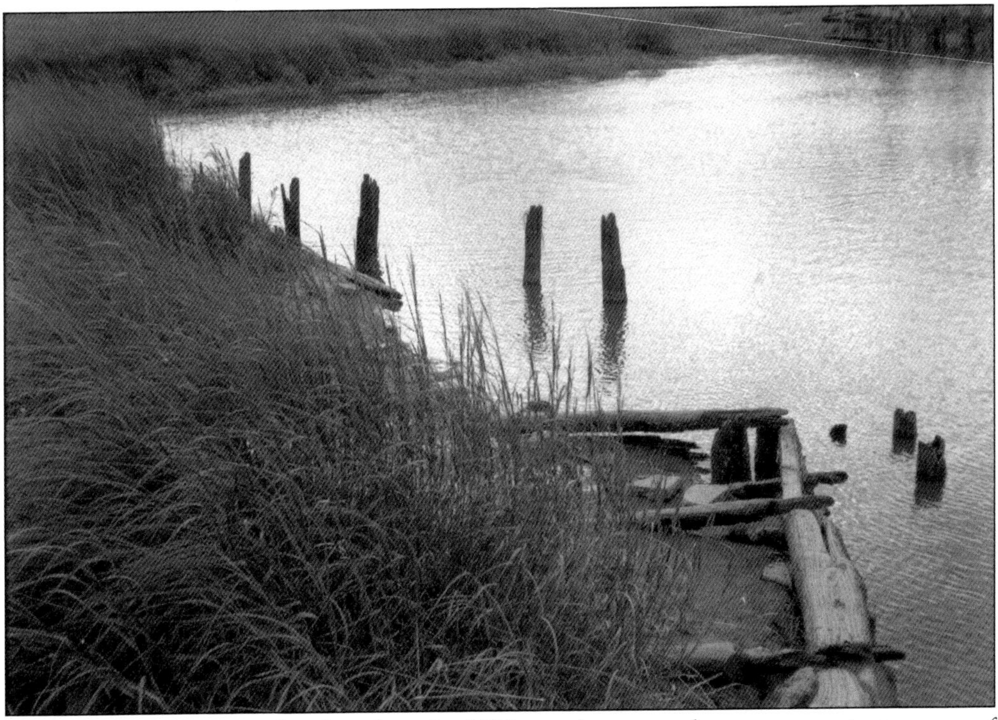

Steamboat Landing was abandoned in the 1920s as cheaper and more convenient means of transportation came about. Today, only a few pilings at the end of Dock Road remind us where it stood. Dock Road is now closed to vehicles, but you can still access it by foot.

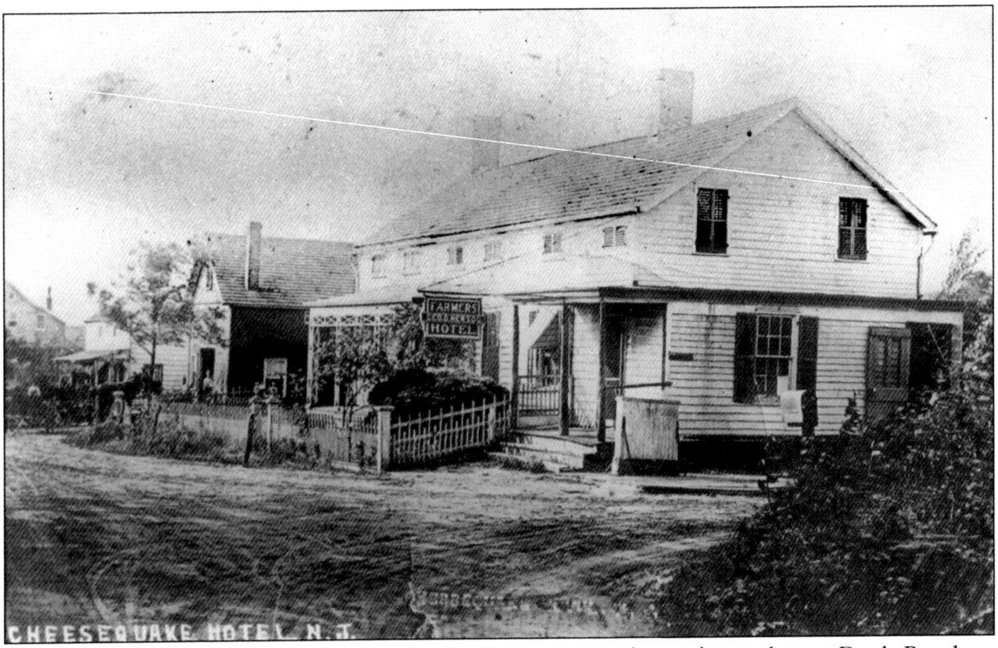

The Cheesequake Hotel, also known as the Farmer's Hotel, was located near Dock Road on Route 34, and many a farmer must have stopped for a bite or drink when transporting their merchandise to Steamboat Landing. The first town meeting was held here in 1869.

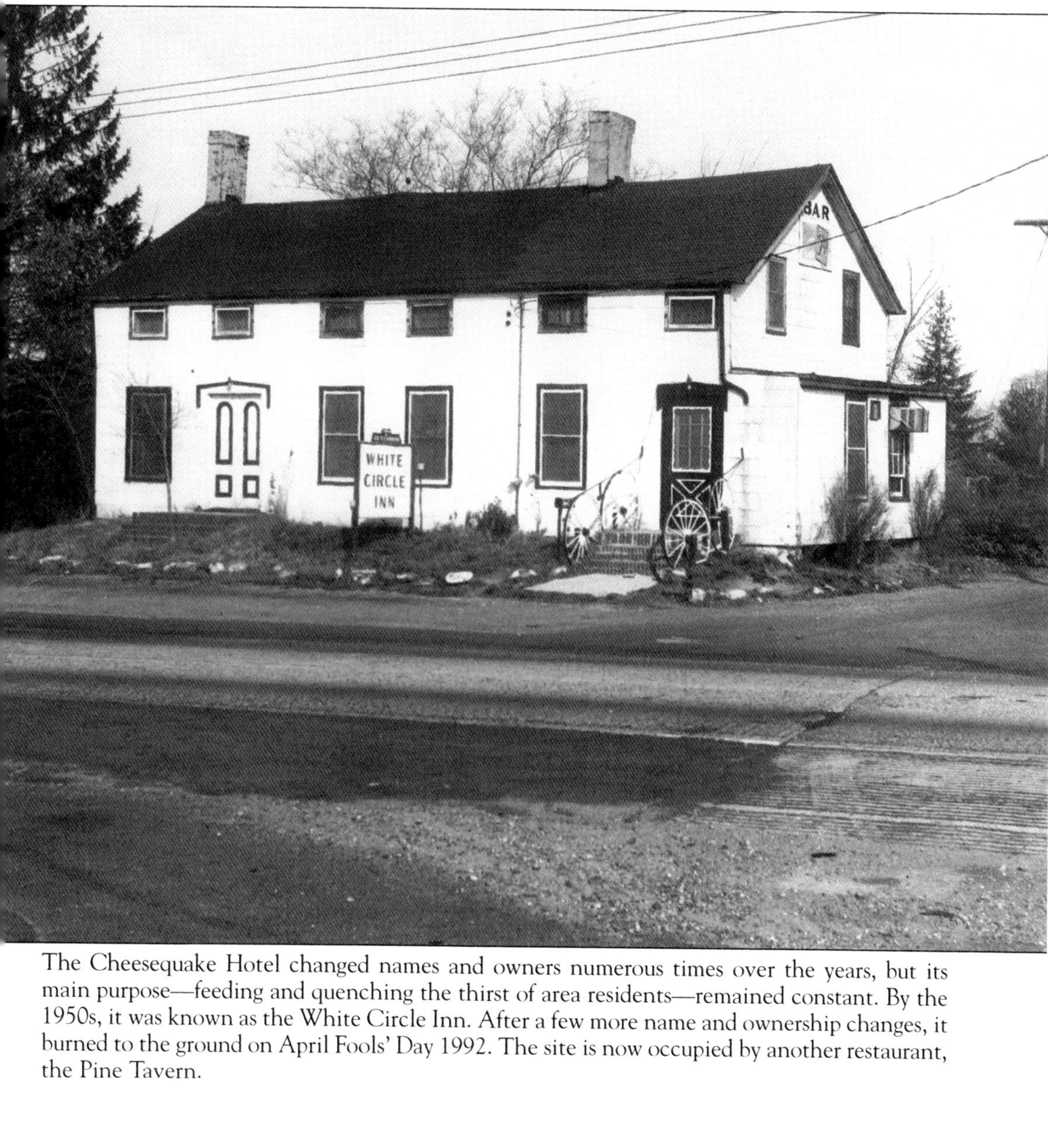

The Cheesequake Hotel changed names and owners numerous times over the years, but its main purpose—feeding and quenching the thirst of area residents—remained constant. By the 1950s, it was known as the White Circle Inn. After a few more name and ownership changes, it burned to the ground on April Fools' Day 1992. The site is now occupied by another restaurant, the Pine Tavern.

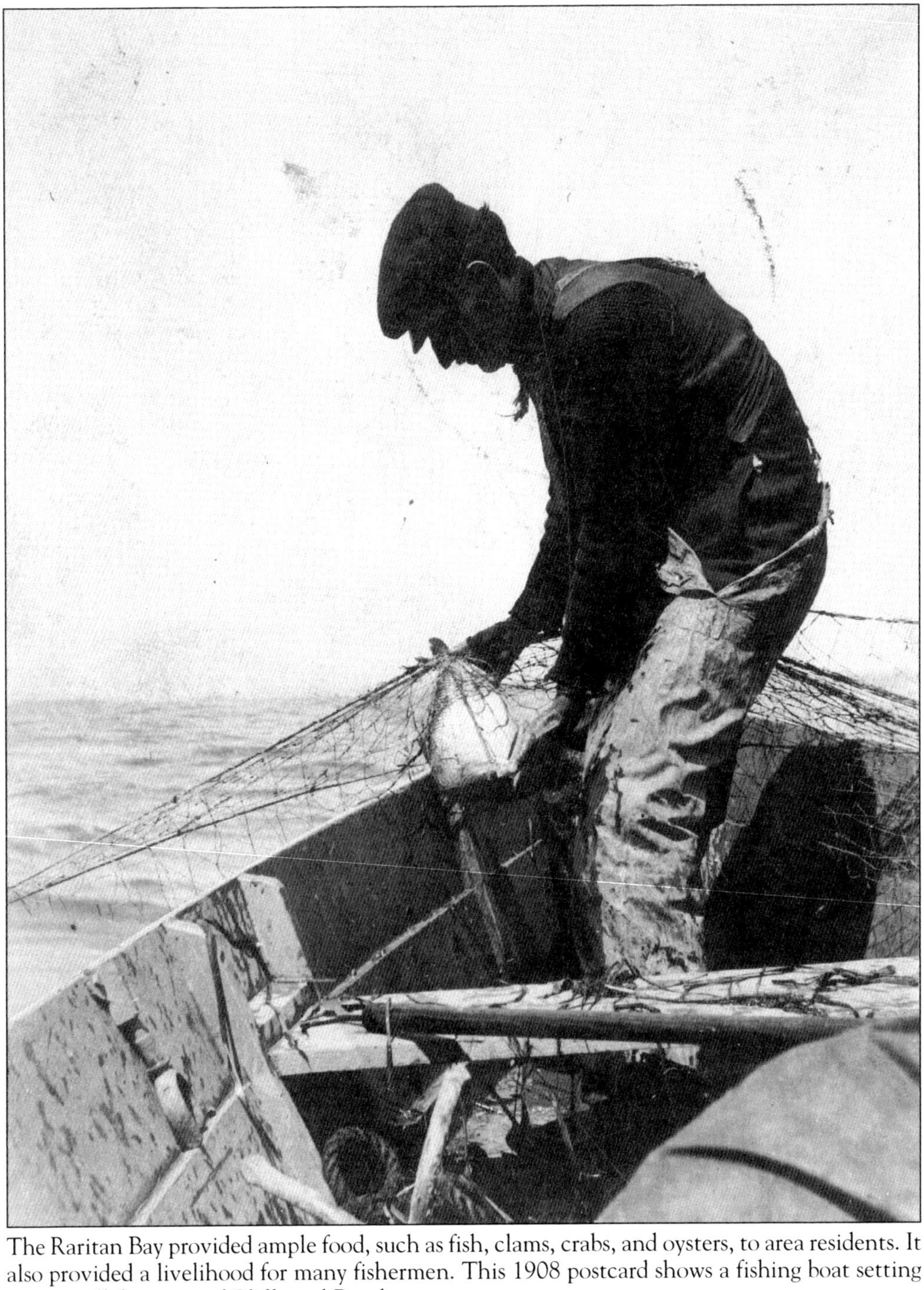

The Raritan Bay provided ample food, such as fish, clams, crabs, and oysters, to area residents. It also provided a livelihood for many fishermen. This 1908 postcard shows a fishing boat setting its nets off the coast of Cliffwood Beach.

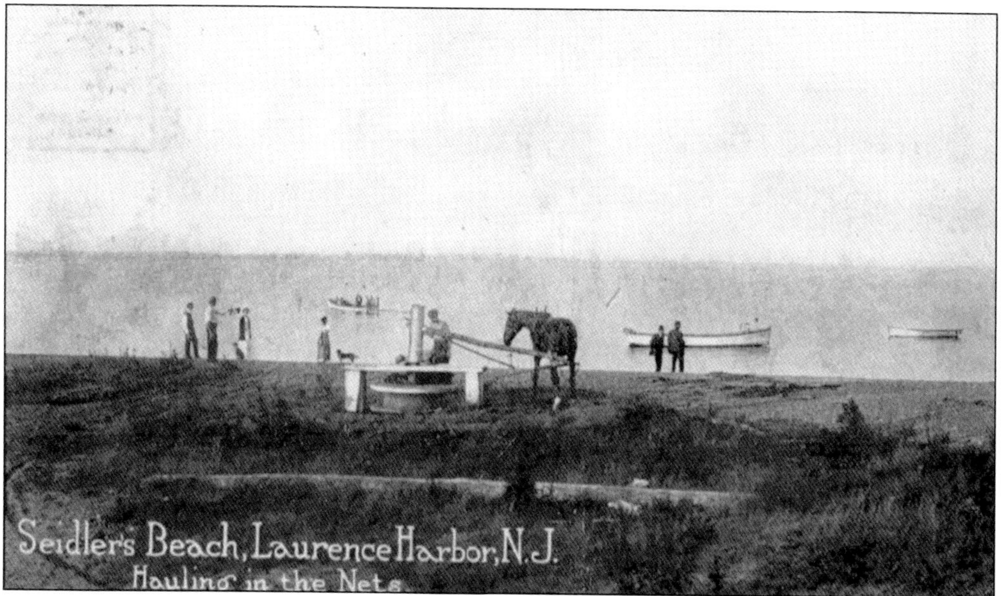

Real horsepower was used to haul in the fishing nets at Laurence Harbor. The sender of this 1914 postcard wrote, "They caught thirty bushels of blue and weak fish this afternoon." Both species are still found in the Raritan Bay today, but not in that abundance.

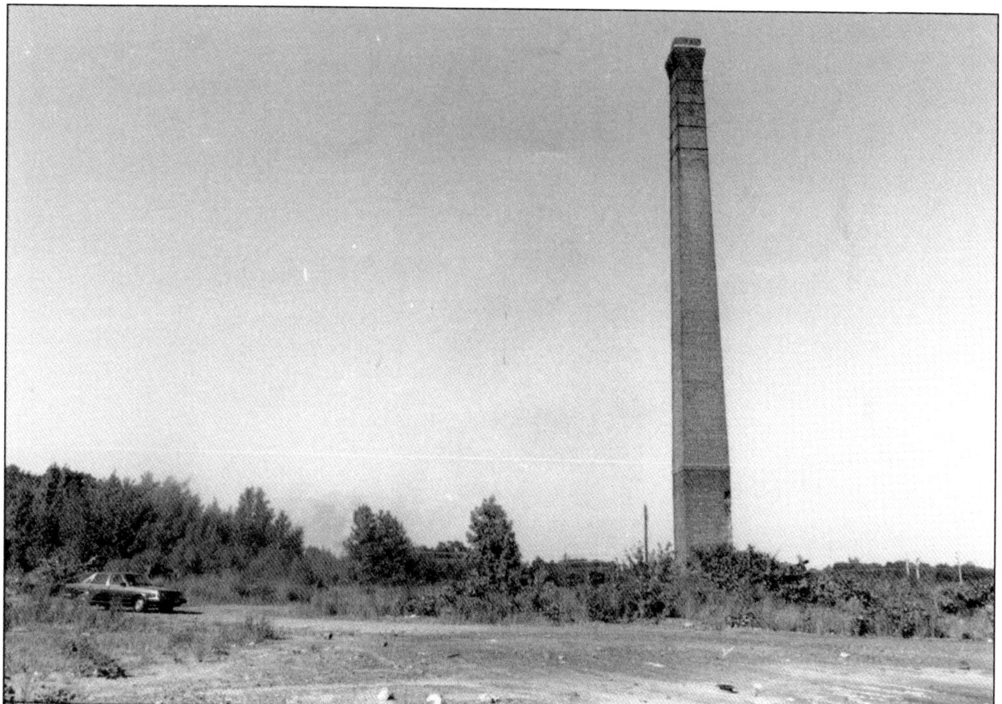
The Ochwald Brickworks in Laurence Harbor began operation in 1910. However, a brickyard existed at the sight at least 30 years earlier. Its 60 workers produced more than 84,000 bricks per day at its height in the early 1900s. It continued in operation until the early 1960s. After a short while, only the tall, red-brick chimney was standing along Laurence Parkway near the railroad tracks. It, too, has vanished, and houses now occupy the site.

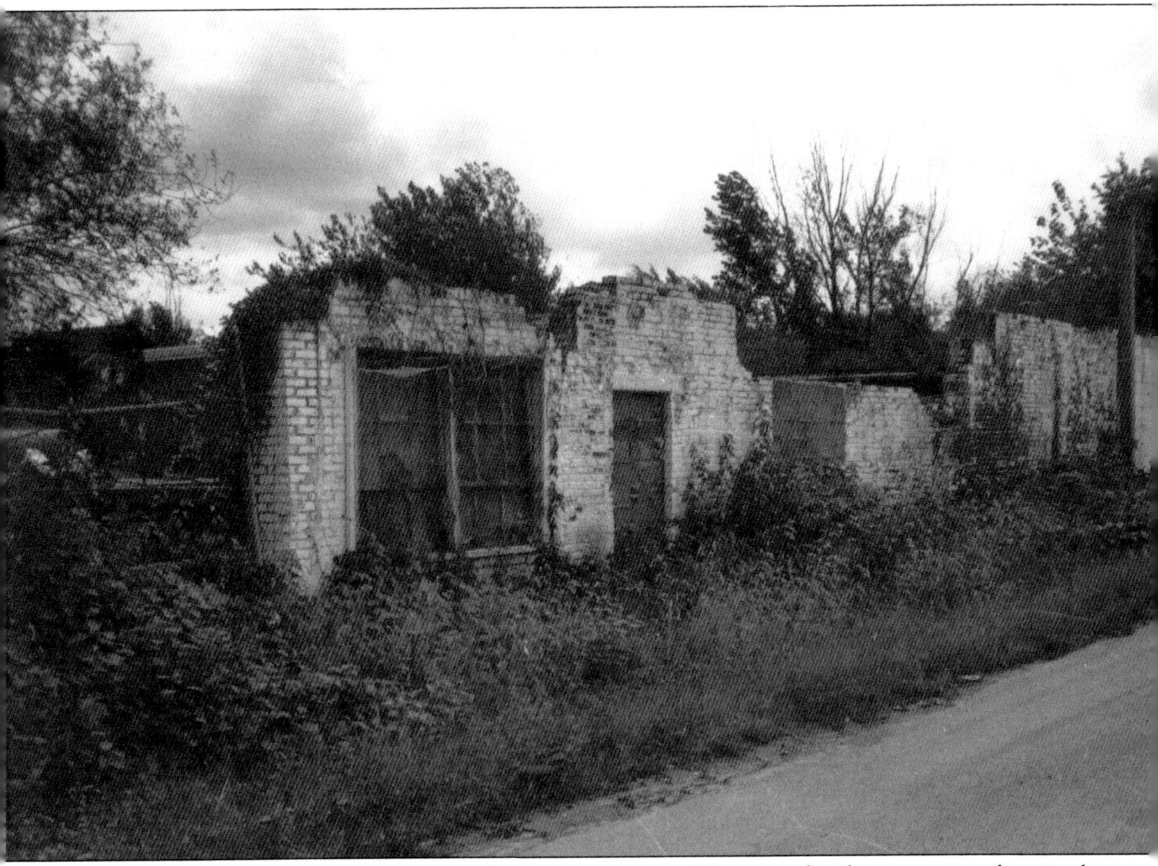

The Kepec Chemical Company in the Genoa section of the township has a unique place in the history of the United States. It was where the Rosenbergs allegedly contacted Russian spies in 1950. The FBI conducted a surveillance of the building in a hidden stakeout at the corner of Biondi Avenue and Gordon Street. Julius Rosenberg was arrested later that year, and his wife, Ethel, soon after. Both were executed in 1953. Only ruins were left when this photograph was taken. Today, just a few bricks remain to mark the location at the foot of Columbus Avenue.

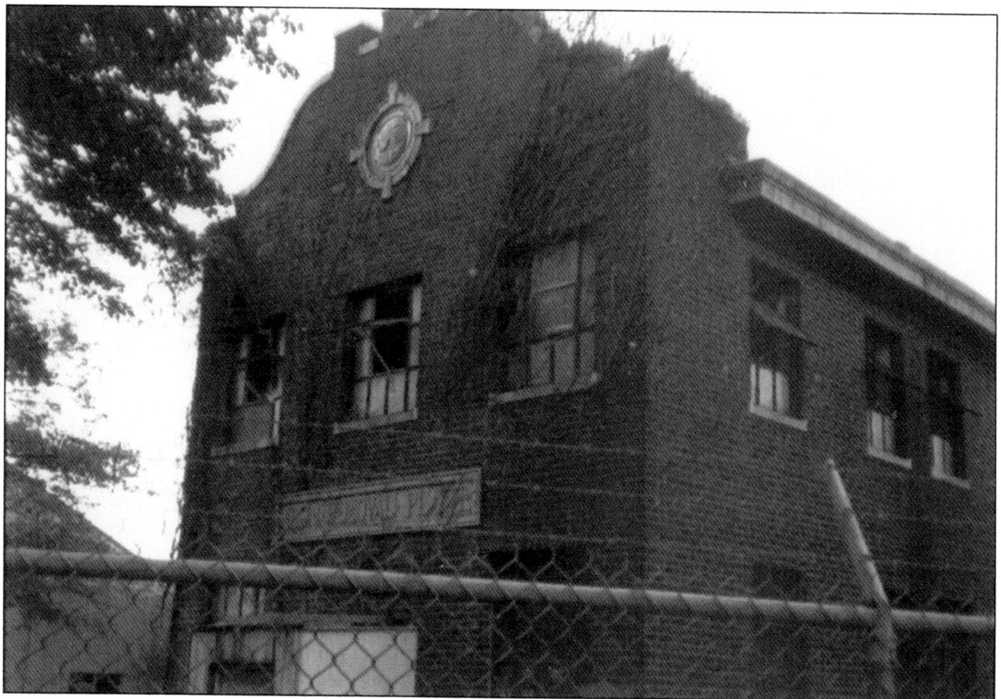

In the 1800s, Perth Amboy purchased the area now known as the Runyon Watershed in order to provide an adequate water supply for its growing population. The city knew it had to look outside its own boundaries for additional sources, and it chose this desolate and mostly uninhabited area in Old Bridge near Route 18. Seen here is one of the water plant buildings built at that time.

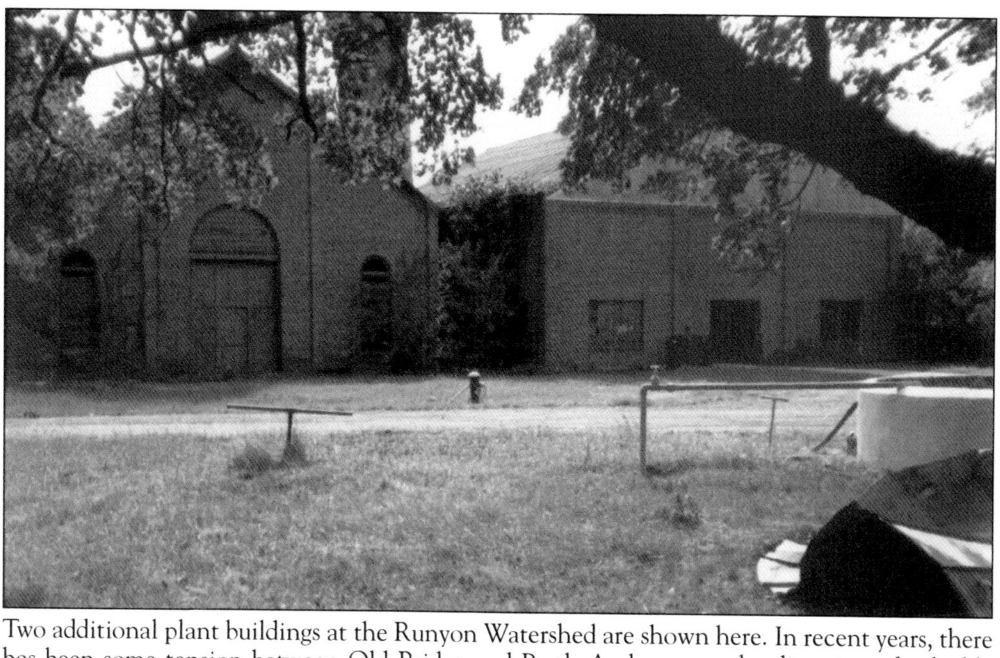

Two additional plant buildings at the Runyon Watershed are shown here. In recent years, there has been some tension between Old Bridge and Perth Amboy over the diversion of valuable water outside the township.

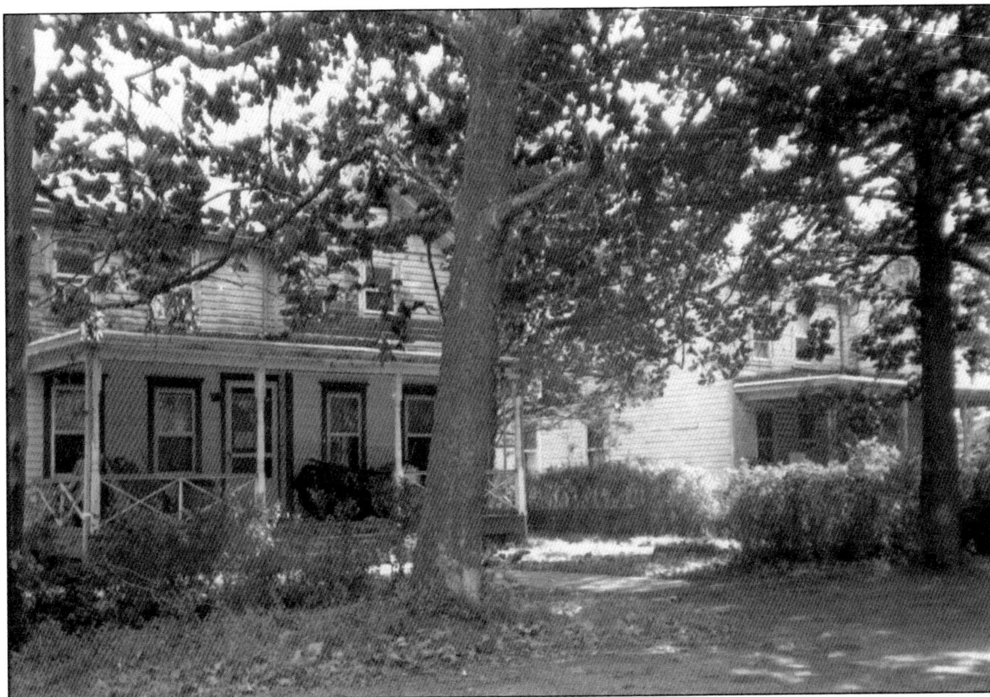

Many of the early employees at the Runyon Watershed lived on the property in houses provided by the city of Perth Amboy. Some of these homes are still standing on the property, though the number is reduced each year. The watershed still provides most of Perth Amboy's water supply.

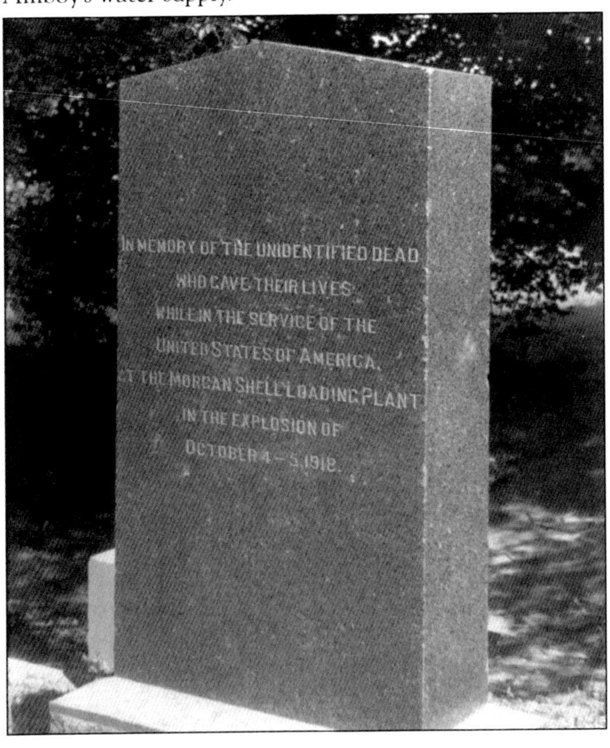

In 1918, the T.A. Gillespie Shell Loading Plant in the Morgan section of neighboring Sayreville exploded, causing shock waves that could be felt as far north as Newark. Thousands were forced to flee their homes and seek shelter elsewhere. An estimated 64 people were killed in the explosion, and the unidentified were interred in a small cemetery off Ernston Road in Old Bridge. This monument was placed there in their honor. Unexploded shells are still occasionally found buried in the surrounding area.

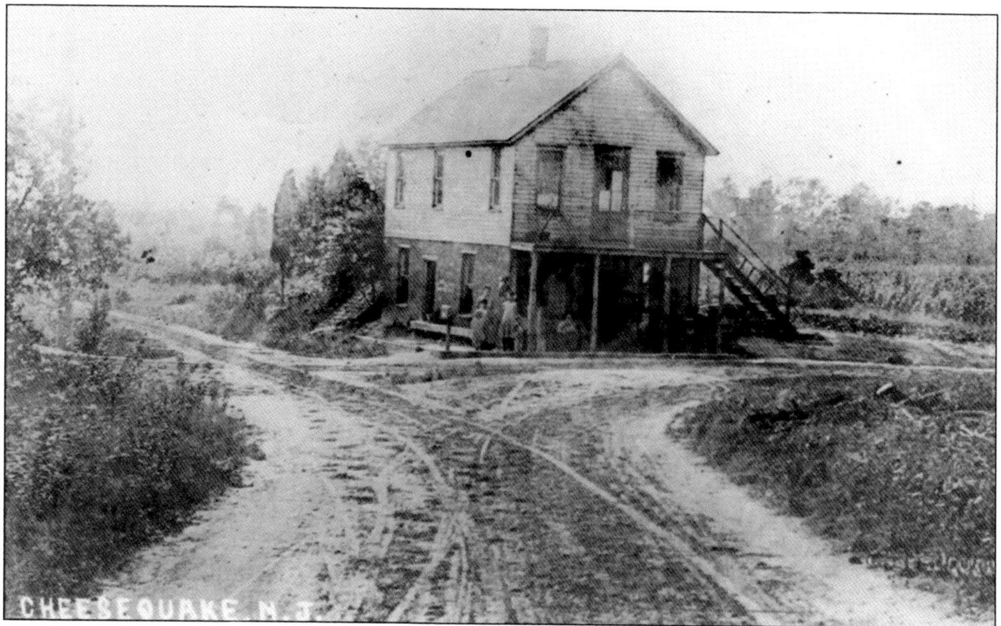

Oscar Caniff operated this small grocery and supply store at the corner of Mill and Springfield Roads. This photograph was taken sometime prior to 1914. On the right is a stairway leading to a separate entrance for living quarters.

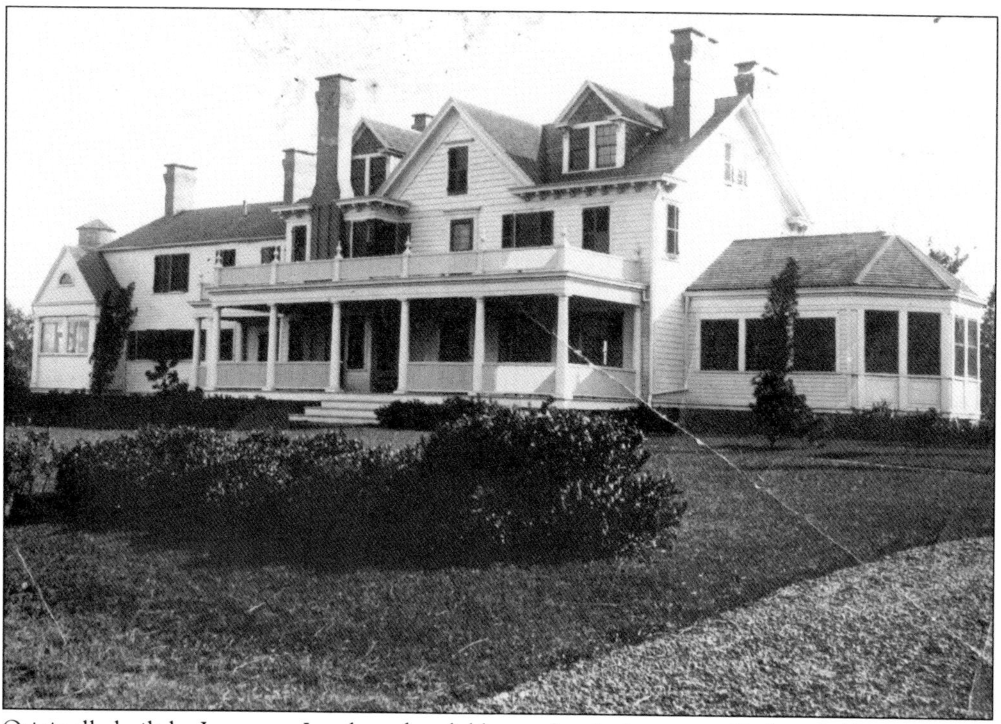

Originally built by Laurence Lamb as the clubhouse for the Laurence Harbor Golf and Country Club, this building was purchased by William Burlew in 1927 and transformed into a restaurant. It became famous for its seafood and was a must-visit for the casual tourist and celebrity alike. Some stars who frequented it were Clark Gable, Ozzie Nelson, Eddie Fisher, and Guy Lombardo.

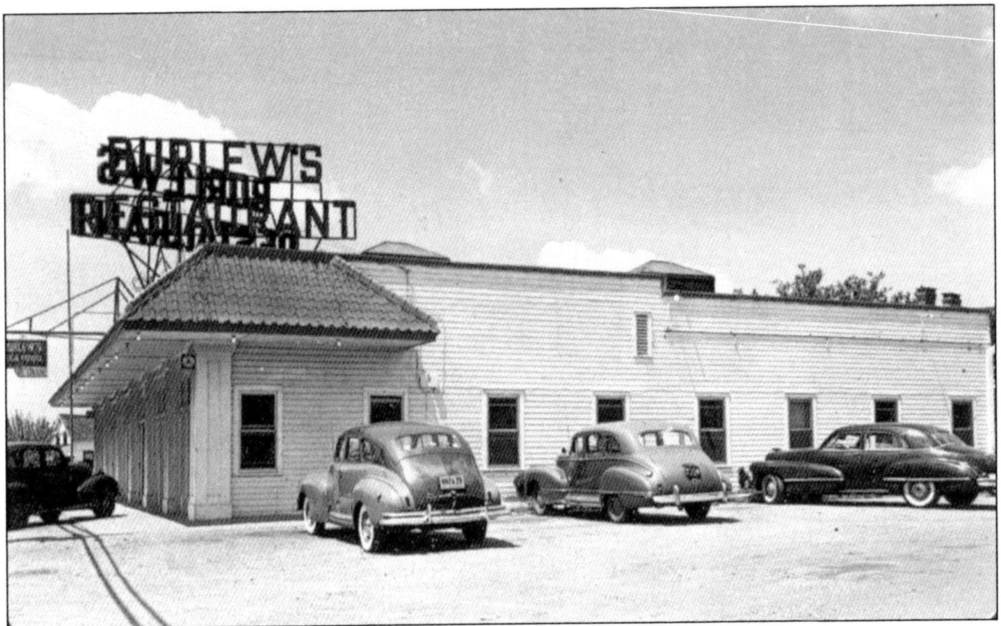

The popularity of his restaurant caused William Burlew to construct a more modern facility on Route 35, in front of the old building. Both buildings were located just south of the Laurence Harbor Circle on the northbound side of the road. Burlew operated both restaurants at the same time.

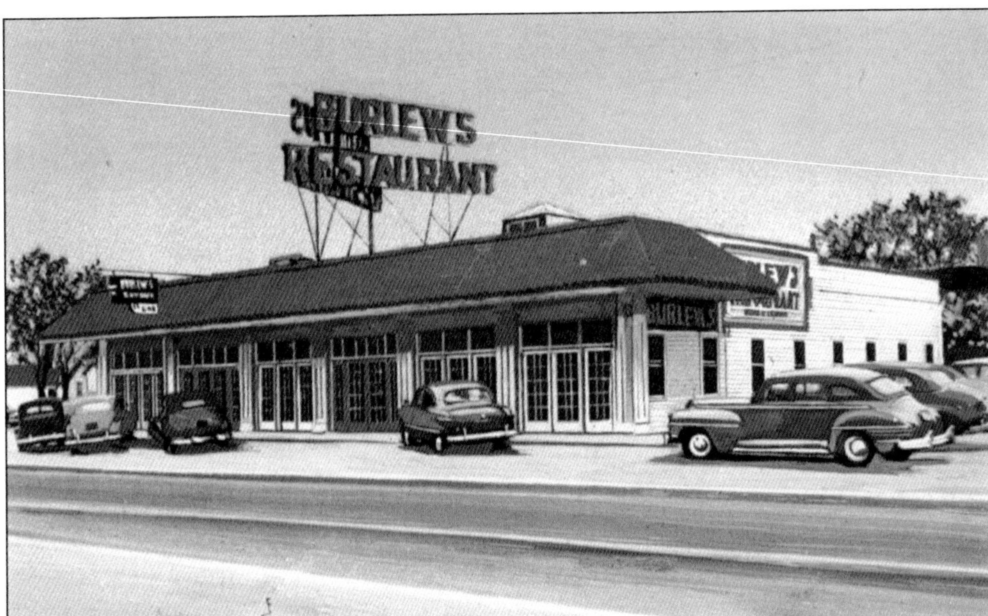

This postcard shows another view of the newer Burlew's Restaurant on Route 35. The restaurant maintained its popularity through the Great Depression, World War II, and the 1950s. The card boasted, "Pioneers in the Seafood Art!"

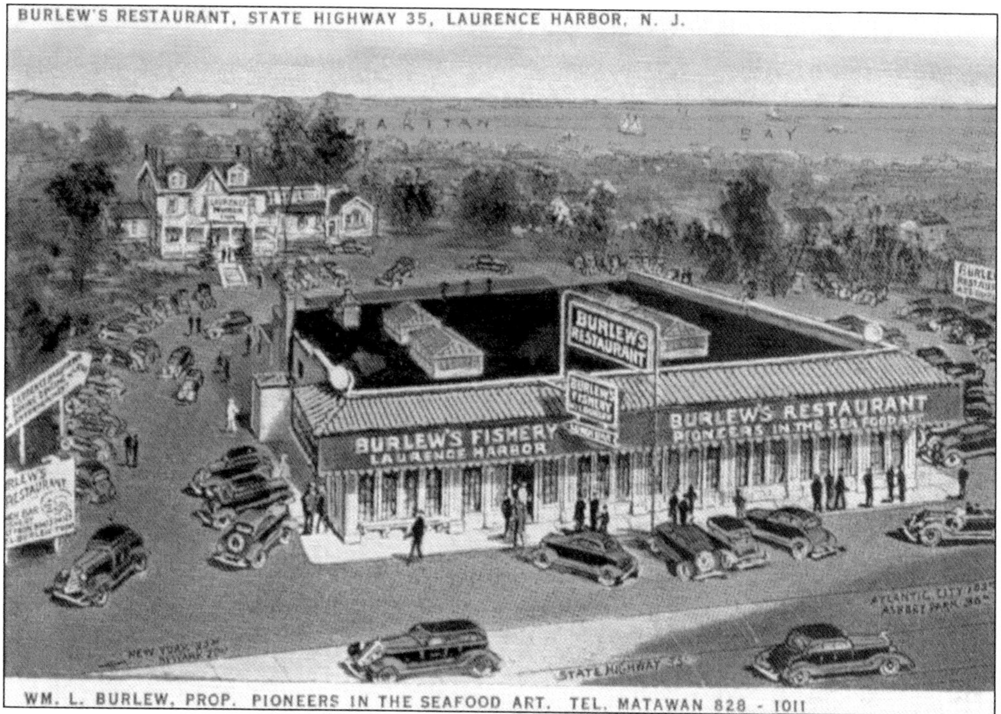

This 1937 postcard shows Burlew's Restaurant with the old clubhouse (then called the Laurence Harbor Inn) behind it. Beyond the clubhouse is where the Laurence Harbor Golf and Country Club once stood. In the foreground of the postcard is Route 35. In the background is the Raritan Bay.

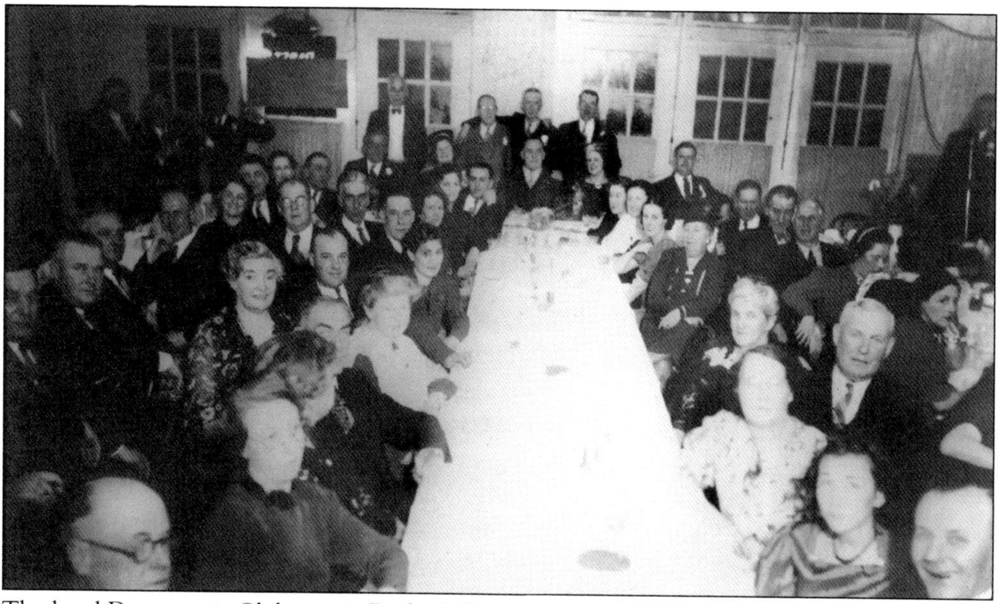

The local Democratic Club met in Burlew's Restaurant in the 1950s. The large windows shown could be swung open to allow for the maximum breeze in the days before air conditioning. The original restaurant was torn down in 1950. The newer building followed 16 years later, a victim of changing tastes and increasing costs. The property remains vacant to this day.

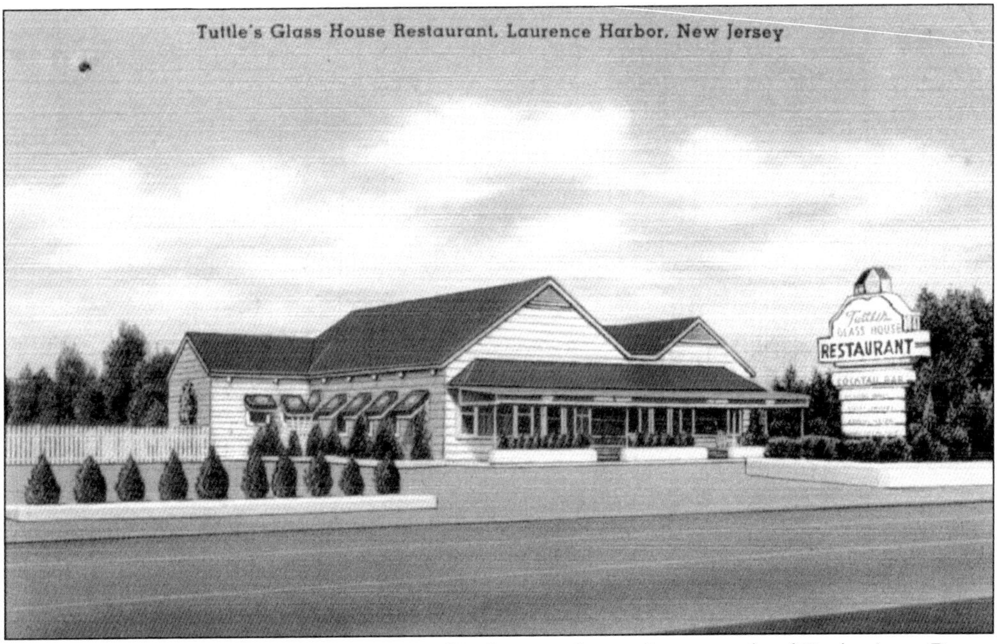

Another popular dining spot in Laurence Harbor was located just north of Burlew's on Route 35. Originally known by the odd name of Tuttle's Glass House Restaurant, it later became McKitrick's, a name it kept for many years. Today, it is called the Harbor Side Pub.

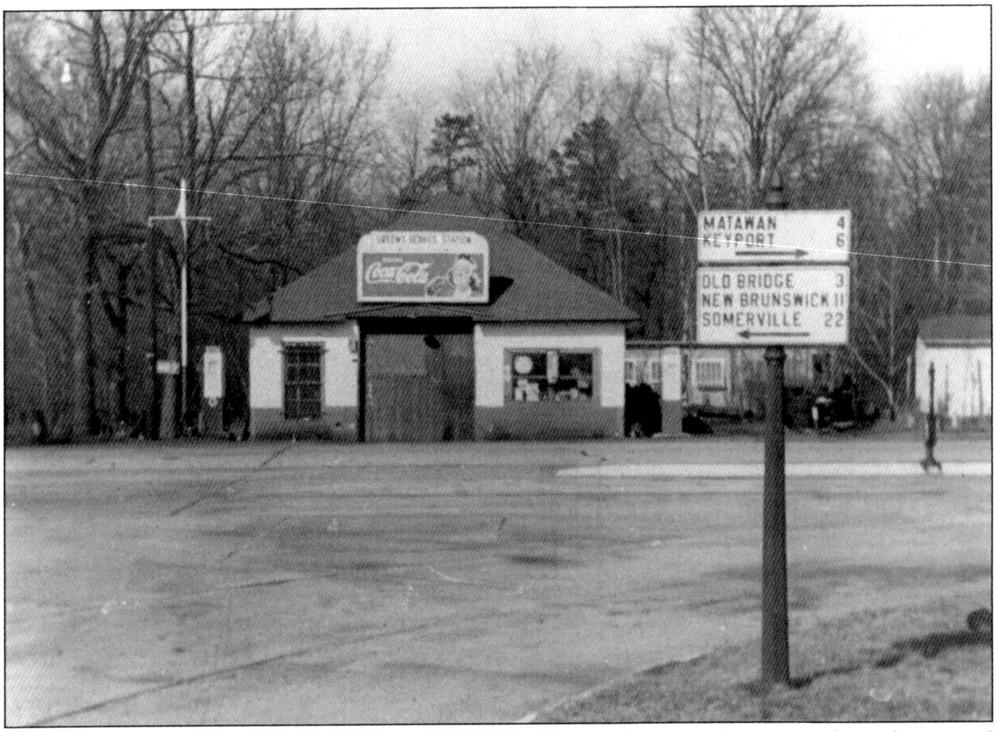

The automobile came into its own as Old Bridge began the transformation from farms and villages to suburban housing. Merrill Green had one of the first service stations in Old Bridge. It was located at the intersection of Route 9 and Route 516.

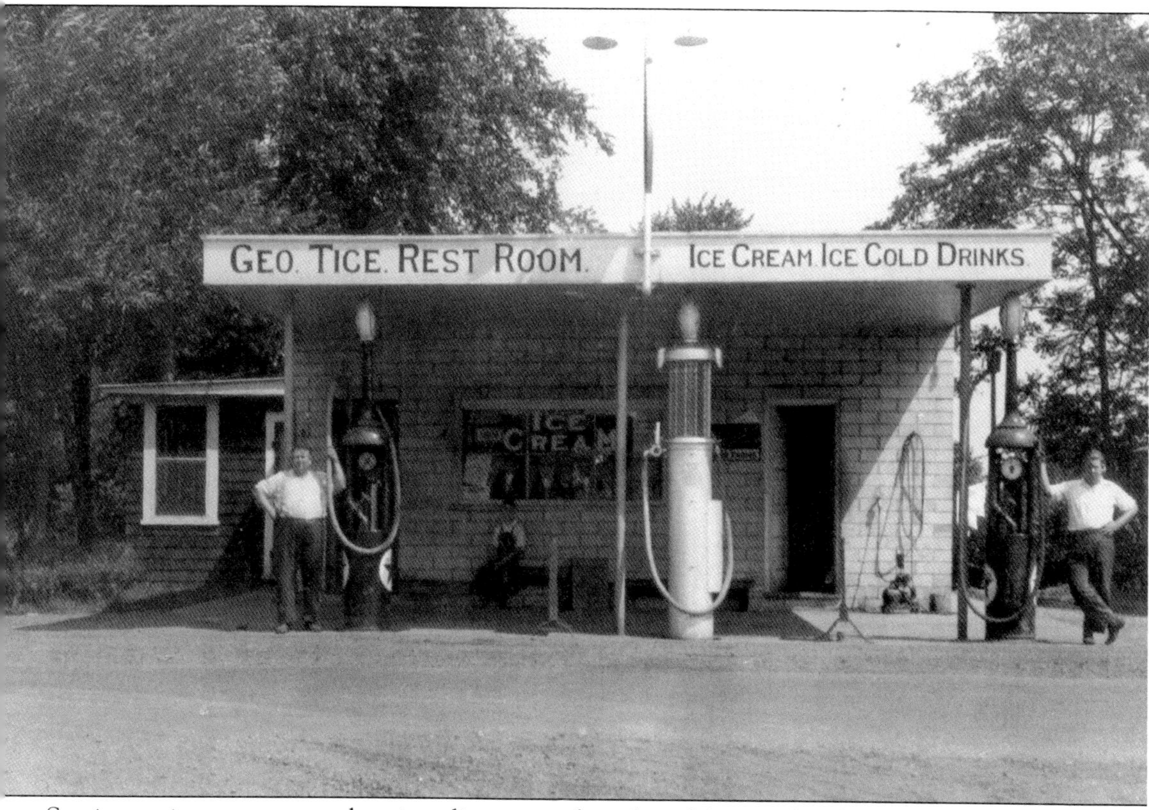

Service stations were more than just dispensers of gasoline. Many replaced the general stores as meeting places for the community. George "Pokey" Tice's (left) station on Route 516 also served as an ice-cream shop. His brother, Hamilton "Hammy" Tice, is also pictured.

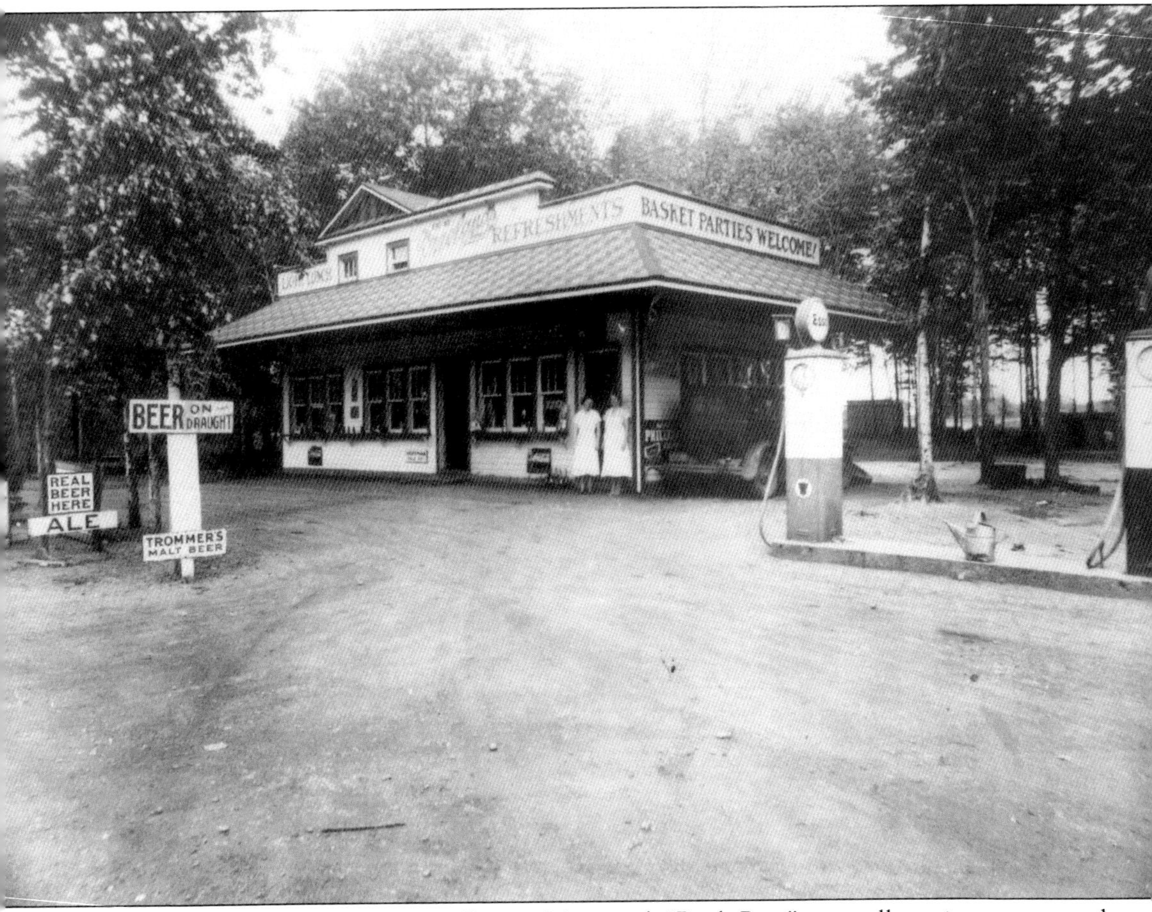

Vreeland's Service Station on Route 34 served "Real Beer" as well as ice cream and refreshments, and "Basket Parties" were welcomed. This photograph was taken just after the construction of the highway. Phoebe Lambertson (left) and Jenny Vreeland are pictured. Note the old Esso gas pumps.

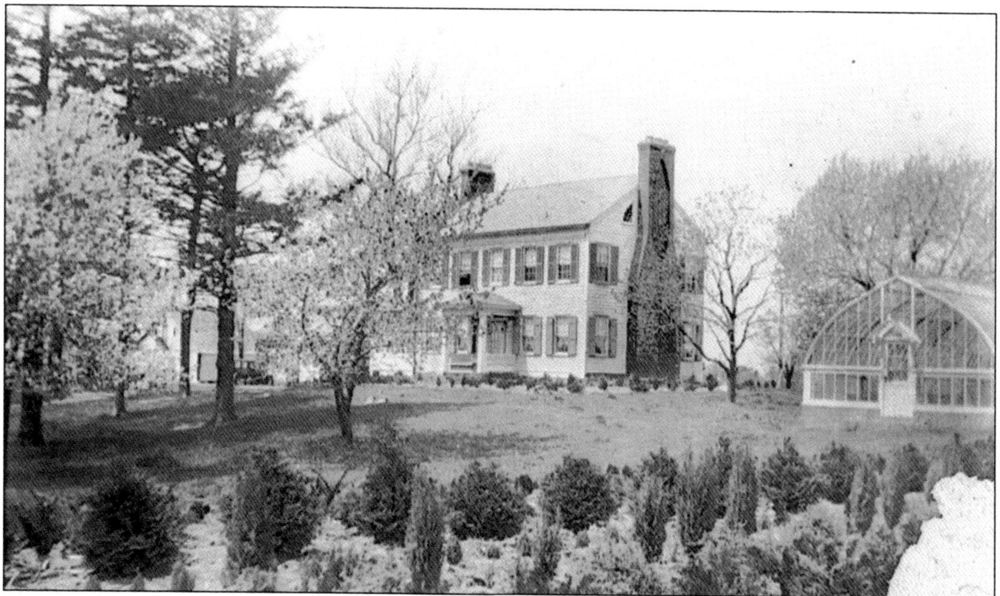

The Cottrell homestead is a landmark in Old Bridge. It was built in 1831, replacing an earlier structure built in 1820 that was destroyed in a fire. This 1925 photograph shows the front of the house and the greenhouse to the left. The home still stands on the northeast corner of Route 516 and Cottrell Road.

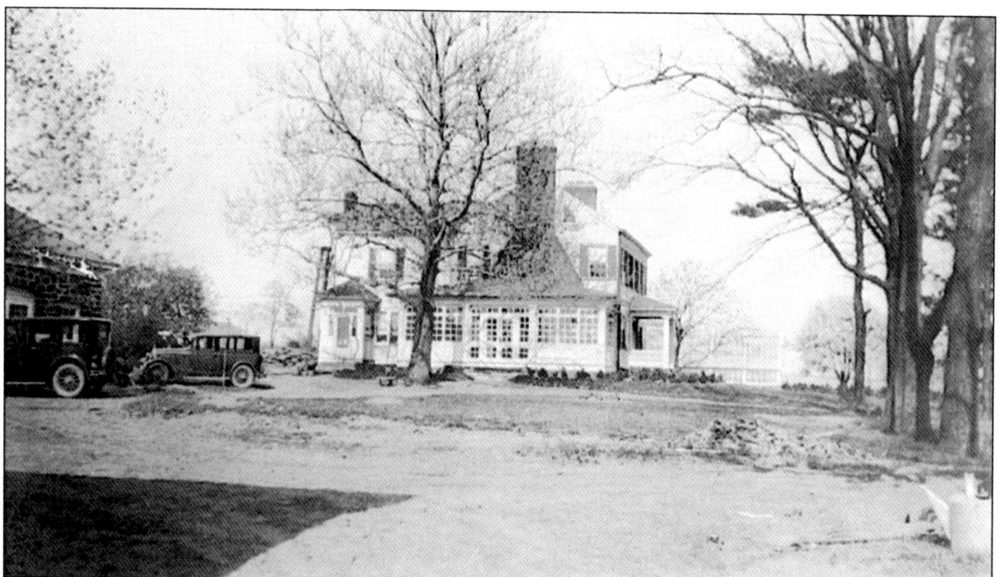

The Cottrells' main crop was apples. In 1904, William H. Cottrell sold the farm to his two sons, Herbert and Franklin. Herbert took sole possession in 1919. This side view of the house shows the impressive chimney brickwork. Note the period automobiles on the left.

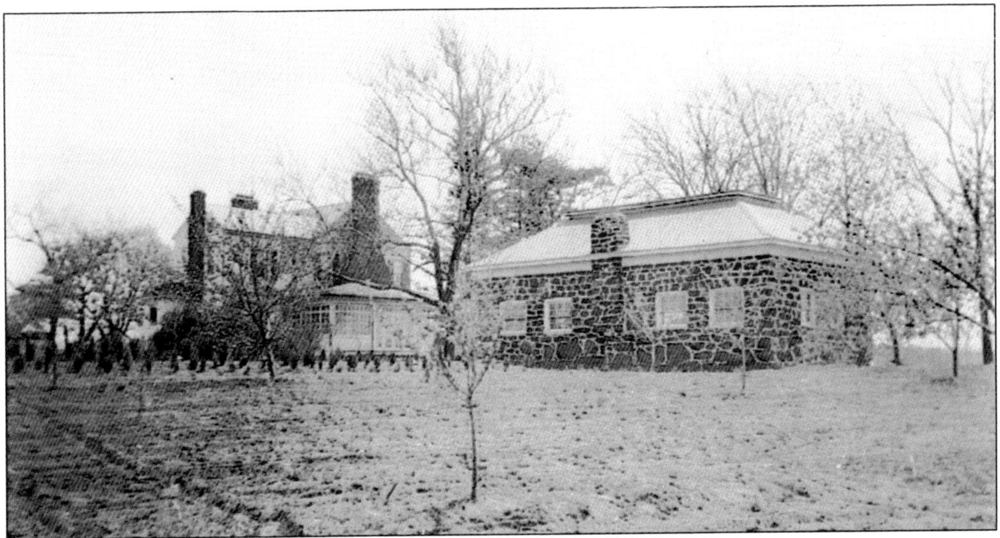

Although stone outbuildings were once quite common in the area, few could match the impressive size of the one pictured here, located behind the Cottrell house. Even fewer are still standing. The house can be seen in the background on the left.

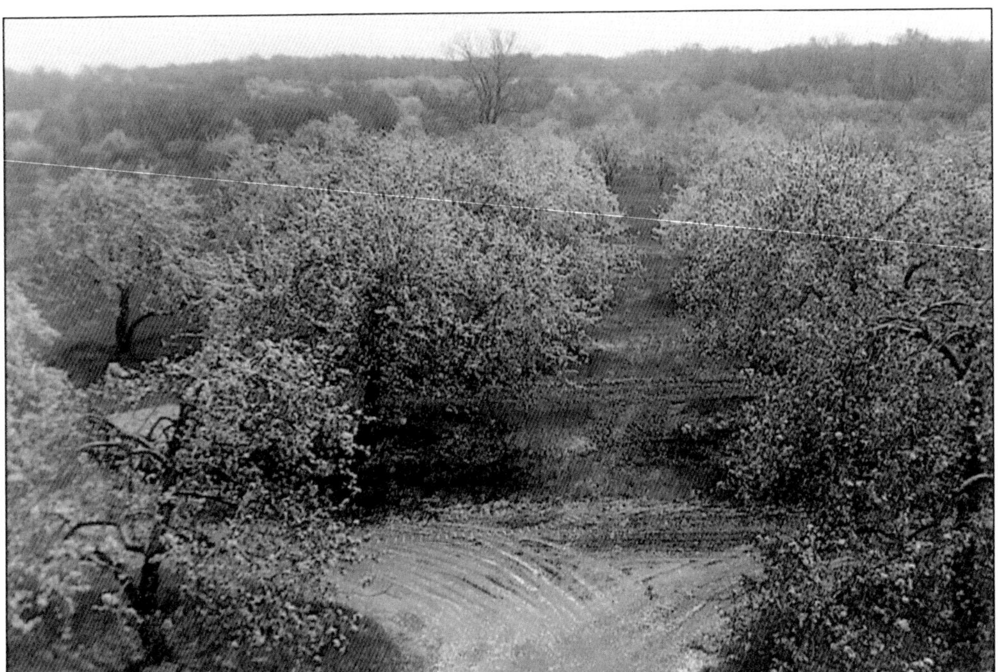

Of course, no apple farm would be complete without an apple orchard. Seen here is the Cottrells' 150-acre apple orchard as viewed from the roof of the cold-storage building across the street from the main house. The photograph was taken in the 1950s. A portion of the orchard still stands on the property.

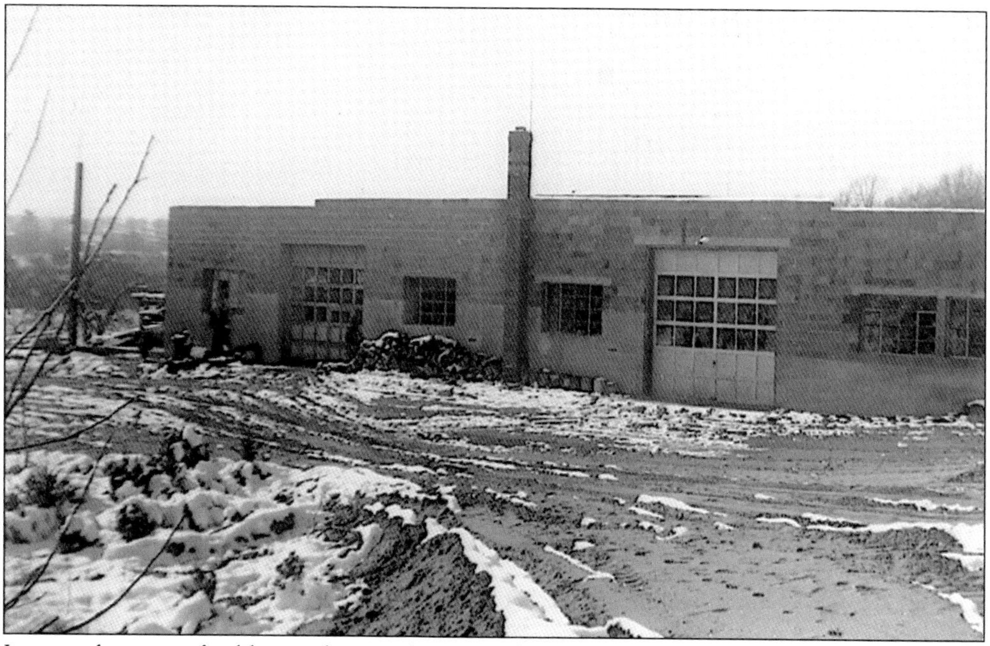

It was always preferable to ship apples immediately after picking, but sometimes it was necessary to keep them in the cold-storage building across the street from the Cottrell house on Route 516. Apples were held in storage at a temperature between 31 and 32 degrees Fahrenheit until they were shipped in order to preserve freshness.

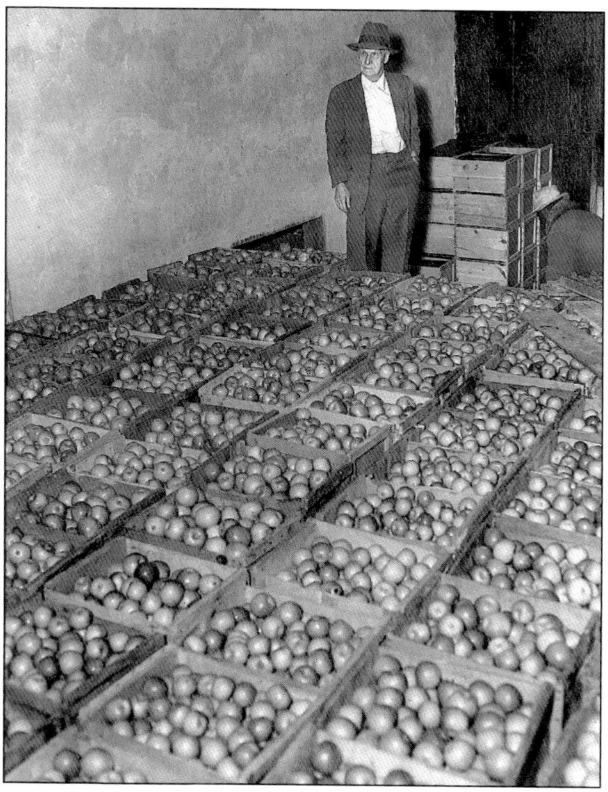

Herbert Cottrell Sr. paid personal and careful attention to every aspect of the apple business. In this 1950s photograph, he is diligently surveying the latest crop awaiting sale in cold storage.

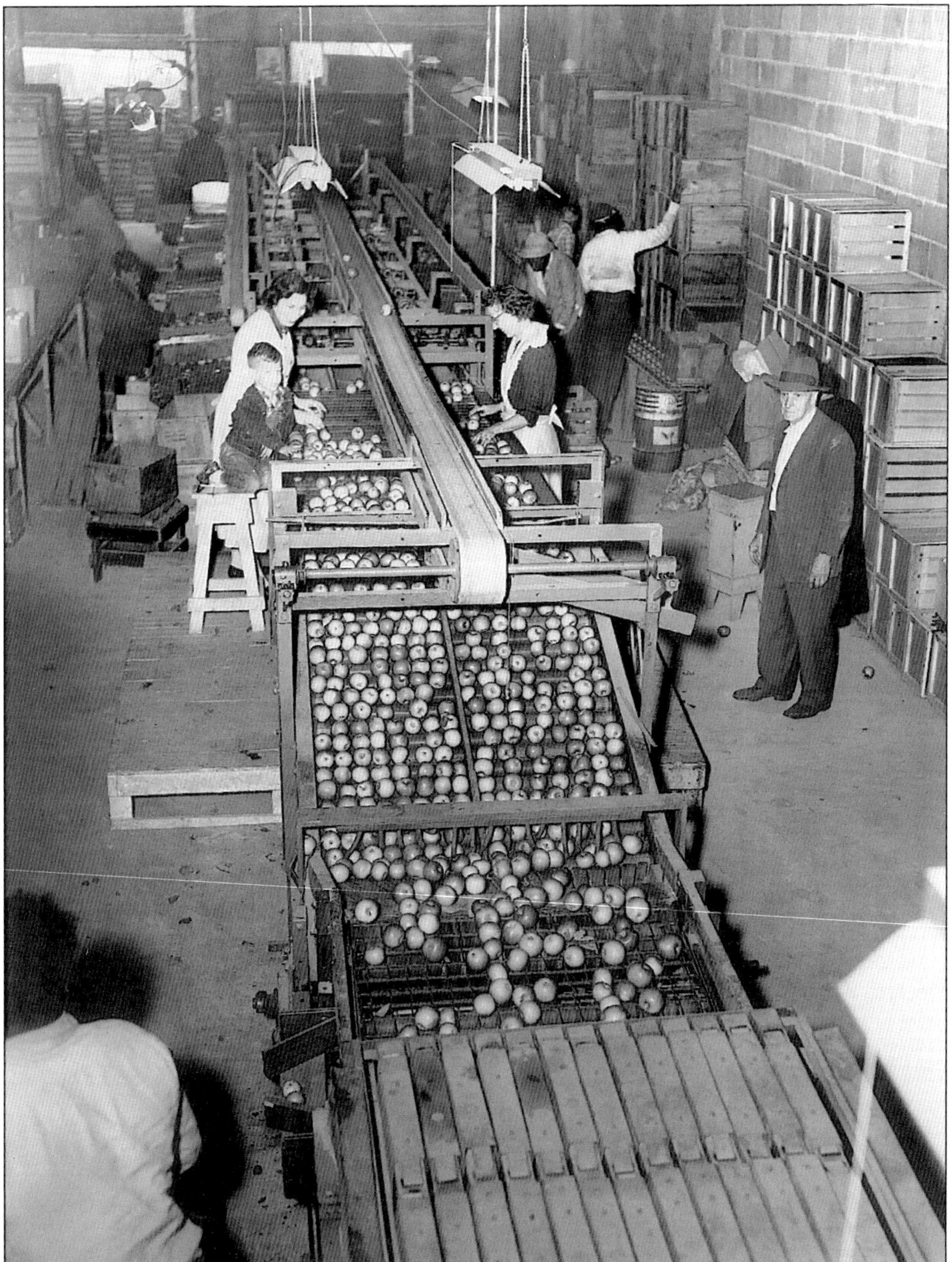

Before the apples could be boxed and sold, they first had to be graded. Here, they make their way through the automatic grading machines under the watchful eye of Herbert Cottrell Sr. Working on the machine are, from left to right, William Cottrell, Rebecca Cottrell, and Pauline Morosco. No apples were wasted on the Cottrell Farm. They found a use for even those that were rejected because of size or quality. Across the street from the cold-storage building, on the southwest corner of Cottrell Road and Route 516, the family built a distillery.

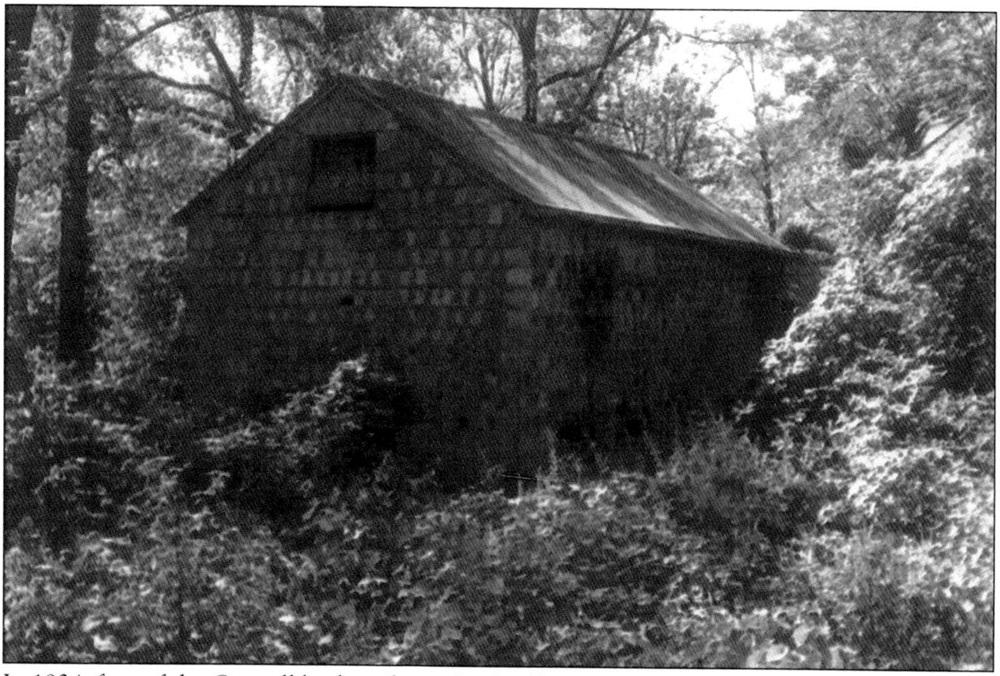

In 1934, four of the Cottrell bothers formed a distillery in the name New Jersey Apple Growers Inc., using the apples from across the street. The apples were pressed into cider and distilled into brandy in large vats. The brandy was then aged in barrels in a bonded government warehouse on the property. This photograph was taken in the 1960s, after the distillery closed.

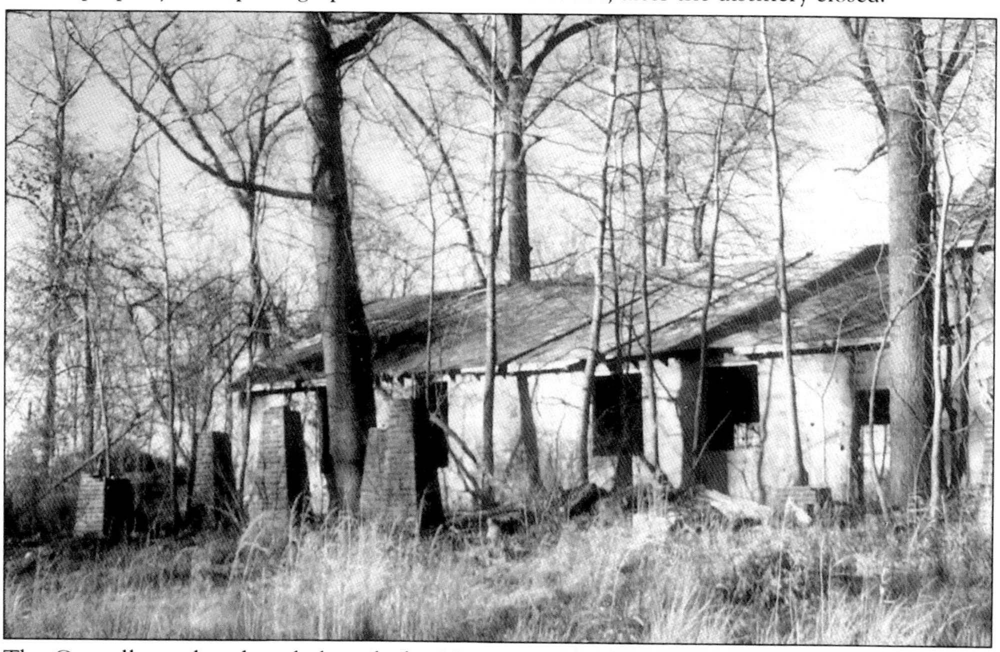

The Cottrells produced apple brandy for 20 years on the farm. It was sold in wholesale lots to distributors or directly to retailers under the brand name Browntown. The business, along with the recipe, was sold to Laird & Company in 1955. By the time this photograph was taken in the 1980s, little of the distillery remained. What was left was razed to make room for a strip mall.

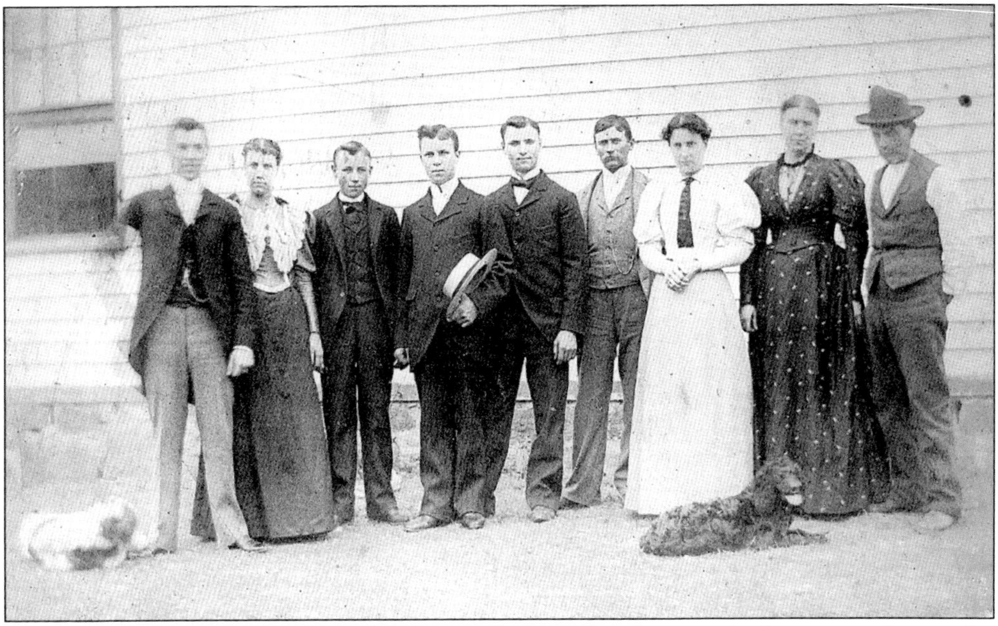

This page shows two generations of the Cottrell clan. The photograph above was taken in the late 1890s outside of the family home. From left to right are Ely Cottrell, Laura Cottrell, Frank Cottrell, Herbert Cottrell Sr., Dr. Willard Cottrell, Ed Zeigler (friend of the family), Emily Cottrell, Louisa Ely Cottrell, and William Cottrell.

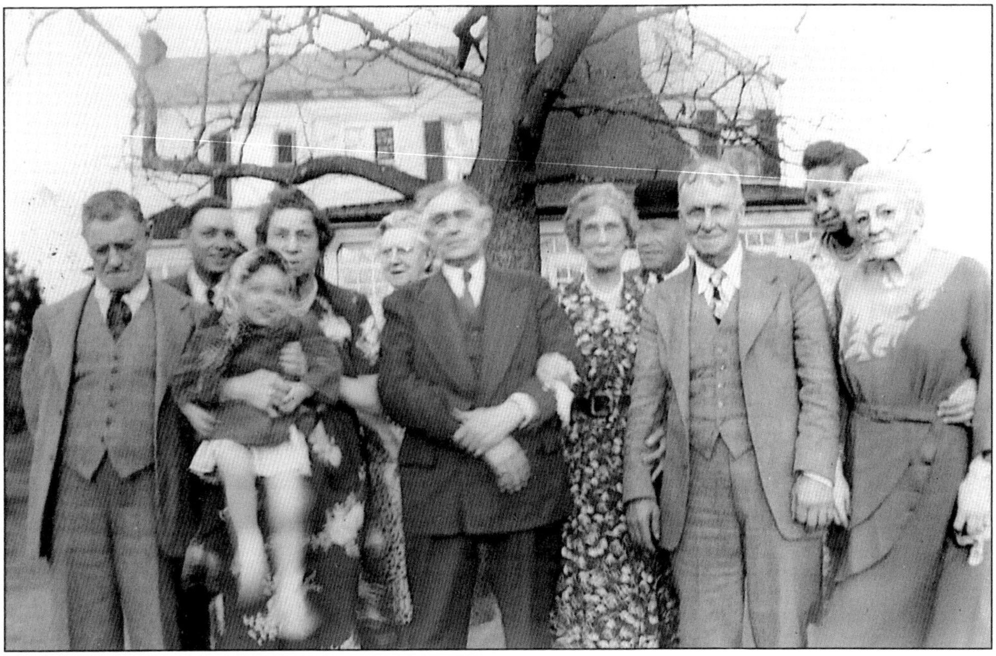

The Cottrell family posed for this picture probably sometime in the 1940s. From left to right are the following: (front row) Wilbur Snyder, Laura Cottrell Woltman, Patricia Cottrell (child), Casler Warne, Emily Cottrell Warne, Herbert Cottrell Sr., and Anna Knoblock Cottrell; (back row) Harvey Warne, Elizabeth Brautigham, Bill Reineker, and Wilhelmina Brautigham Cottrell.

Four

FAITH AND EDUCATION

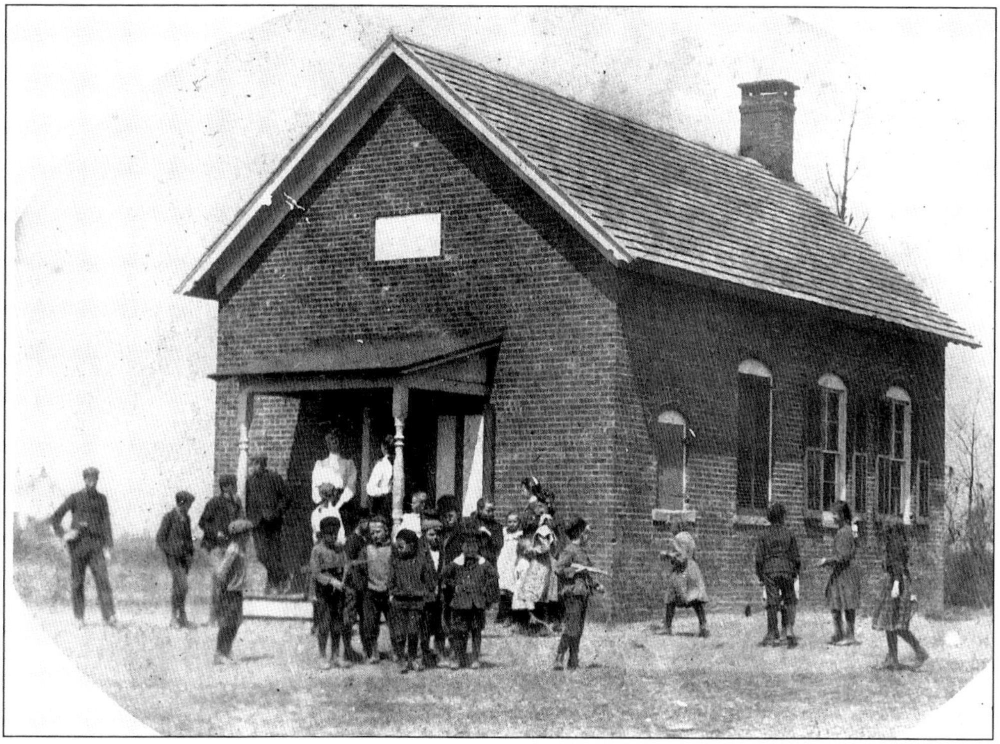

The Morristown School (Public School No. 1) is believed to be the first school in Old Bridge Township. It is located in the Morristown section of the township, near Cheesequake State Park. The original structure on the site burned to the ground in 1897. It was replaced by the brick building shown in this 1906 photograph. Standing on the porch is Marguerite Winter, the teacher.

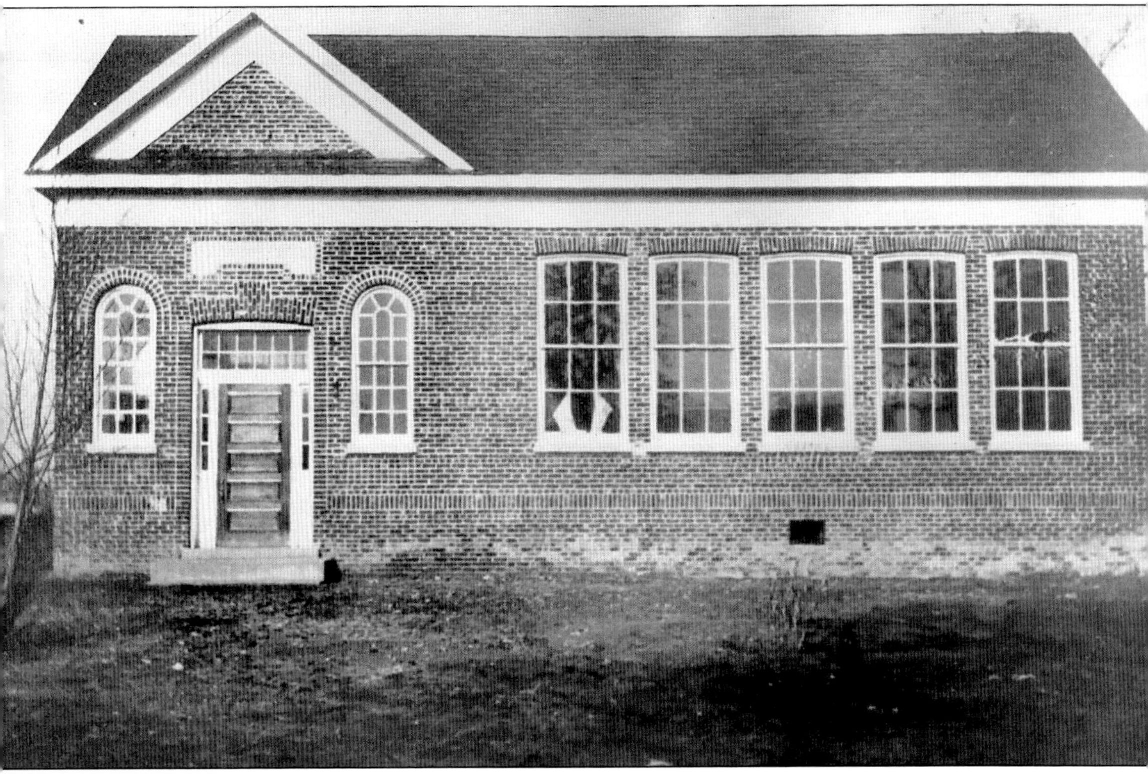

In 1917, the Morristown School was expanded with a brick extension at a cost of $5,272, plus $128 for the furnace. If you look closely, you can see the old building on the left incorporated into the new addition. The school finally closed in 1948, after 160 years of education.

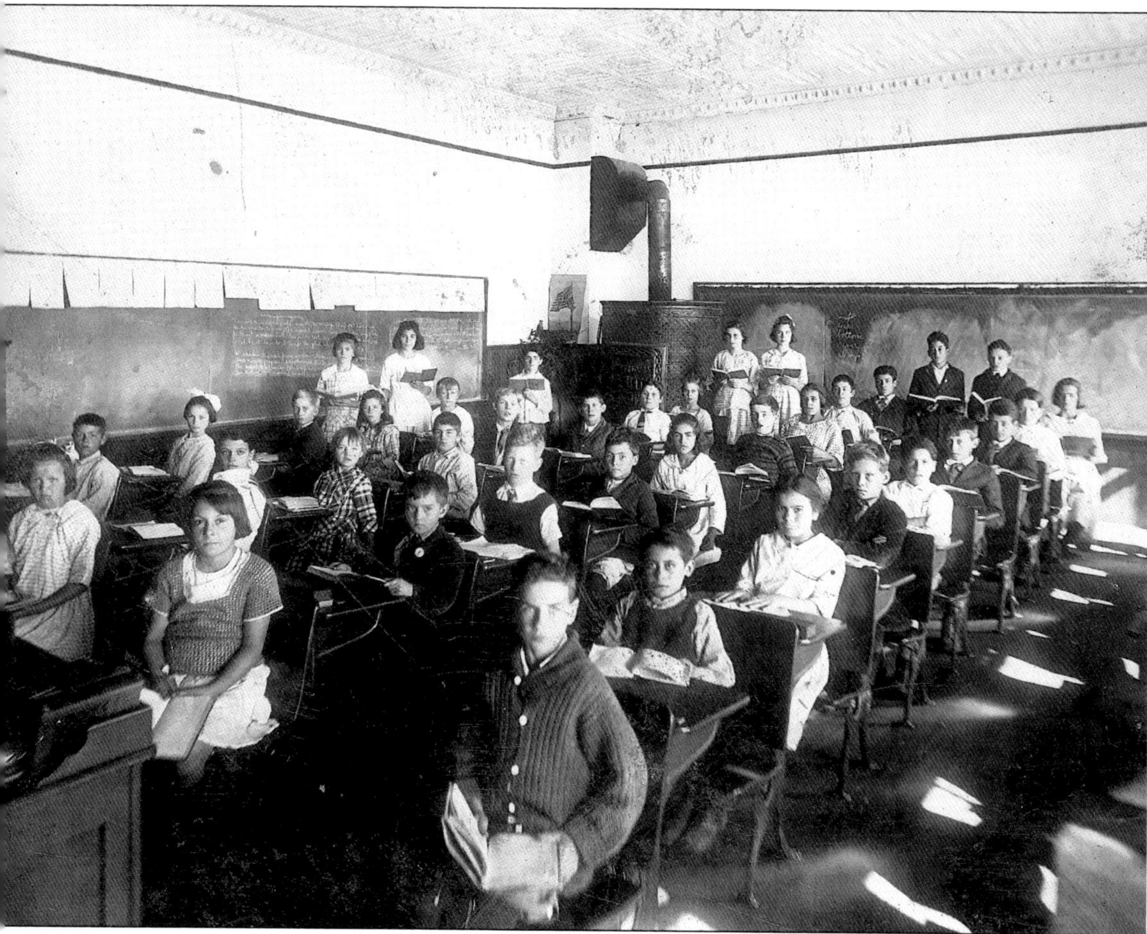

The interior of the Morristown School is shown after the 1917 expansion. This photograph was taken in 1923. The classroom is typical of its time period. The children standing on the left and rear of the classroom usually sat at the desks on the right, just out of the picture.

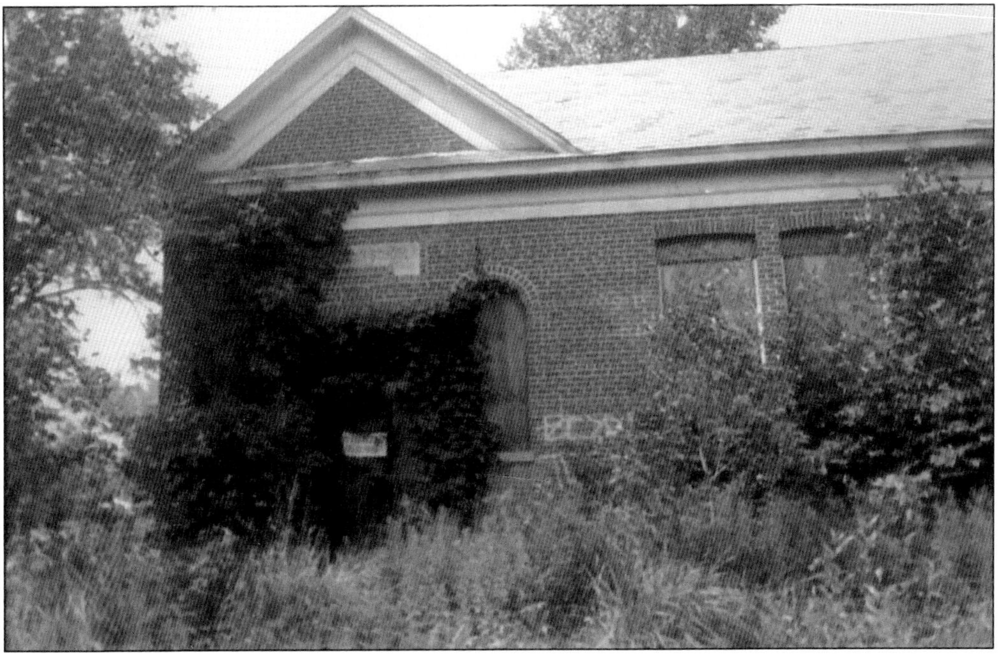

By the 1960s, the Morristown School was abandoned by the board of education after its use for storage for a number of years after its closing. The building still stands on School House Road, but it is in imminent danger of collapse. Many efforts have been made to preserve the building, but none have been successful.

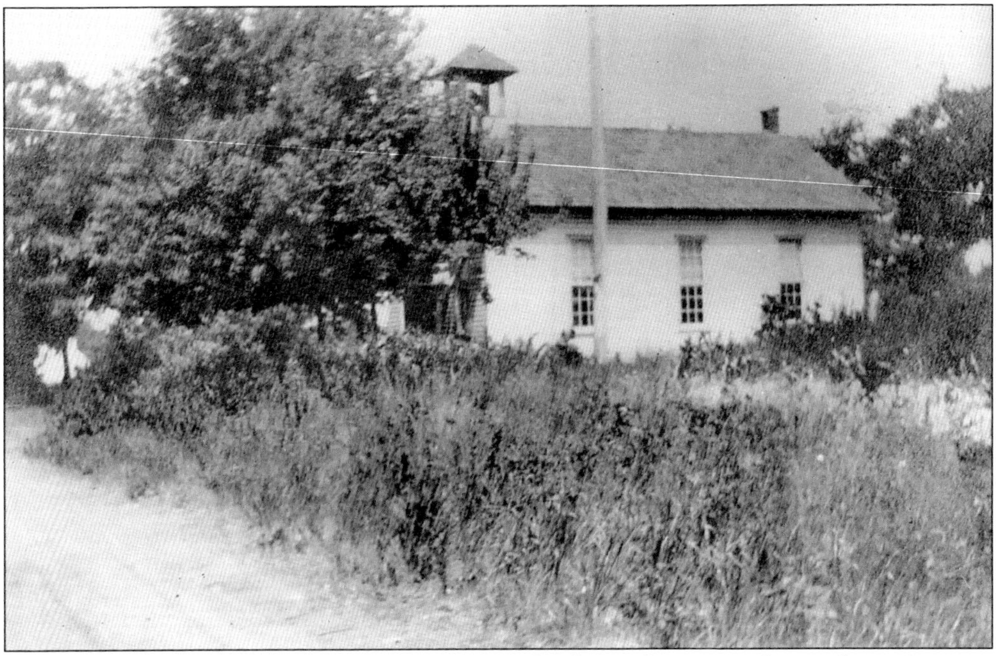

The first site of the Cheesequake School (Public School No. 2) was on a dirt road near Route 9. In the 1870s, a new school was built on Route 34. It was soon overcrowded by the growing school-age population, and a replacement was planned. To make room for the new school, the building was sold in 1915 and moved to Cottrell Road, where it still stands as a private residence.

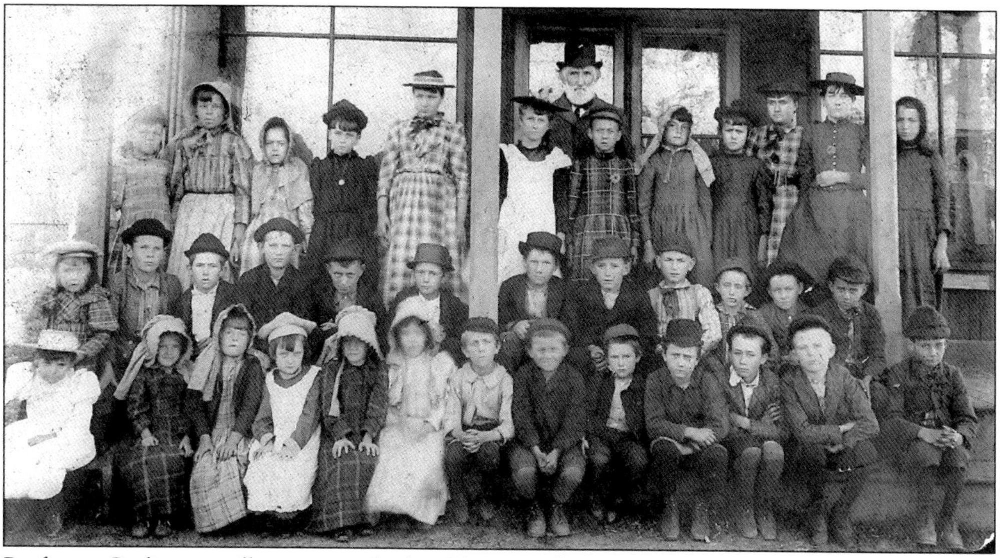

Professor Carliss proudly poses with the Cheesequake Class of 1890. He looks every bit the serious educator with his top hat and full beard.

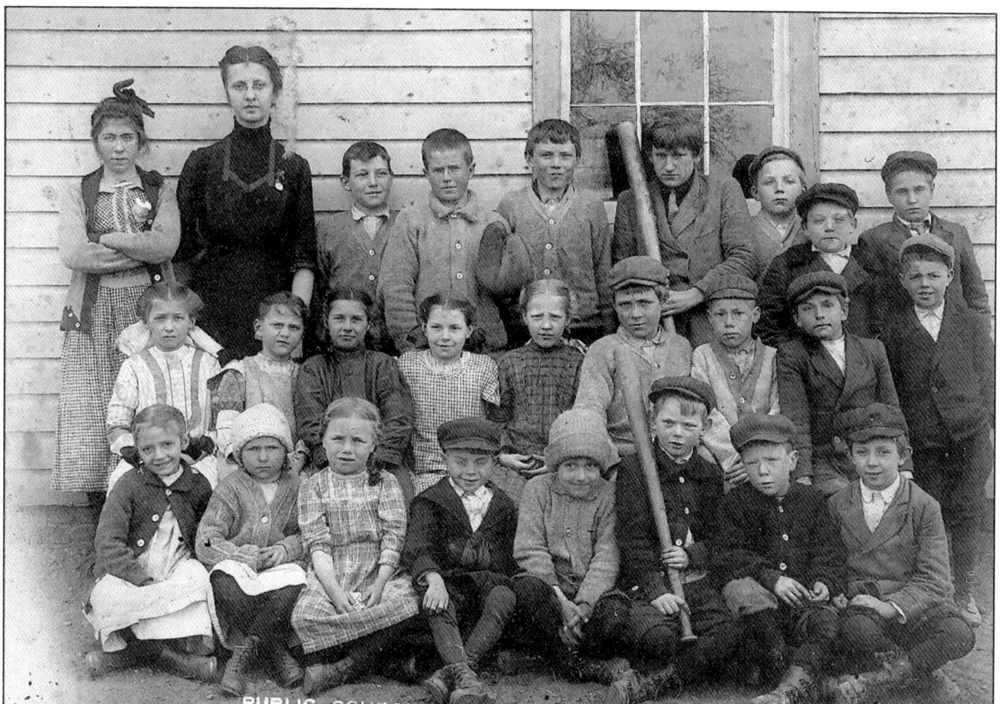

The Class of 1913 poses in front of the Cheesequake School. The teacher was Josie Gordon (back row, second from left). The scowling baseball-bat bearers look ominous, but they are probably just members of a local ball team.

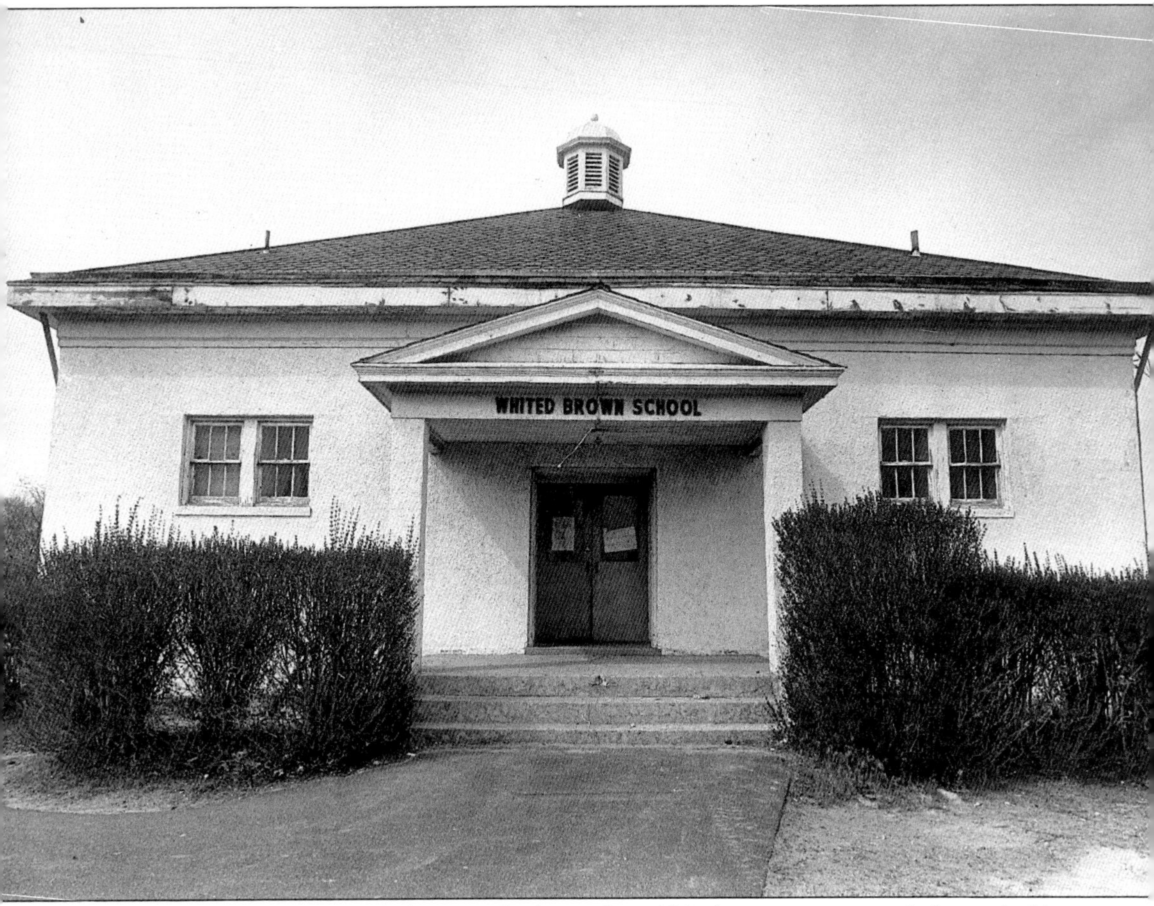

The Cheesequake School that was built in the 1870s became overcrowded, much like its predecessor, and was replaced in 1915 by a new building. This time they planned for the coming crowds and constructed a two-room school. In 1948, it was named for Whited Brown, the son of Lewis Brown. Whited Brown was killed in World War II.

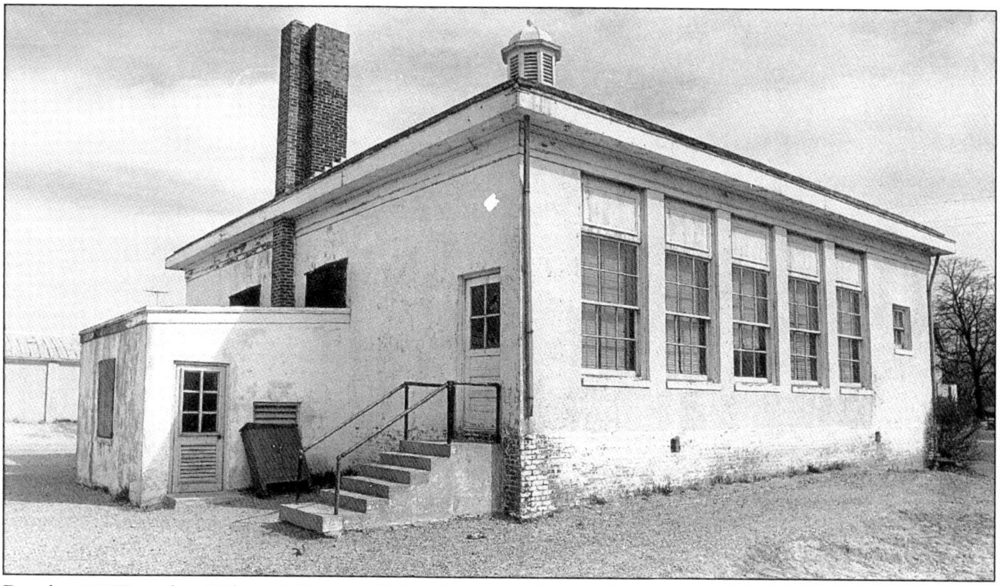

By the 1950s, the Whited Brown School was suffering from overcrowding, and yet another new school was planned. It was demolished in the 1970s and replaced with the present-day Cheesequake School, which was built on the same site.

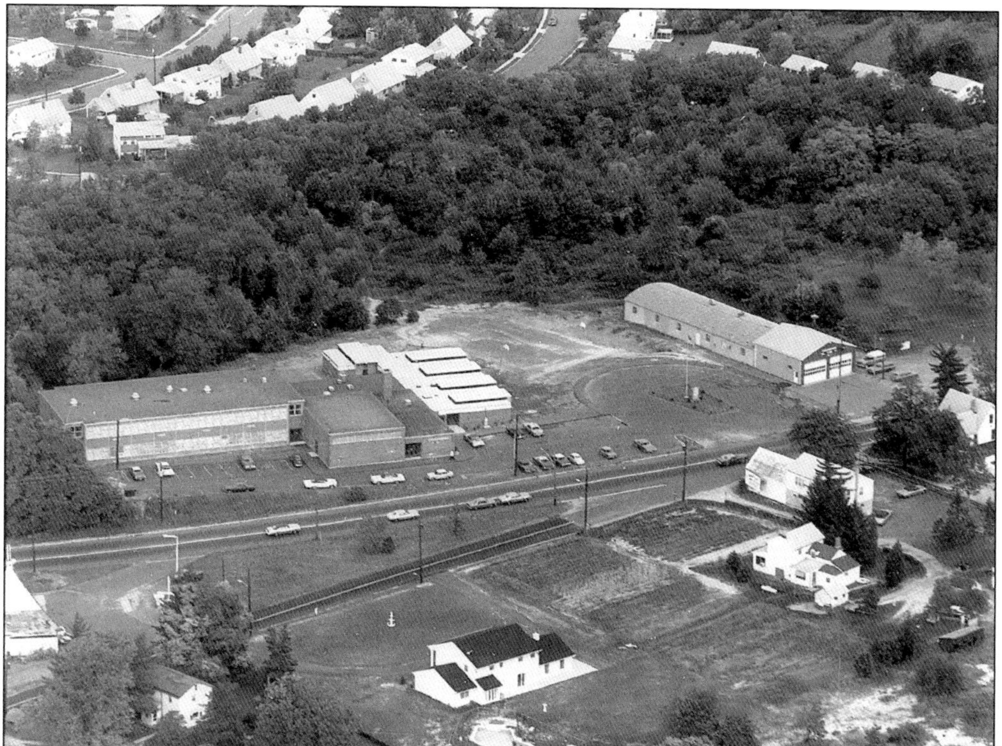

The present-day Cheesequake School is shown shortly after its completion. Today, the area around it is much more developed. Route 34 runs from left to right in the center of the photograph. The Cheesequake Firehouse is on the right. (Courtesy of the Old Bridge Board of Education.)

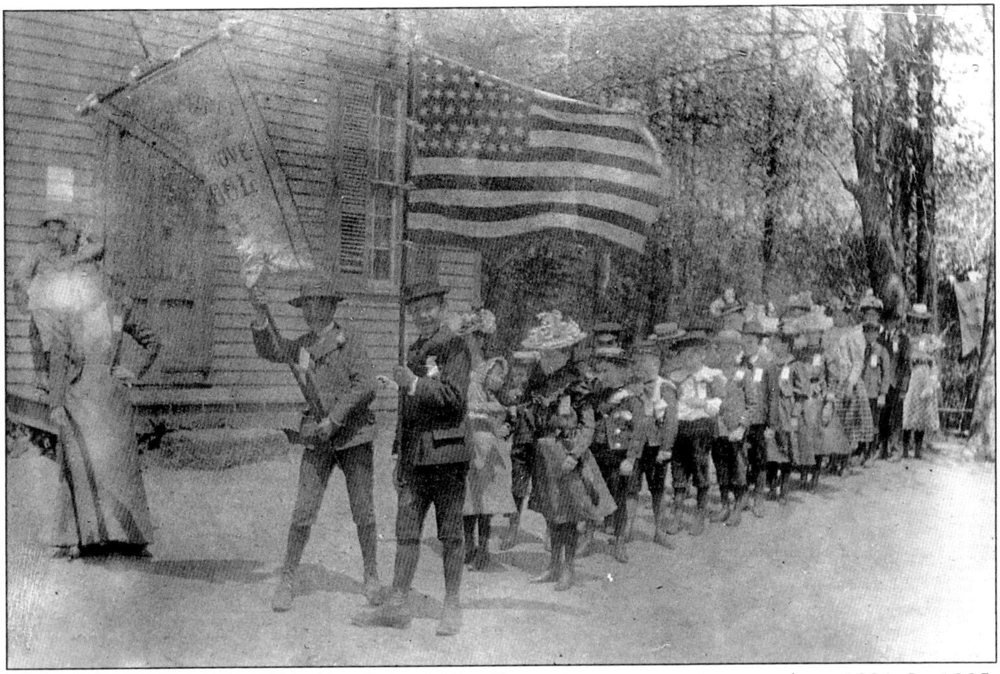

The Cedar Grove School (Public School No. 3) was known to exist as early as 1821. In 1885, a new school building was constructed that still stands today and serves as the home of the Madison Township Historical Society on Route 516. This 1890s photograph shows the Cedar Grove students marching in honor of the annual celebration of School Day at the Herbertsville School. Bessie Warne is the teacher.

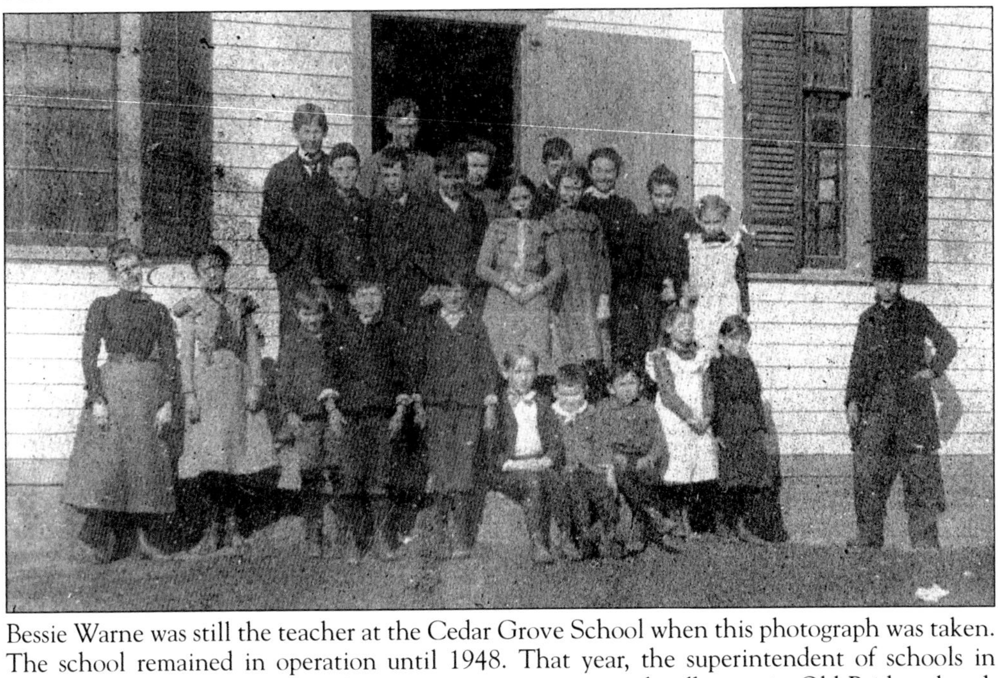

Bessie Warne was still the teacher at the Cedar Grove School when this photograph was taken. The school remained in operation until 1948. That year, the superintendent of schools in Middlesex County ordered the three remaining one-room schoolhouses in Old Bridge closed. In 1976, the school was placed on the National Register of Historic Places.

The Browntown School (Public School No. 4) dates from before 1850, when it was located on present-day Throckmorton Lane. Sometime before 1893, the structure shown here was built on Route 516, near Route 9. Note the flagpole and the rooster weathervane.

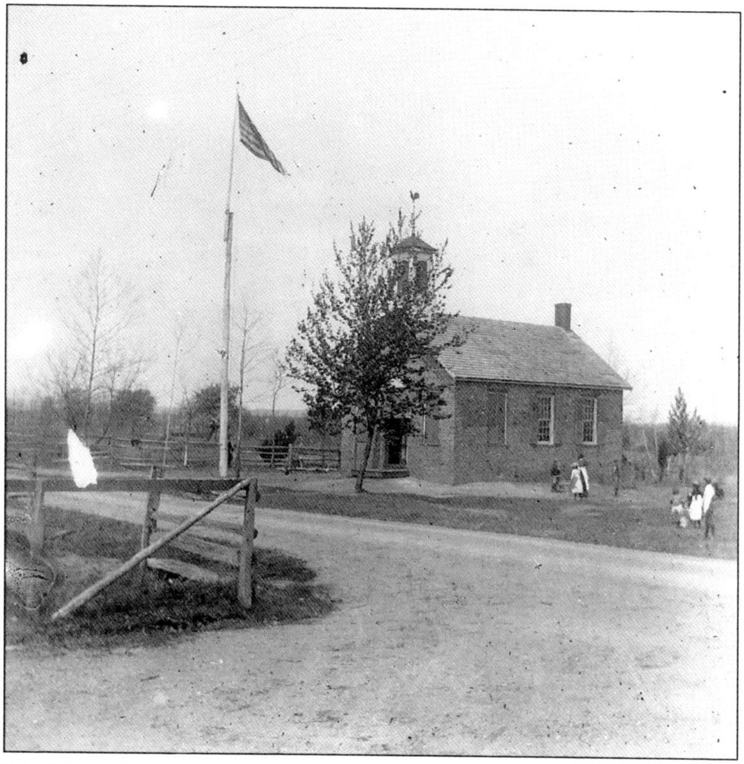

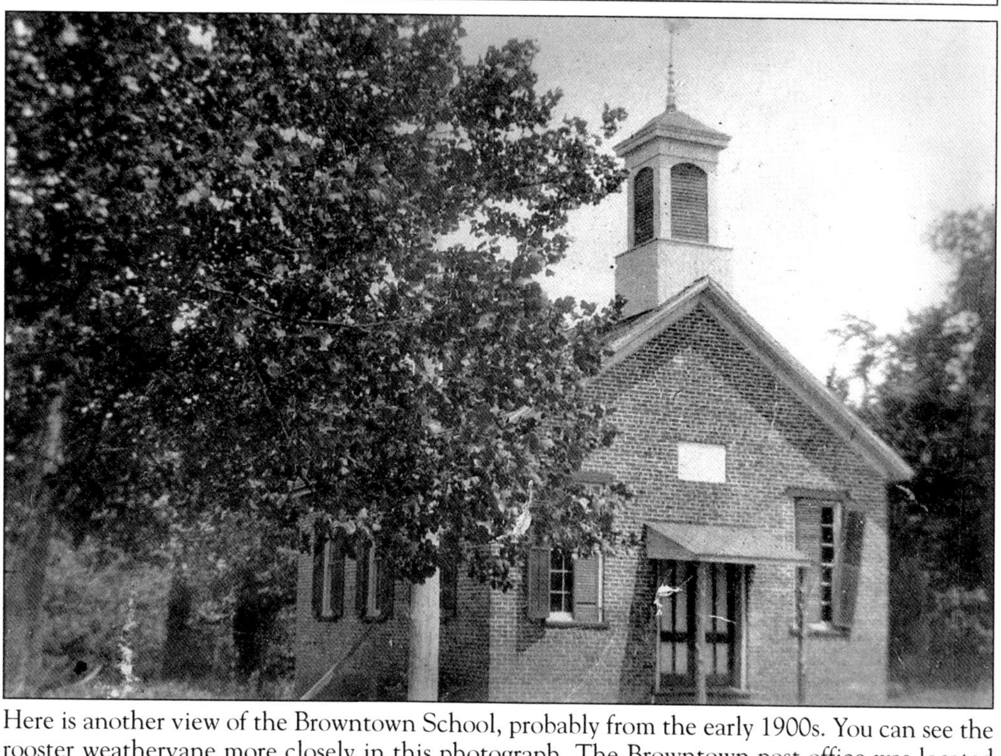

Here is another view of the Browntown School, probably from the early 1900s. You can see the rooster weathervane more closely in this photograph. The Browntown post office was located directly across the street.

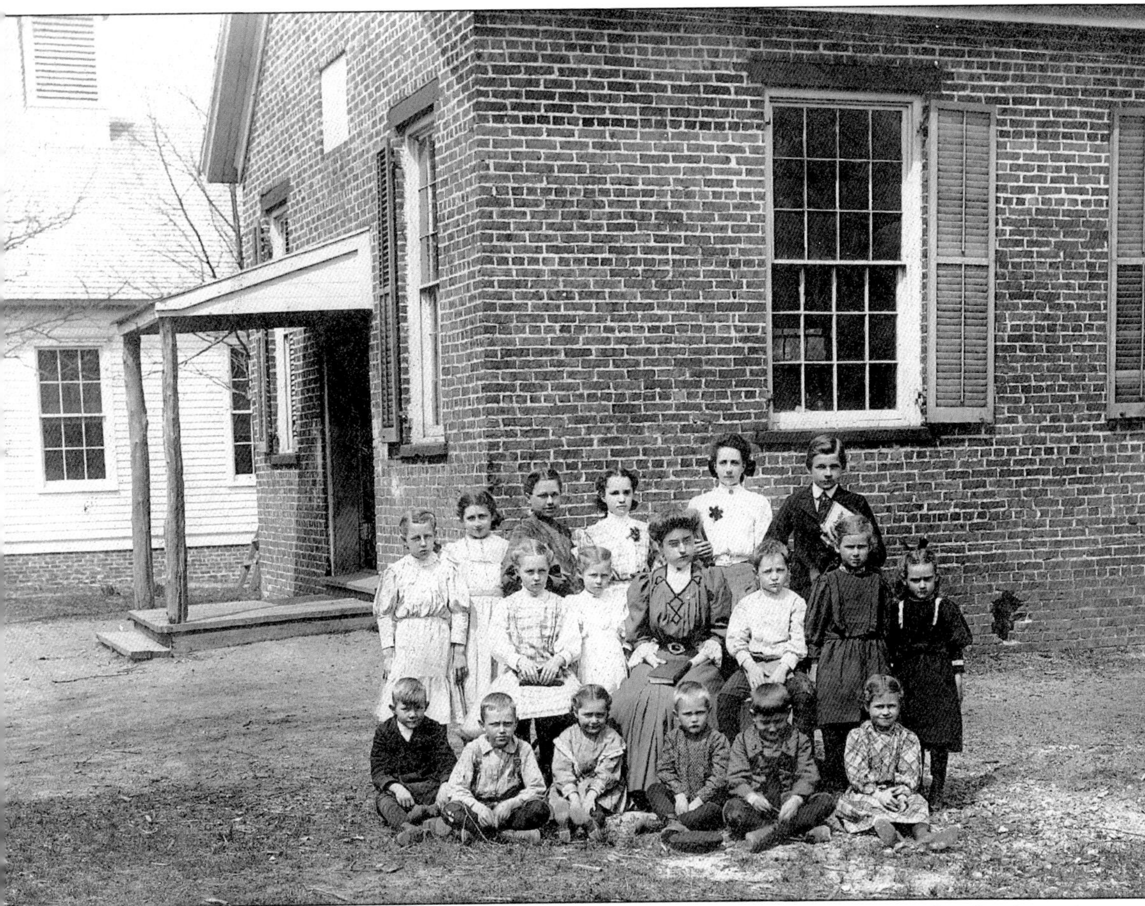

Grace Bayliss of New Brunswick was the teacher at the Browntown School when this photograph was taken in 1908. In the background is the Browntown Union Sunday School, which also served as a community center and a place of worship for various denominations. The Browntown School was expanded in 1917.

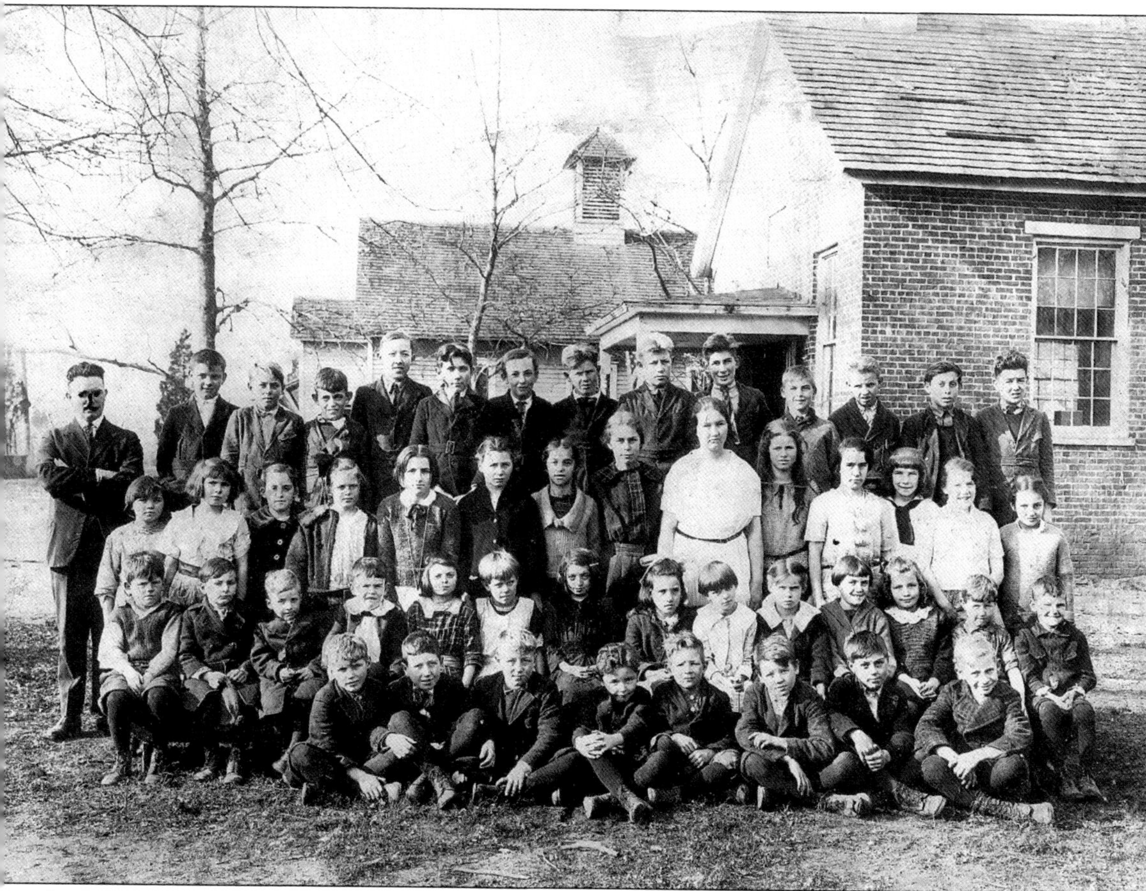

In 1923, the Browntown School looked similar to the original building even after the 1917 expansion. As you can see, the student population had increased greatly. The Browntown Union Sunday School in the background now serves as the Browntown Volunteer Firehouse.

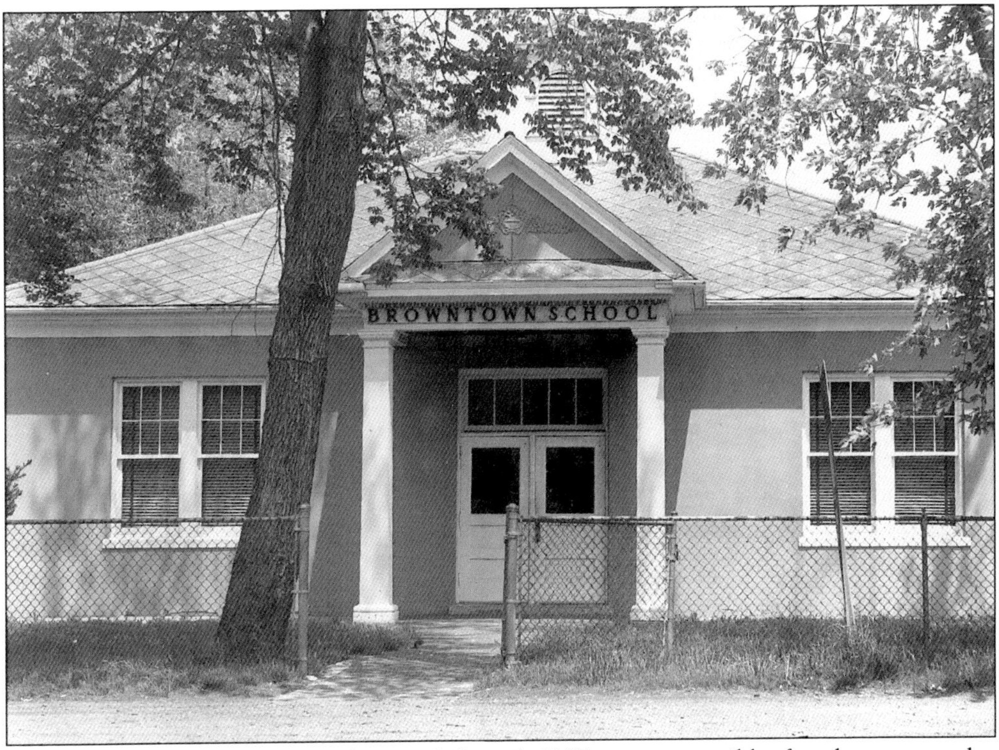

The additional expansions made in 1947 and 1957 are responsible for the present-day appearance of the Browntown School, which still stands on Route 516. The building is still used for educational purposes and serves the township as an adult high school.

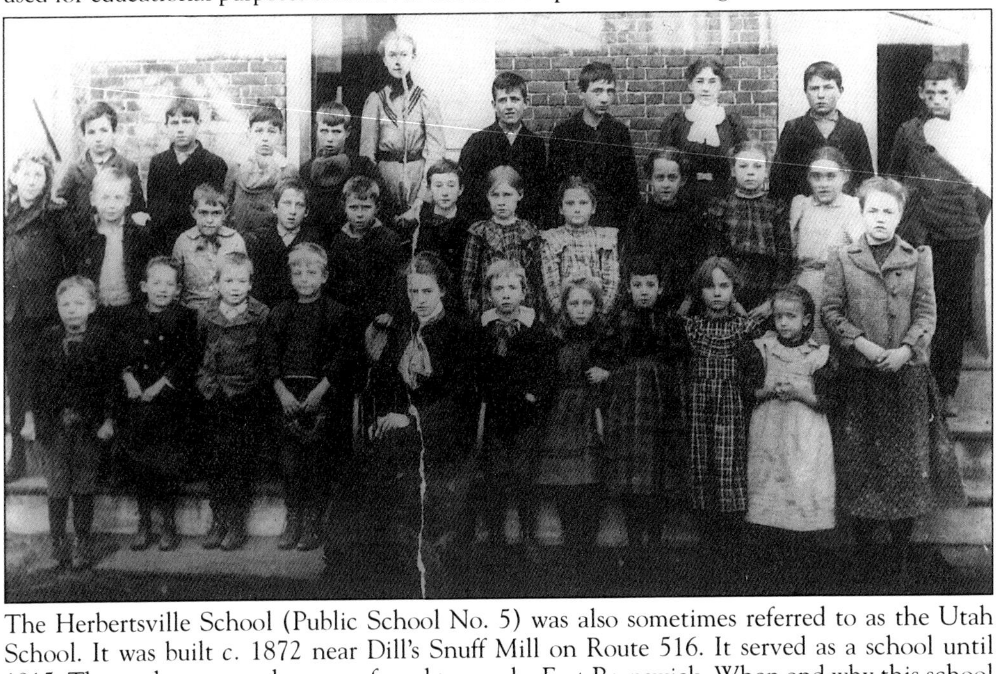

The Herbertsville School (Public School No. 5) was also sometimes referred to as the Utah School. It was built *c.* 1872 near Dill's Snuff Mill on Route 516. It served as a school until 1915. The students were then transferred to nearby East Brunswick. When and why this school became known as the Utah School is unknown. The date of the photograph is 1899.

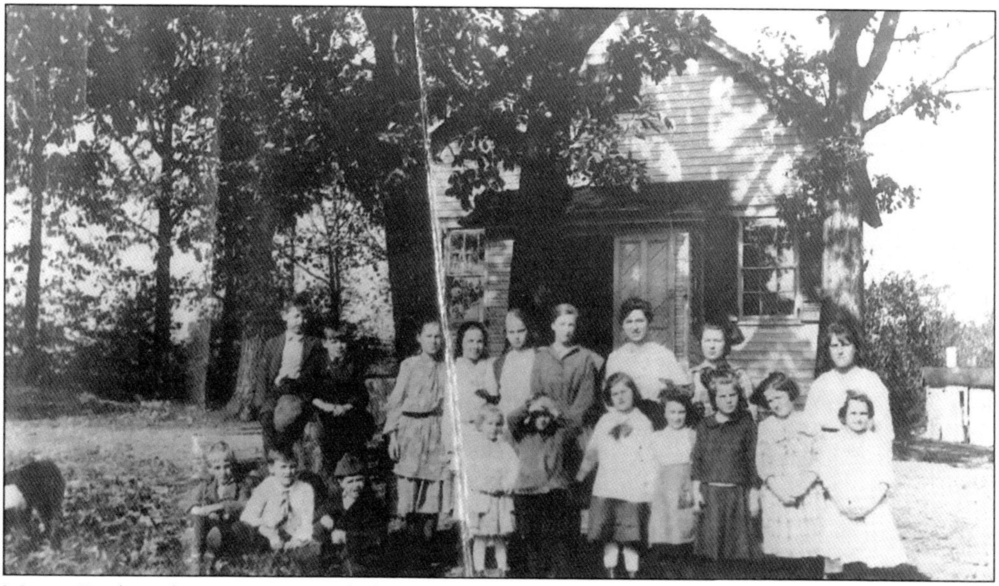

Marie Gaub is shown posing with her class at the Hillsboro School (Public School No. 6) in 1920. The school was built in 1839 and expanded in 1900. It closed in 1948, along with the other remaining one-room schoolhouses still operating. In 1949, the building was moved across the street from its original location on East Greystone Road and converted into a private home. It is still standing.

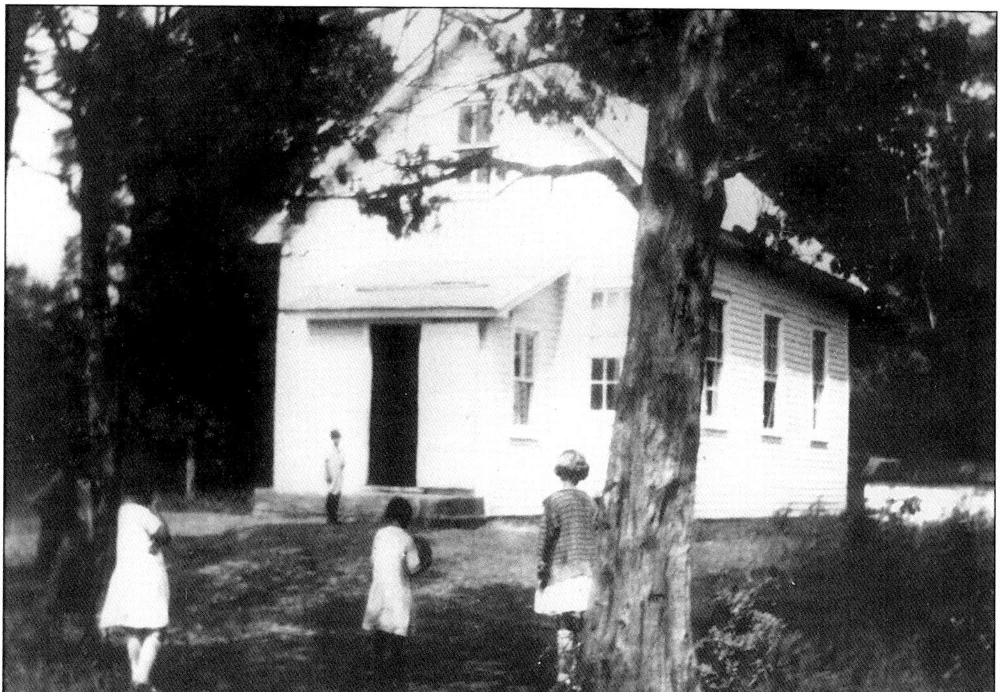

The Millbridge School (Public School No. 7) was located on Texas Road. It was originally built in 1865. The school underwent extensive renovations after a fire c. 1903. This photograph was taken after the renovation in the late 1920s.

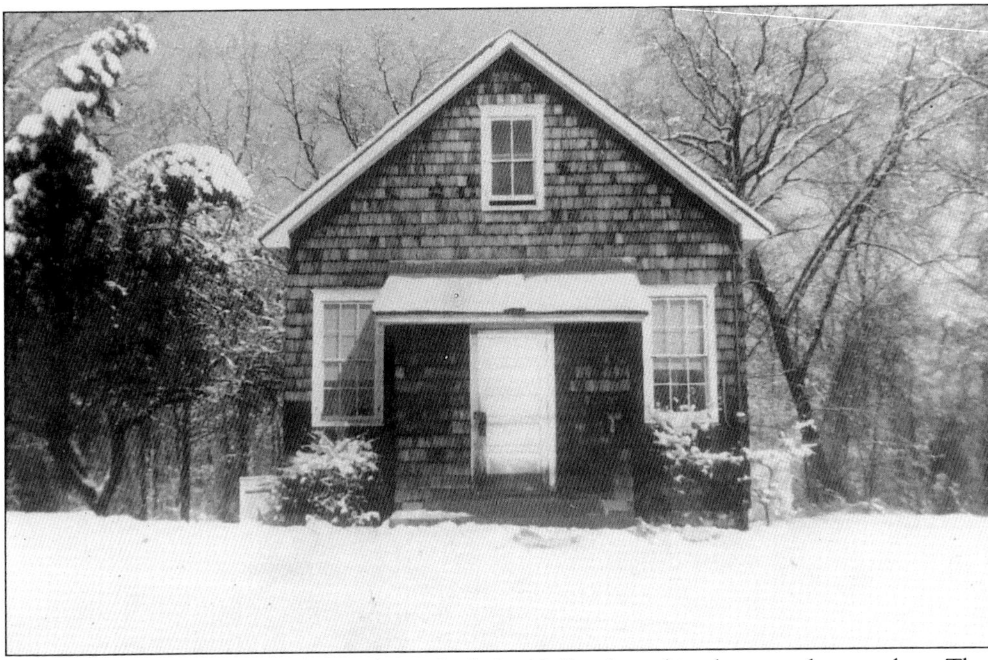

The Millbridge School had changed very little by 1948, when this photograph was taken. That year, the school was closed, along with the Cedar Ridge and Hillsboro Schools. The building was moved soon after by the Middlesex Monmouth Friendly Association to Old Dutch Neck Road, near Route 130, in Hightstown.

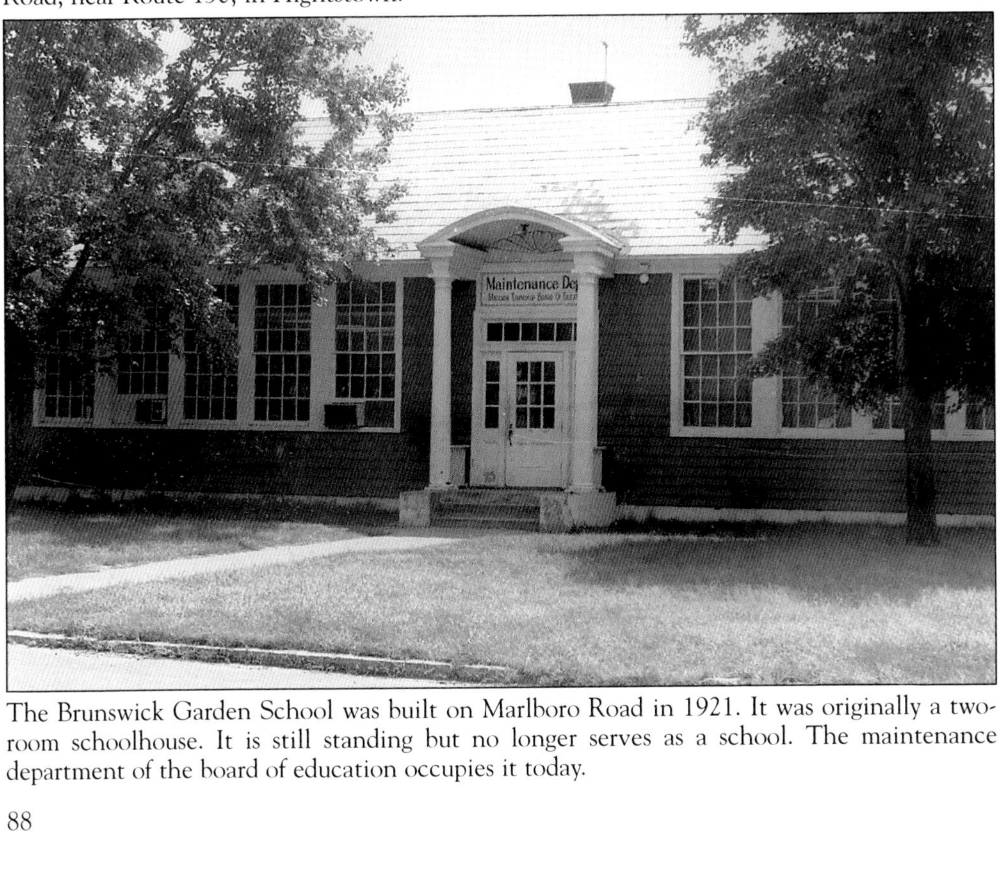

The Brunswick Garden School was built on Marlboro Road in 1921. It was originally a two-room schoolhouse. It is still standing but no longer serves as a school. The maintenance department of the board of education occupies it today.

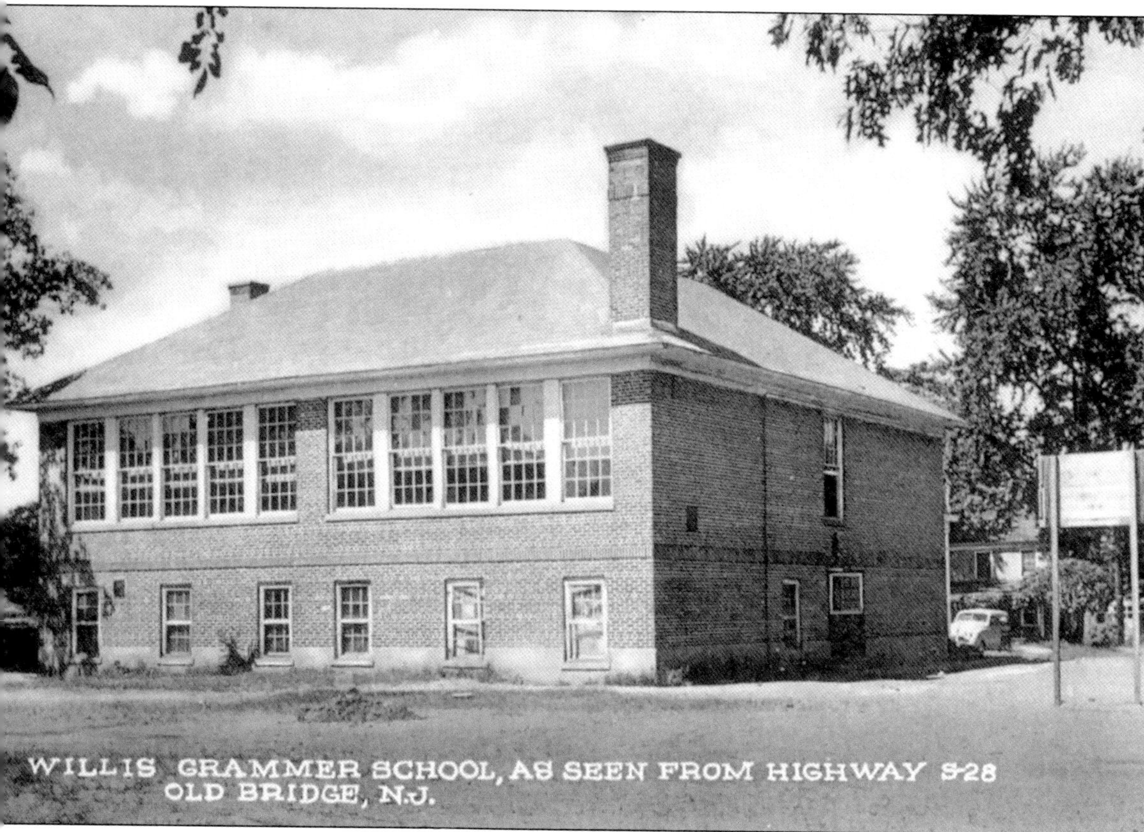

Located in the Old Bridge section of the township, the Willis School was a three-room brick building that was built in 1923. The cost of construction was $25,500. Its first principal was Elizabeth Palmer. Alberta Appleby and Judida Conover Pettie were the first teachers.

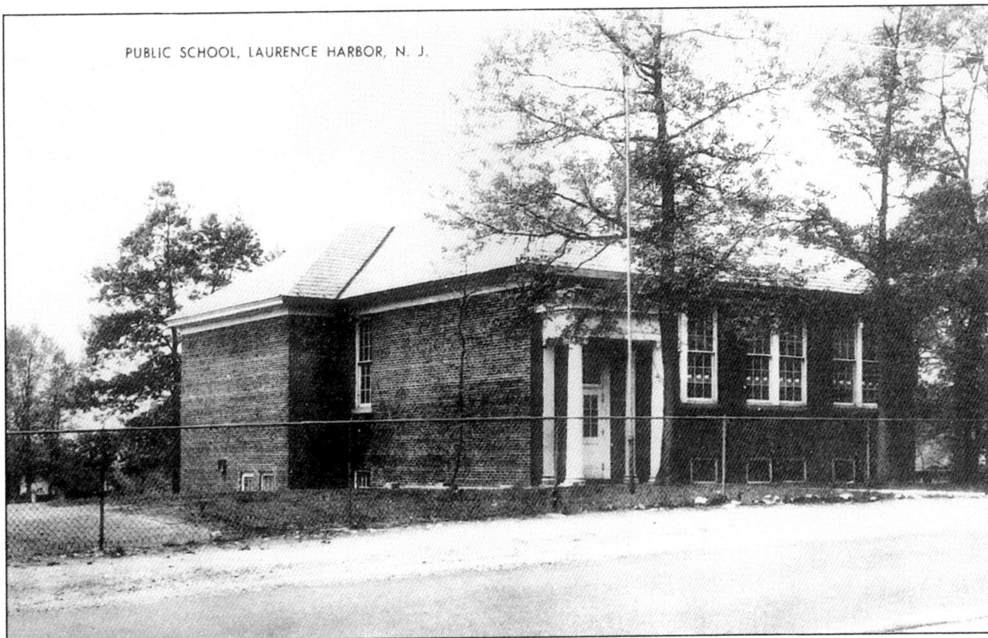

The Laurence Harbor School (Public School No. 9) was built in the early 1900s on Laurence Parkway. For a short time, it also served as the home of Laurence Harbor Volunteer Public Library, which was housed in the basement before moving to its current location.

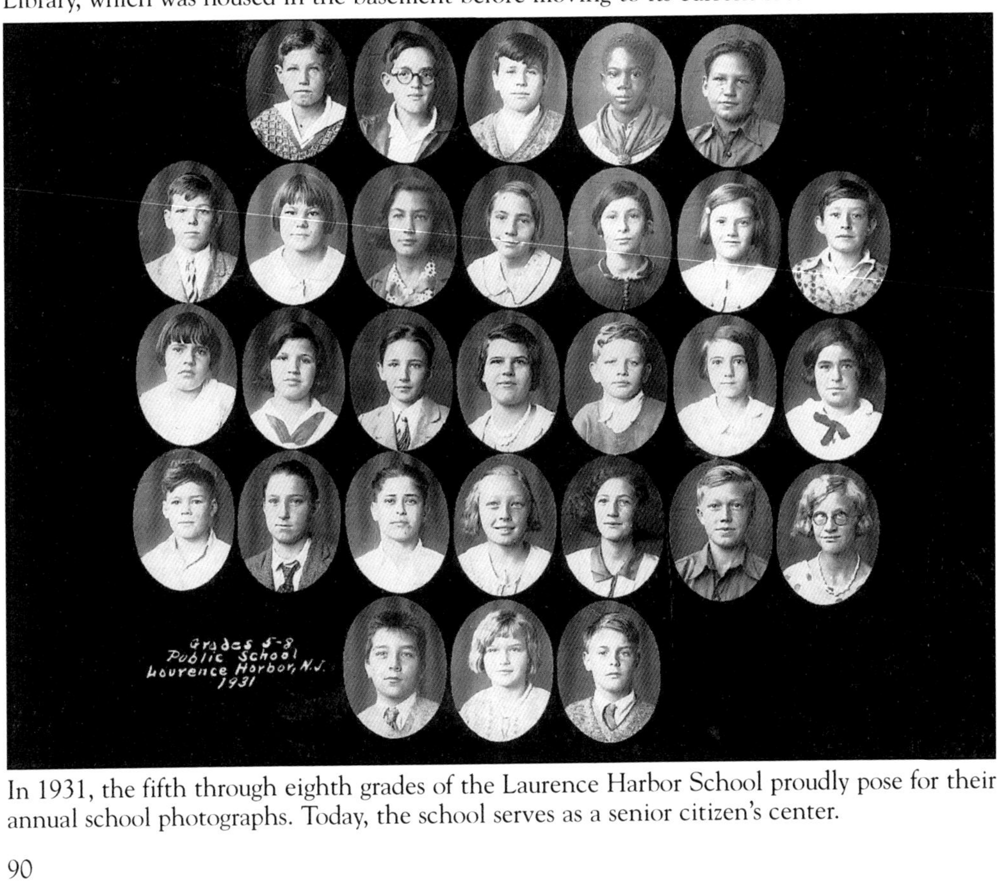

In 1931, the fifth through eighth grades of the Laurence Harbor School proudly pose for their annual school photographs. Today, the school serves as a senior citizen's center.

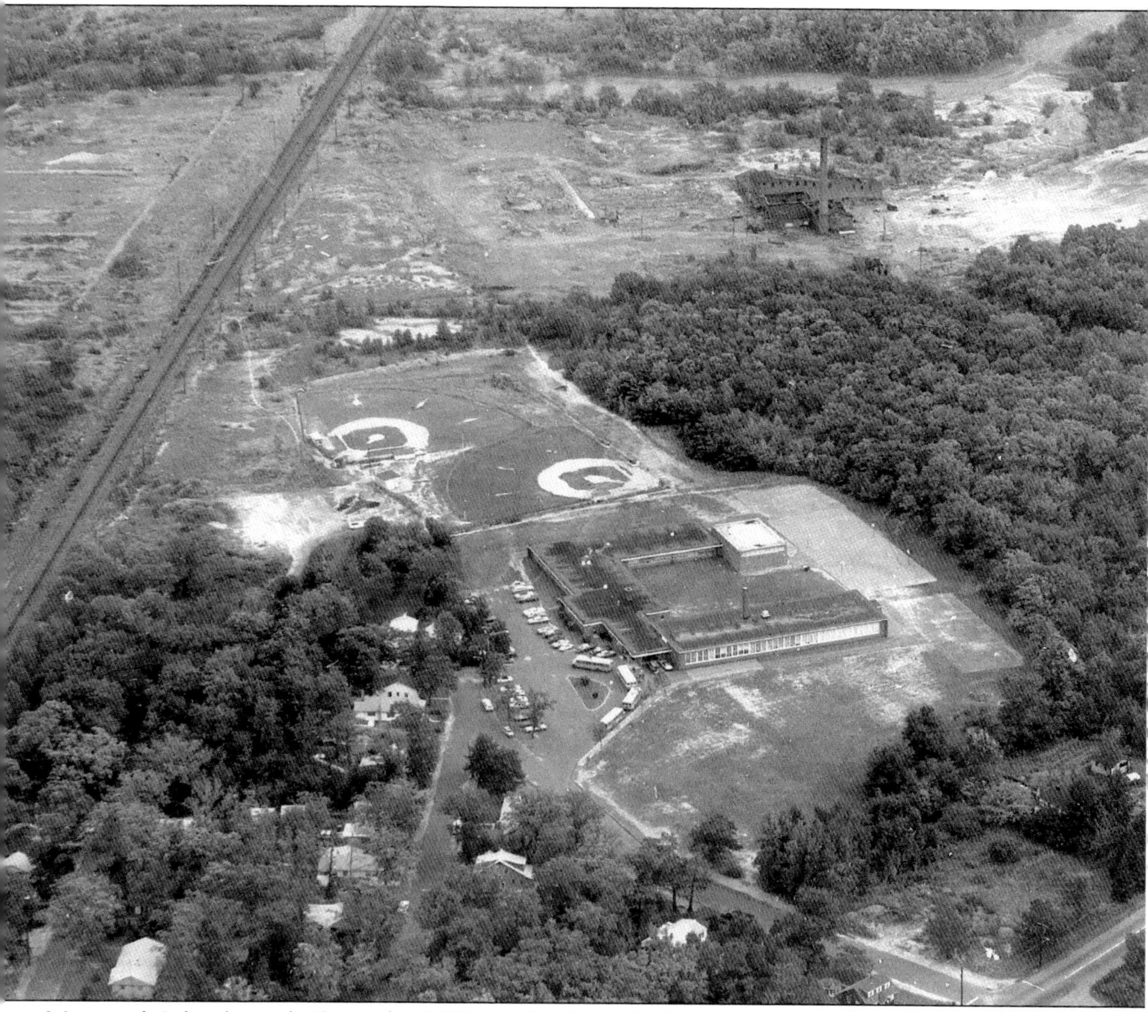

Memorial School was built in the 1950s at the foot of Ely Avenue to replace the Laurence Harbor School. This photograph was taken soon after its completion. The school has since been expanded. The baseball fields in the photograph are the home of the Laurence Harbor Little League. Today, there are five fields and a clubhouse. There is a condominium development currently located where the trees are on the right. The New Jersey Department of Transportation is planning to construct a commuter station near the tracks on the left. (Courtesy of the Old Bridge Board of Education.)

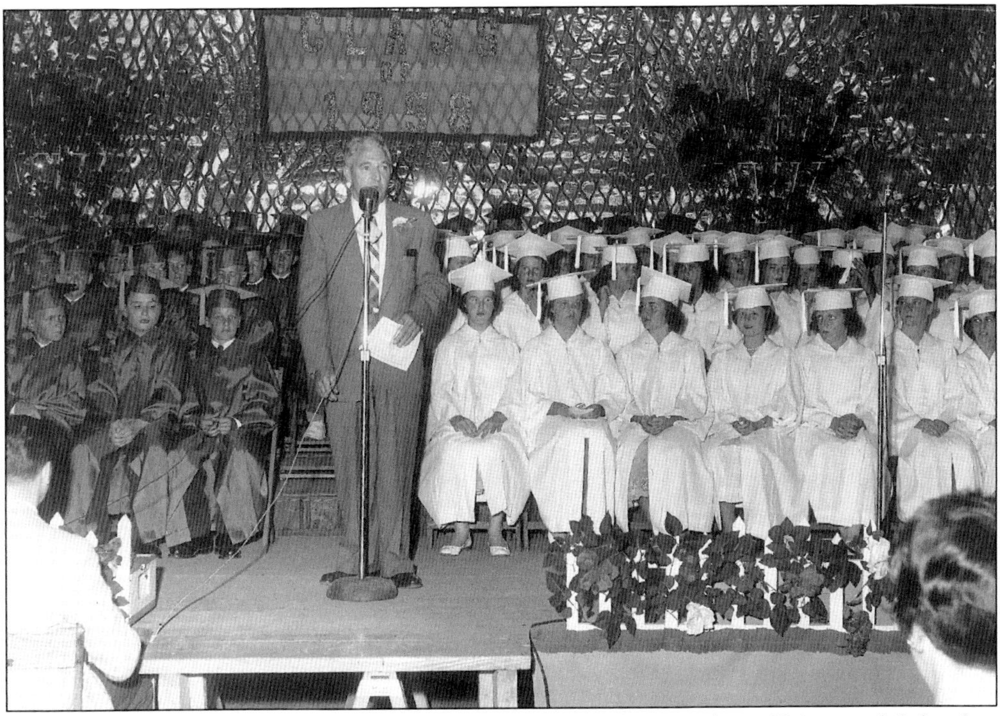

The president of the board of education addresses the graduating class of Memorial School in 1958. The event was held at the Casino on the boardwalk in Laurence Harbor.

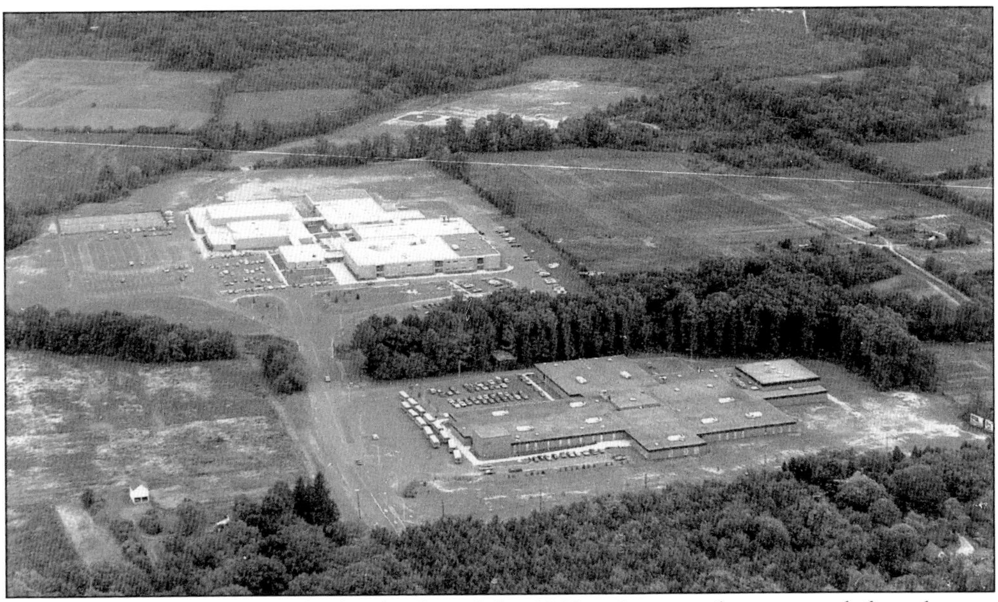

Old Bridge Township had no high school until the 1960s, when population growth forced a new wave of school construction. Prior to then, all of the township's high school–aged children were bused to schools in the neighboring communities. The Cedar Ridge High School, now called the Old Bridge High School East Campus, is shown shortly after its completion on Route 516. Carl Sandburg Middle School is the building in the foreground. The schools are located on the former Hauser farm. (Courtesy of the Old Bridge Board of Education.)

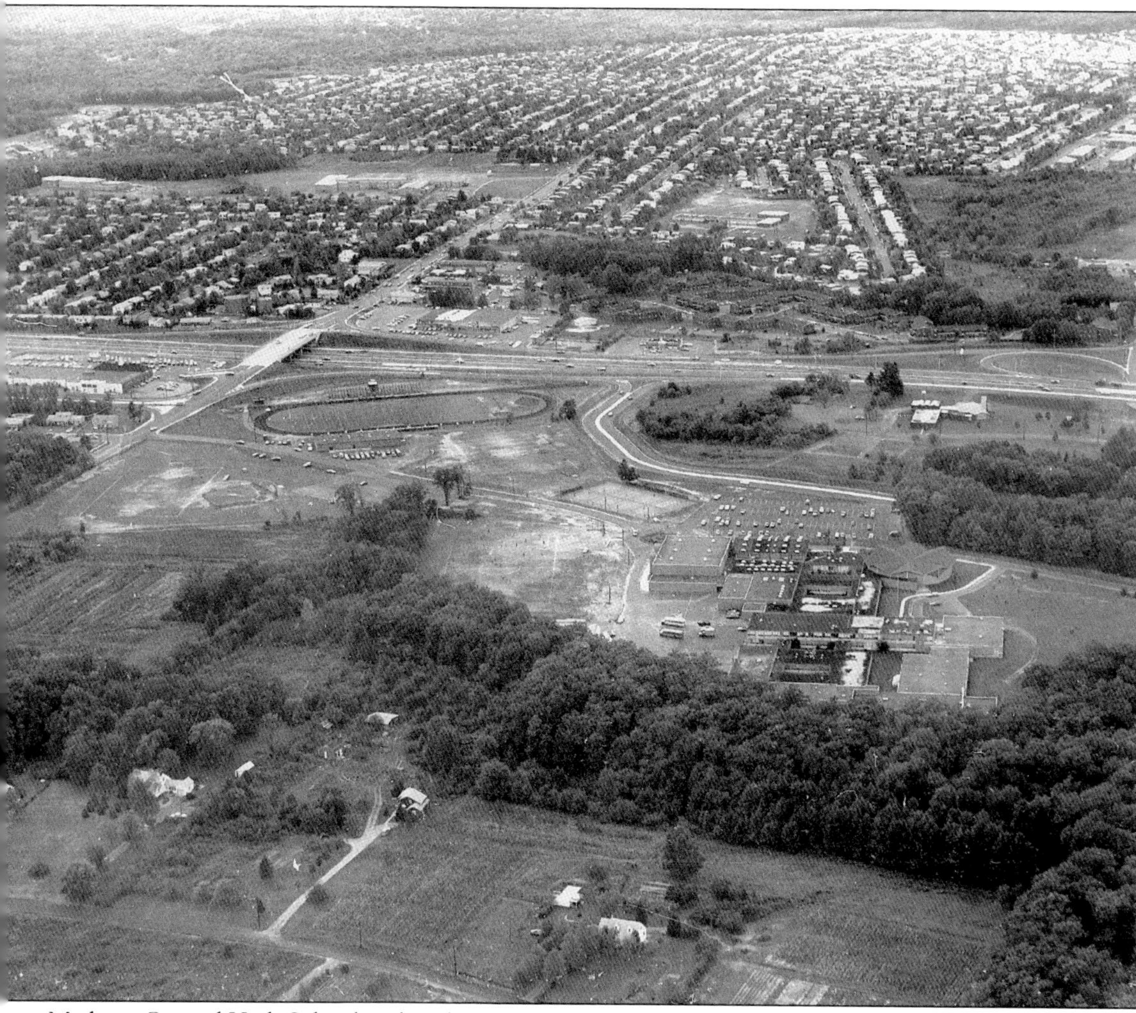

Madison Central High School and Cedar Ridge High School were located just a few miles apart from each other on Route 516. The latter school opened its doors in 1967 to help deal with a growing student population. The two schools were operated as separate facilities until the 1990s, when they were combined. The schools are now known as the east and west campuses of the Old Bridge High School. Route 9 runs from left to right in the center of the photograph. (Courtesy of the Old Bridge Board of Education.)

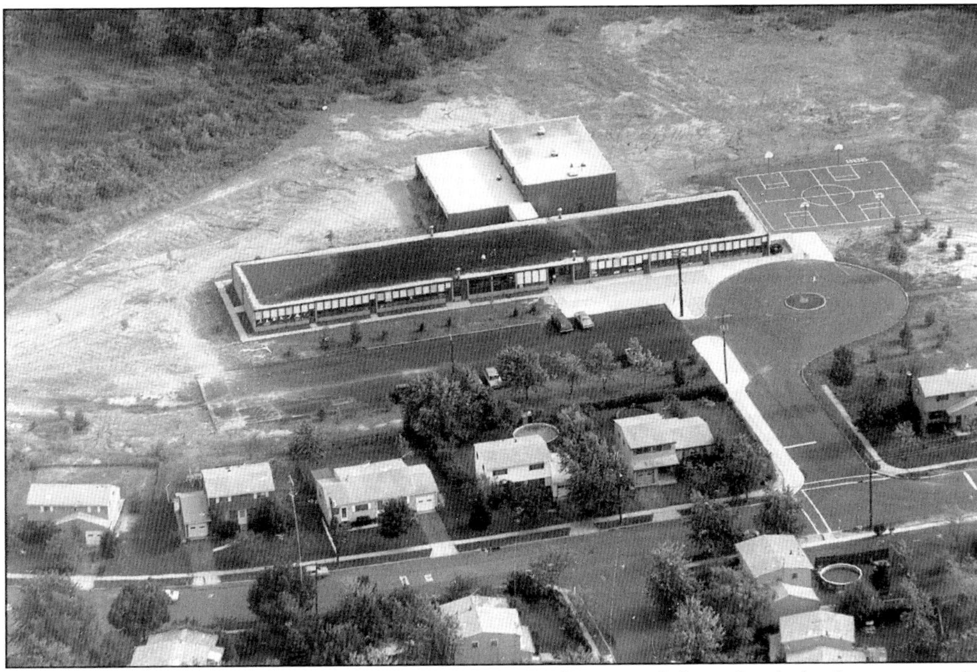

The Grissom Elementary School is representative of many of the schools built to meet the exploding population of the township in the 1950s and 1960s. It was built in the Sayrewoods South development on Sims Avenue in 1960. The school is named after astronaut Virgil Grissom. Many of the schools built in the same era were also named after astronauts, including John Glen, Alan Shepard, and Walter Schirra. (Courtesy of the Old Bridge Board of Education.)

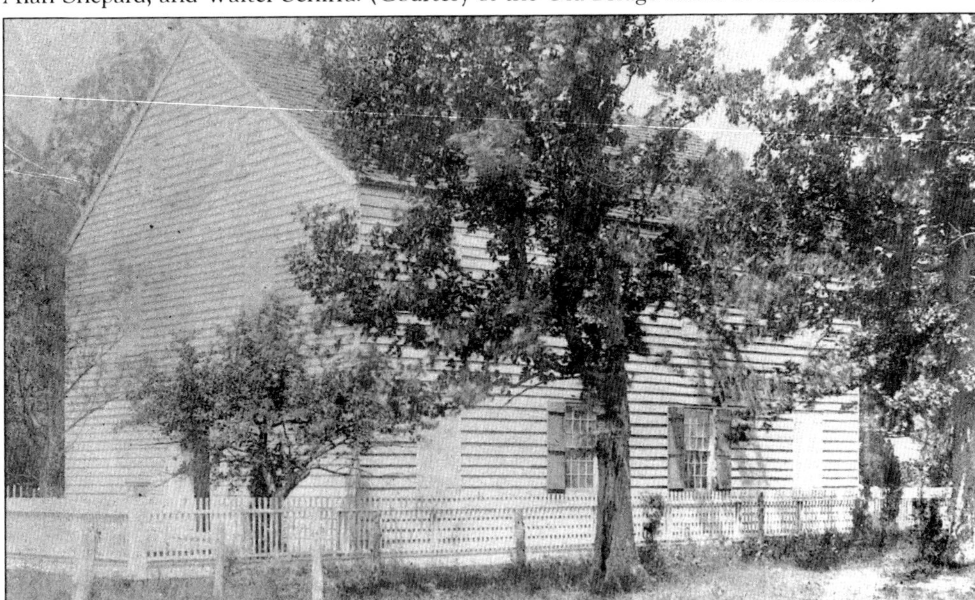

The Cheesequake Baptist Church was one of the earliest houses of worship in the area. It was located on Route 34. The first pastor was Rev. Able Morgan (1713–1785), who was known for his fierce support of the American Revolution. He preached at a log cabin at the church site from the 1740s. In 1832, the cabin was replaced by the building shown here.

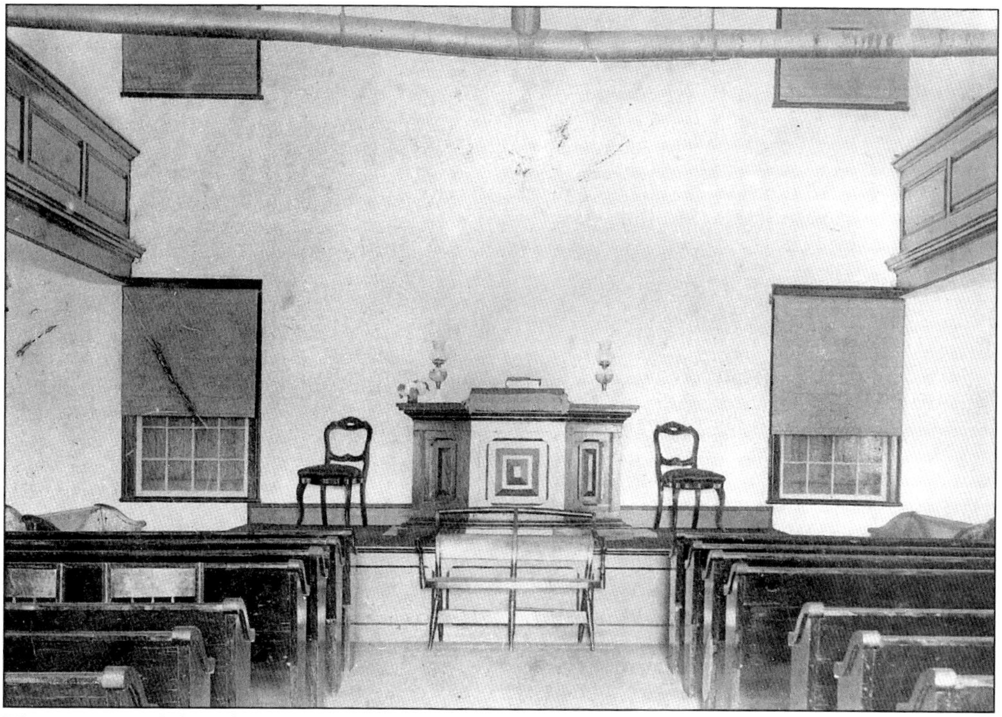

The interior of the Cheesequake Baptist Church was sparse and austere, befitting for a place of worship attended by modest farmers and townspeople. As the largest building in the area, the church was also used for secular purposes. School functions, town meetings, and other local events were held there.

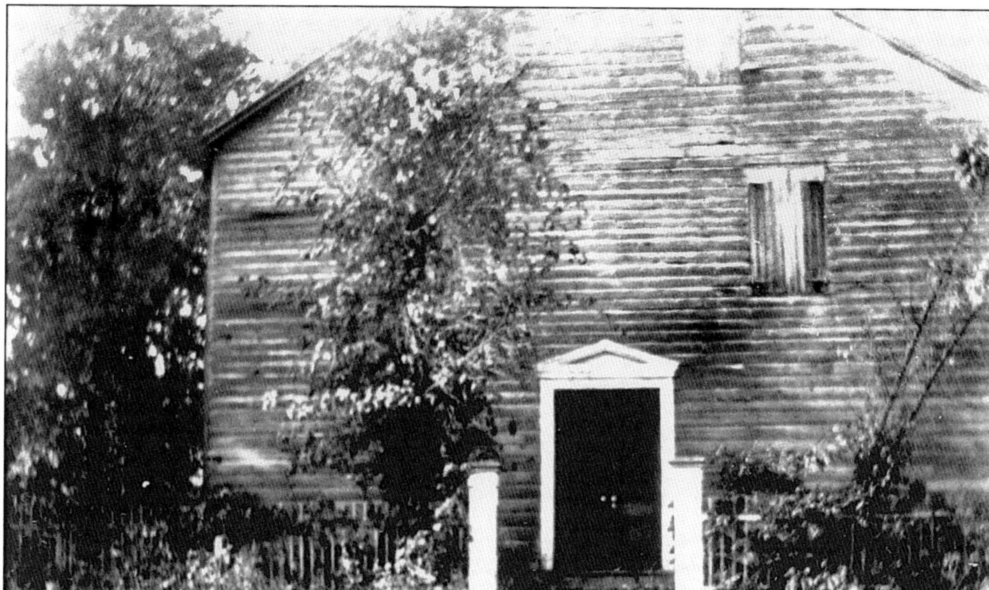

By the 1930s, the Cheesequake Baptist Church was deserted and crumbling. This may have been one of the last photographs taken of the building. The church burned to the ground in 1932, after 100 years of service.

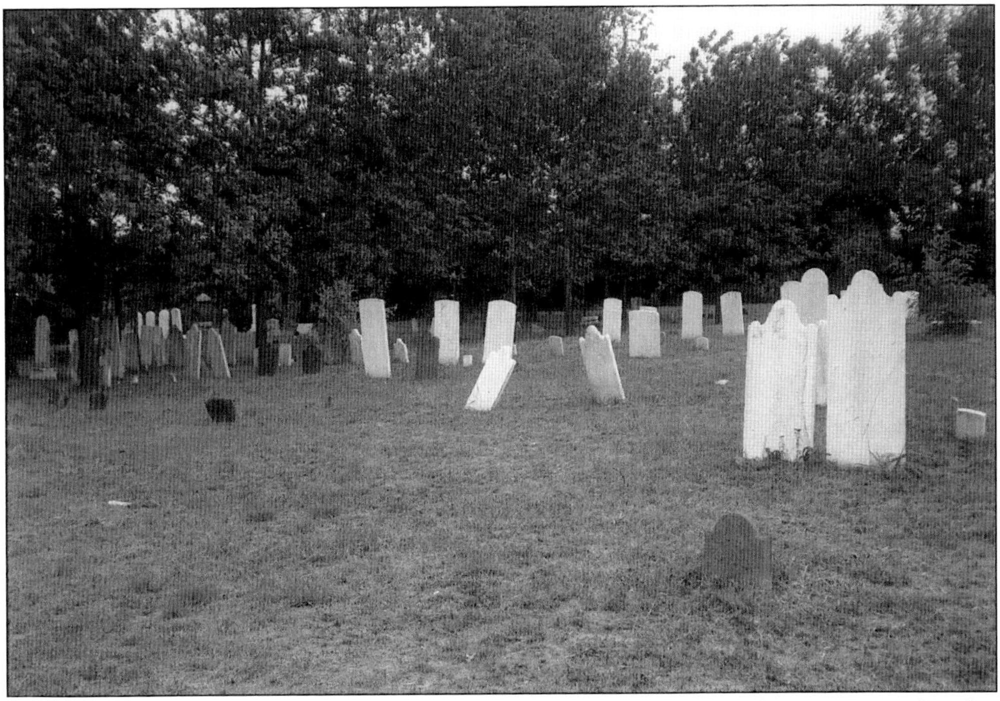

All that remains of the Cheesequake Baptist Church site is a small cemetery and a few crumbling foundation stones. Many of the parishioners of the early church are buried there, and the founding families are well represented. The Old Bridge Historical Commission has erected a plaque at the site to identify it.

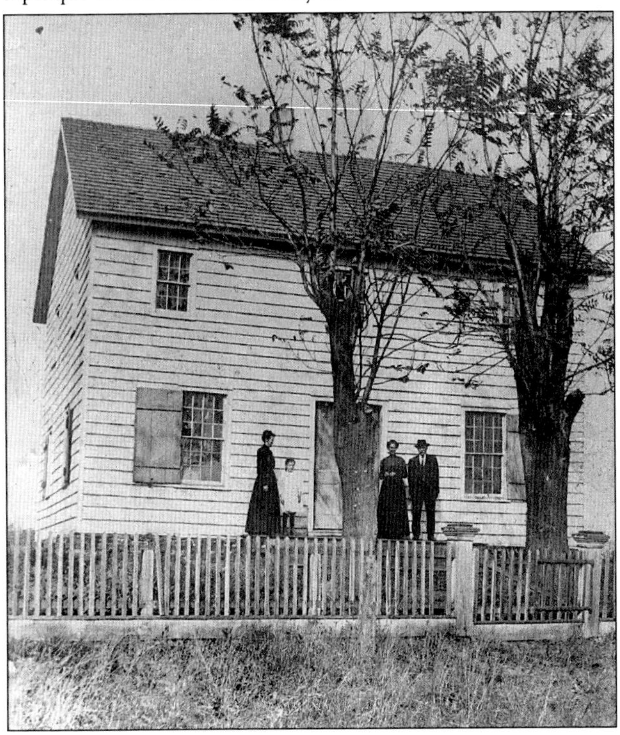

Just west of the Cheesequake Baptist Church, on Route 34, the Methodist Episcopal church was built in 1806. Prior to its construction, members of the congregation used the Baptist church for services and its cemetery for burials. Its location was not appreciated by J. Leonard Giler, who described it at a New York East Methodist Conference. Giler said, "I stood in the midst of a sand-field, one of the most God-forsaken spots on earth I ever saw, where neither bird, beast, reptile or insect could have extracted nutrition sufficient for the most ephemeral existence."

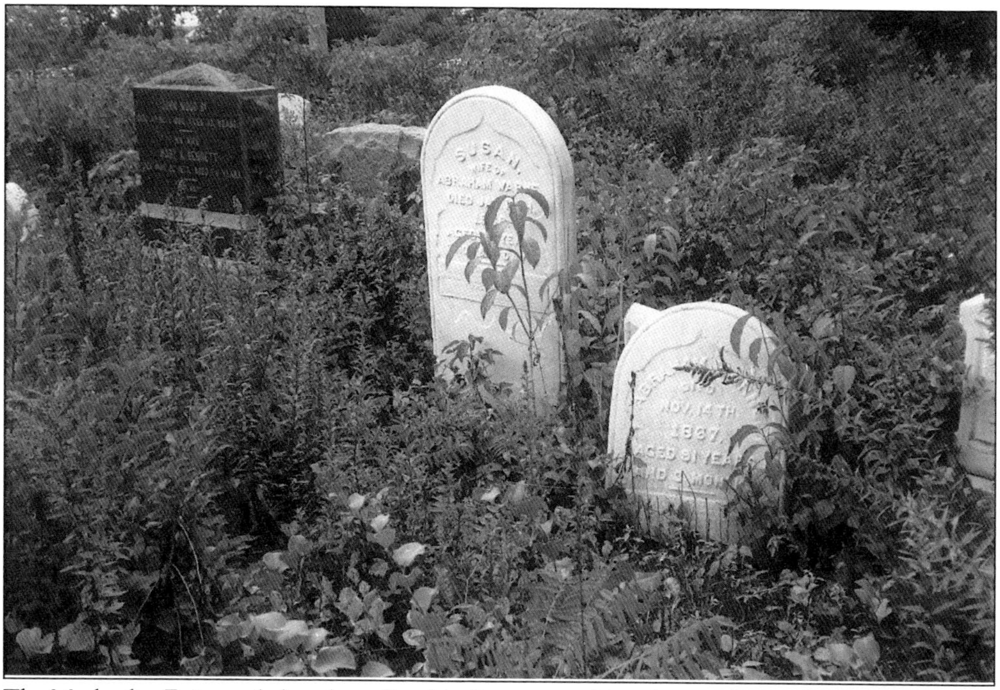

The Methodist Episcopal church outlived its Baptist neighbor, but not by too long. It succumbed to fire in 1956, after being closed in 1924. Like its neighbor, all that remains is a small cemetery and a barely recognizable building foundation. The Old Bridge Historic Commission has also placed a plaque at this site.

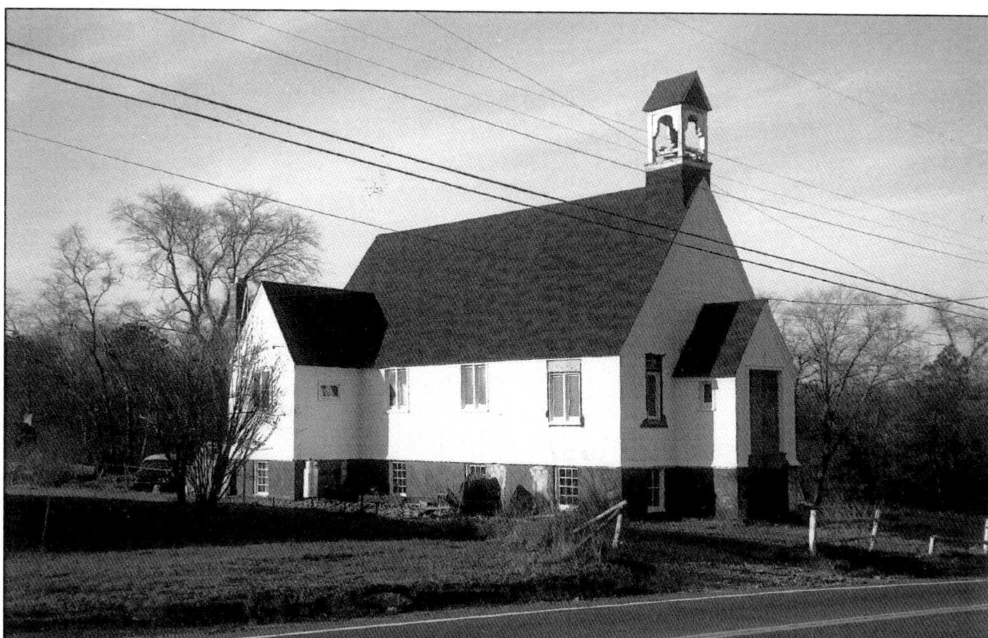

Built in 1901, Christ Our Savior Church is located on Cottrell Road between Route 34 and Route 516. When this photograph was taken in the 1960s, the church was abandoned and beginning to deteriorate. It has since been renovated and converted into a private residence.

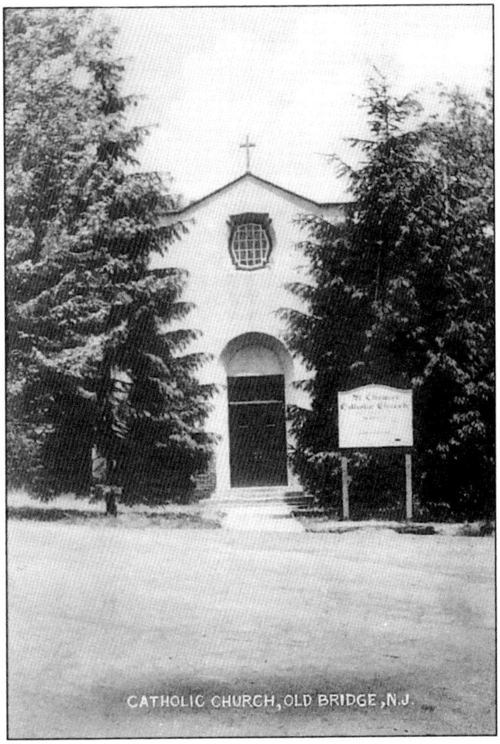

St. Thomas Roman Catholic Church was originally located on the Old Bridge Turnpike, just across the border in East Brunswick. That first building, shown in this postcard, was sold to a Greek Orthodox congregation when St. Thomas moved to its new, larger facility on Route 18 in Old Bridge.

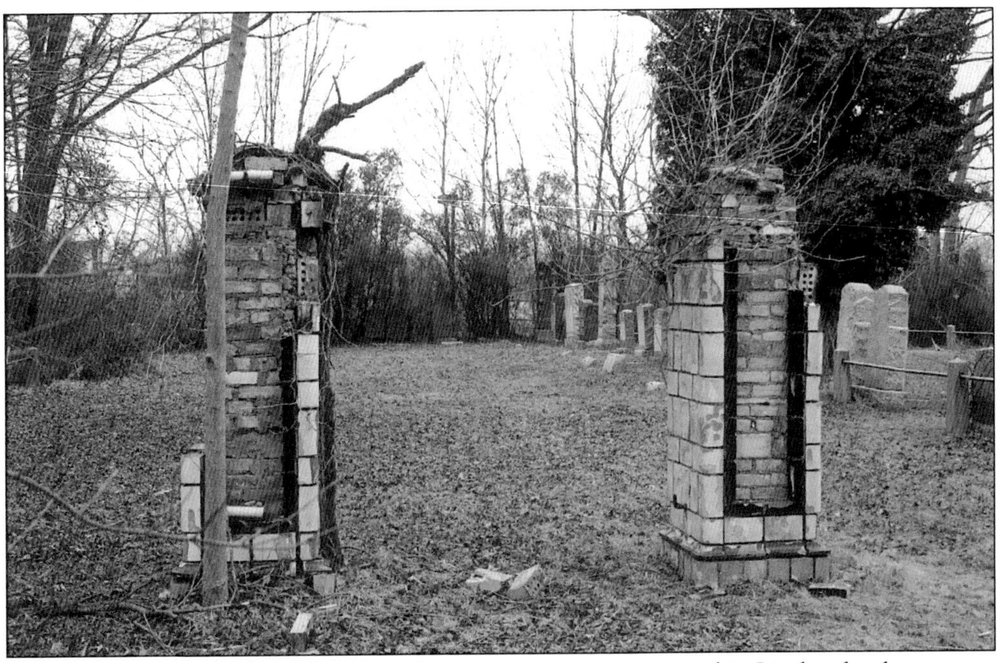

In 1928, the Mount Hebron Cemetery Association was incorporated in Linden for the purpose of acquiring property for a Jewish cemetery. It is believed they chose this location on Morristown Road, near Route 34, because the township was willing to grant the necessary permits. Since then, approximately 100 people have been interred on the property. The gateposts shown here could use some work, but the cemetery is very well tended to and still active.

Five

Fun and Relaxation

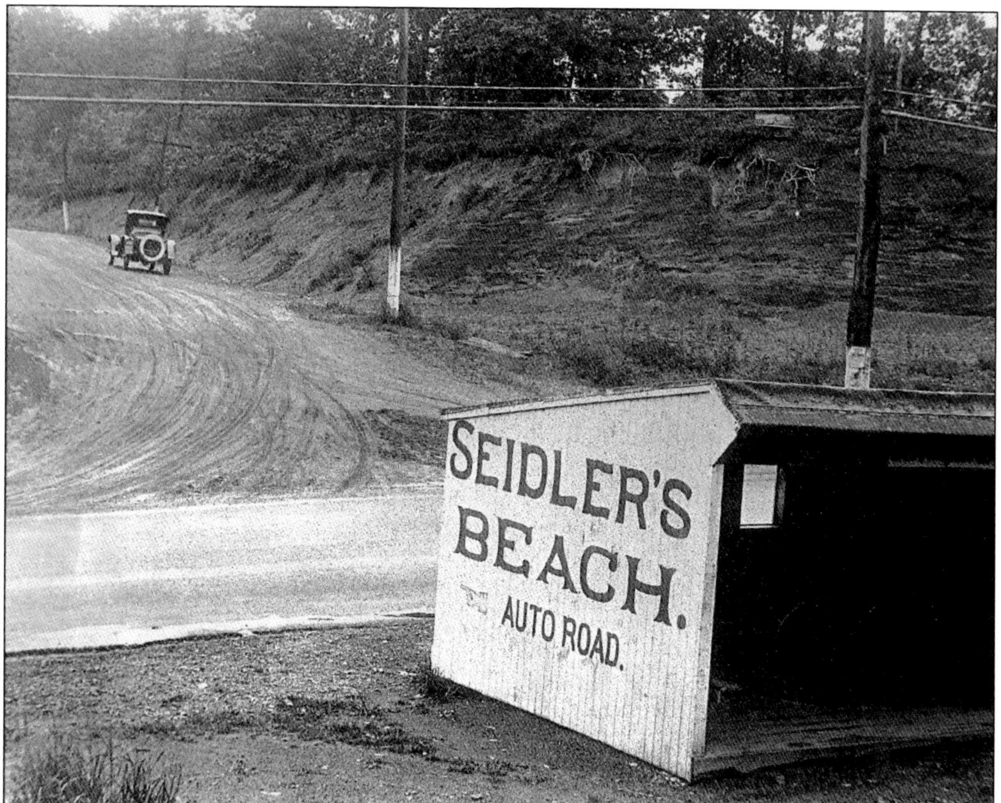

Perhaps the oldest and most famous recreation site in Old Bridge is Seidler's Beach on the Raritan Bay. Situated between Laurence Harbor and Cliffwood Beach, Seidler's Beach offered cool breezes, calm waves, and plenty of sun for visitors. Native Americans used this shoreline for swimming, fishing, and clamming long before the first European settlers arrived. For many years, the road leading from Route 35 to Seidler's Beach was a welcome site to hot summer arrivals.

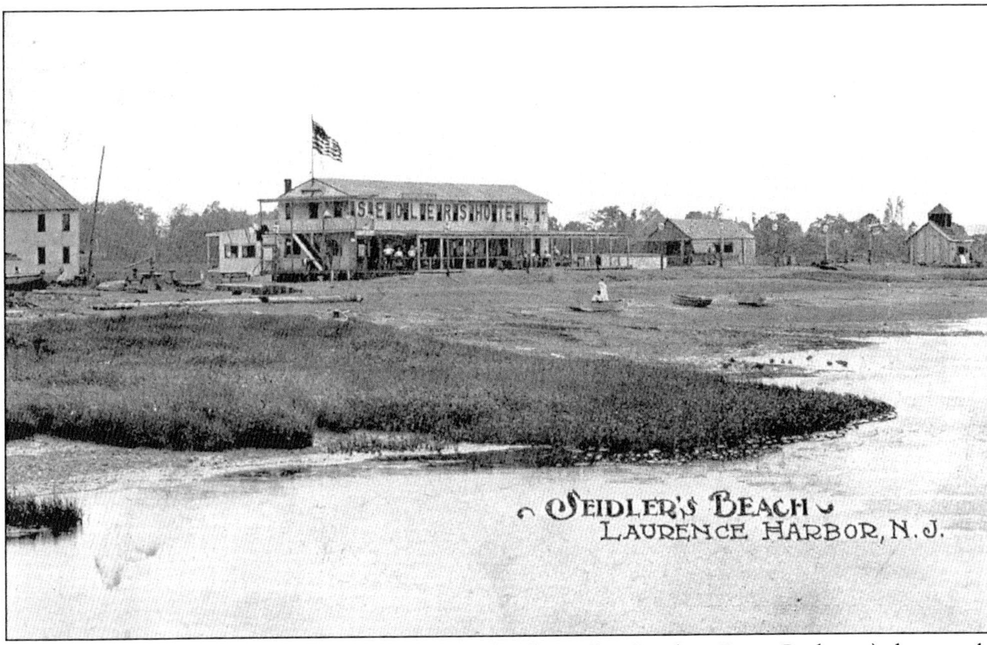

Prior to the construction of major highways (such as the Garden State Parkway) that could more easily funnel families to towns located farther south along the Atlantic Ocean, the Raritan Bay was considered the Jersey Shore for many visitors in the cities to the north. This postcard, dated 1909, shows how Seidler's Beach looked at the beginning of the 20th century. The building in the center is a hotel. The view is looking north toward Laurence Harbor.

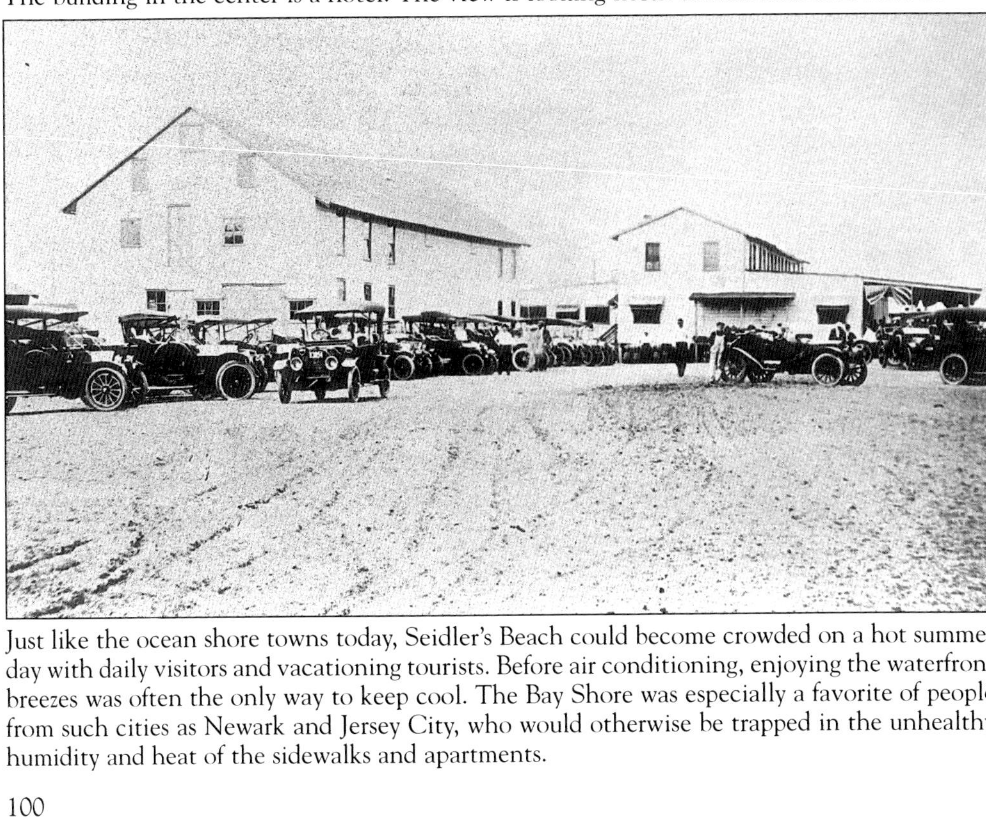

Just like the ocean shore towns today, Seidler's Beach could become crowded on a hot summer day with daily visitors and vacationing tourists. Before air conditioning, enjoying the waterfront breezes was often the only way to keep cool. The Bay Shore was especially a favorite of people from such cities as Newark and Jersey City, who would otherwise be trapped in the unhealthy humidity and heat of the sidewalks and apartments.

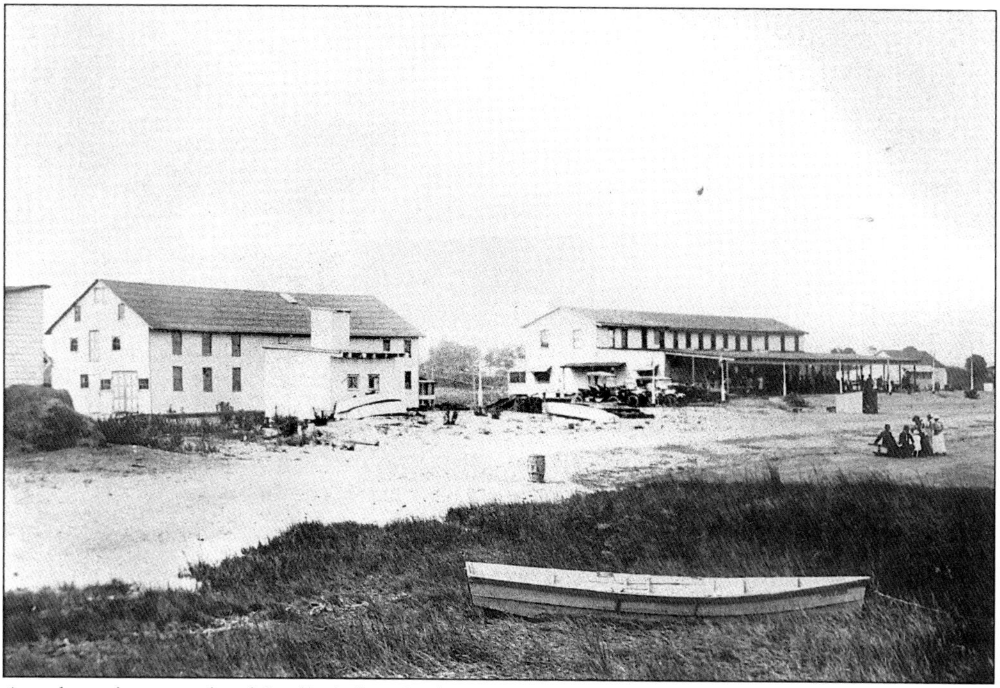

Another photograph of Seidler's Beach shows a much less crowded scene, perhaps in the off-season. The small boat in the foreground could be used for fishing, crabbing, or just relaxing on the water.

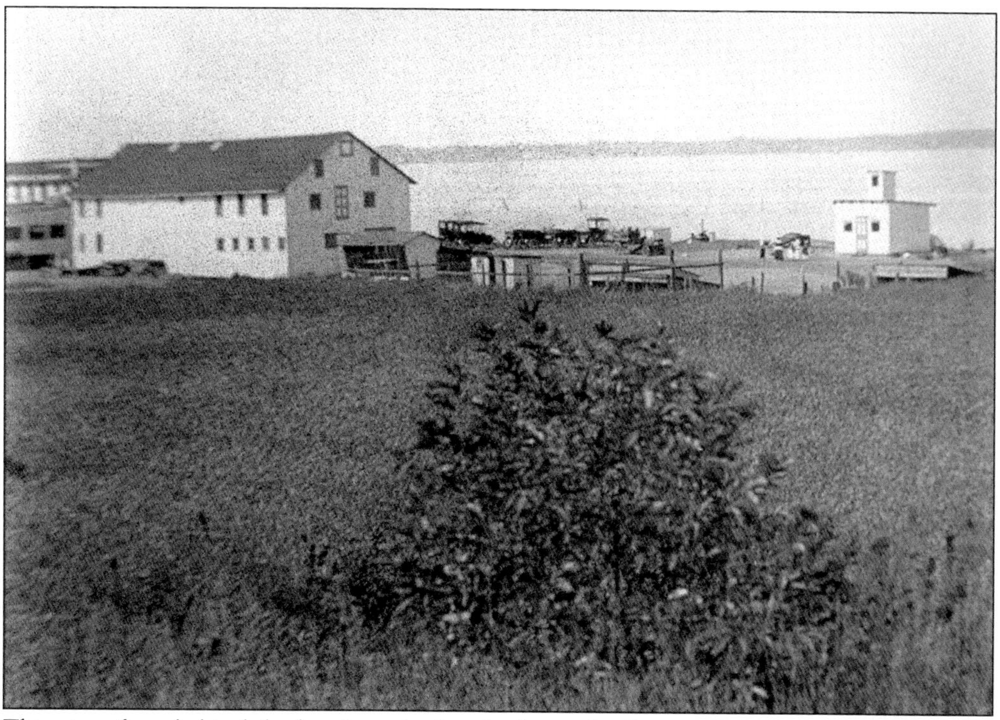

This view, from behind the hotel on the beach, shows the Raritan Bay. Staten Island is in the background. The calmness of the scene makes you appreciate what drew visitors to the area.

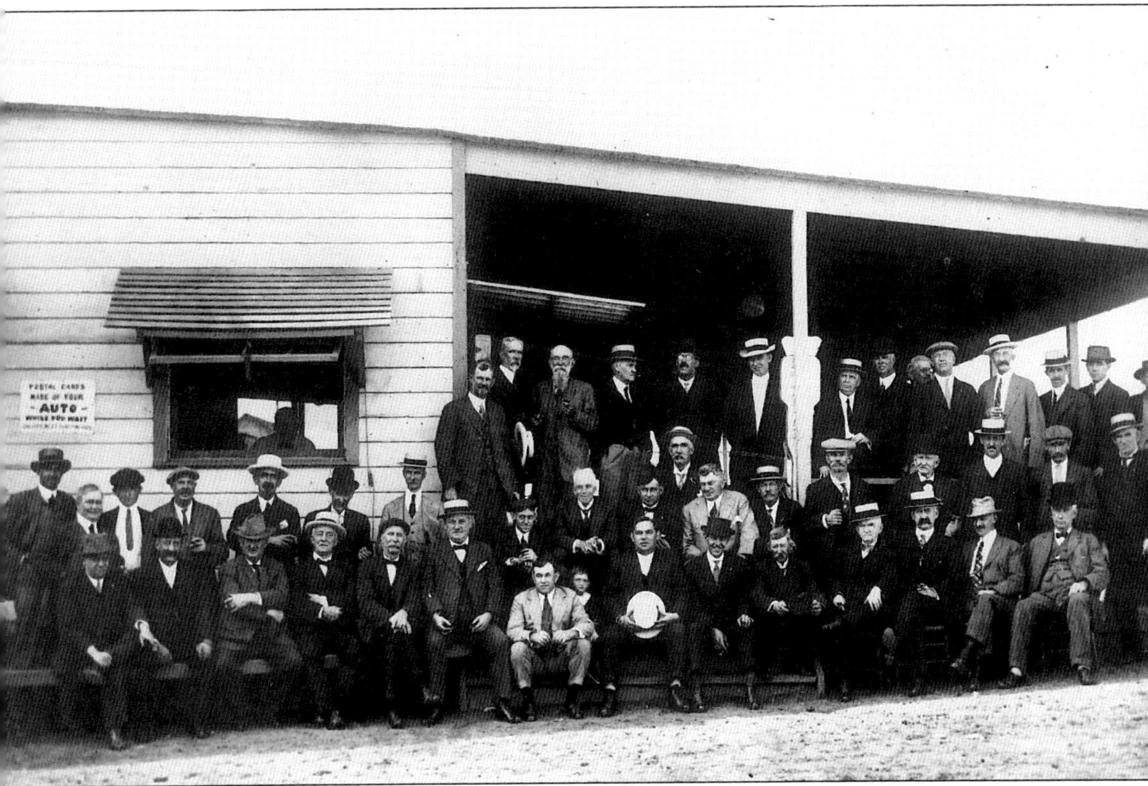

Like Atlantic City and other shore towns, Seidler's Beach also served as a meeting place for civic and government organizations. The Middlesex County board of freeholders met there in 1920. The sign on the left on the building reads, "Postal cards of your auto while you wait."

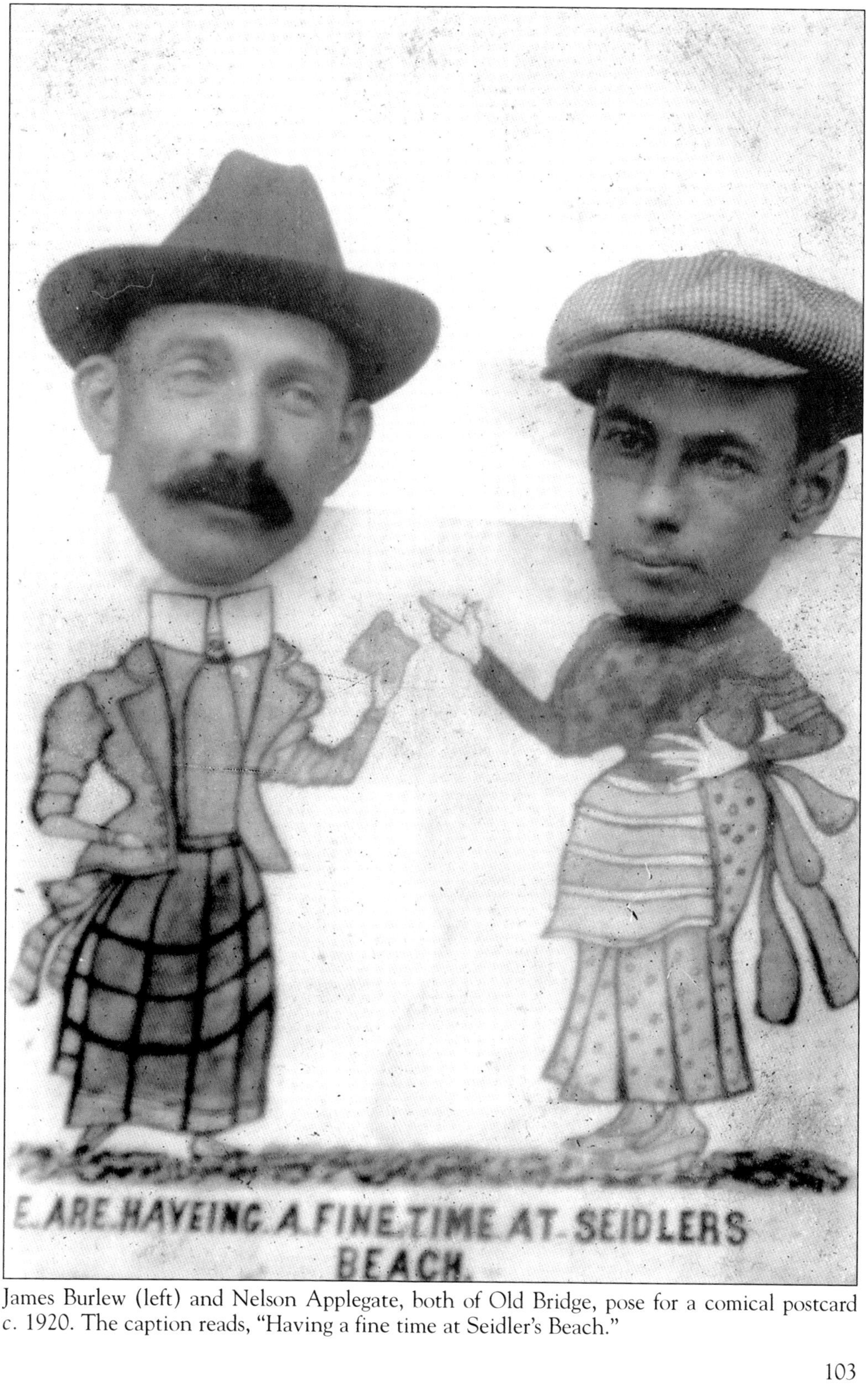

James Burlew (left) and Nelson Applegate, both of Old Bridge, pose for a comical postcard c. 1920. The caption reads, "Having a fine time at Seidler's Beach."

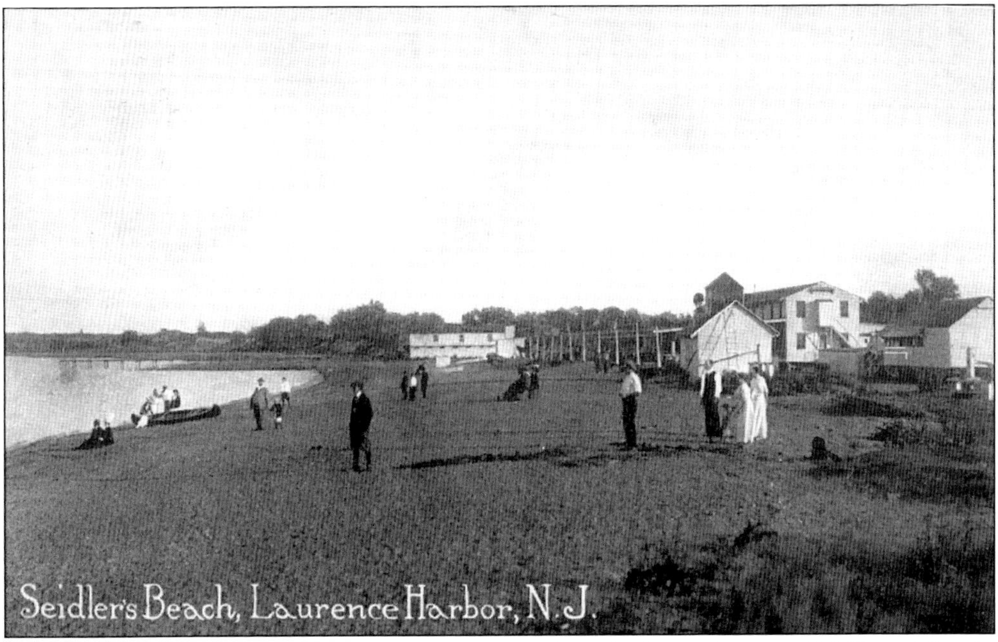

Seidler's Beach is shown in this 1924 postcard view, which looks south toward Cliffwood Beach. Note the canoe on the shore. What is everyone looking at?

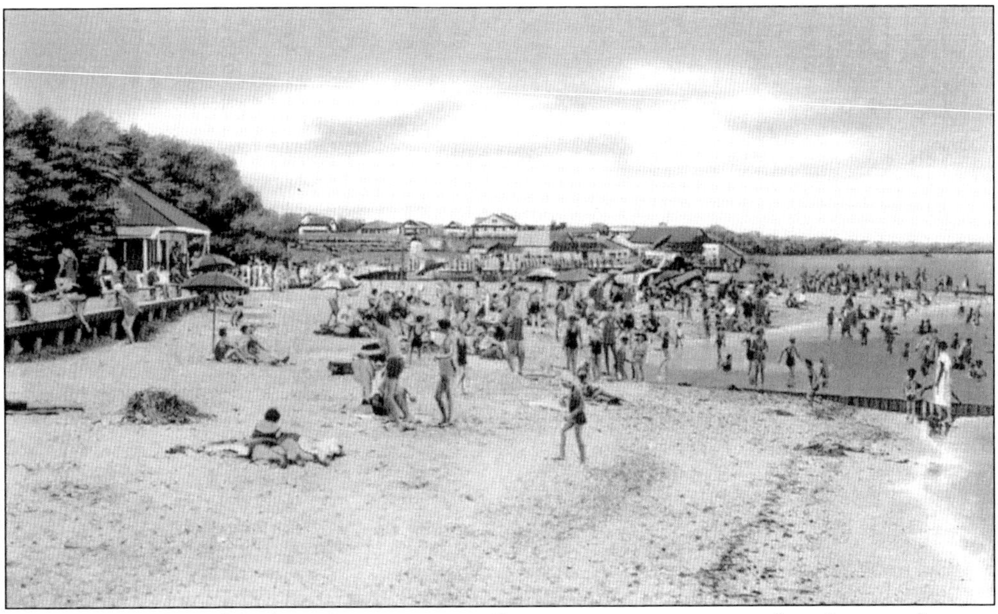

The large hotels and bathing houses eventually gave way to a more relaxed atmosphere at Seidler's Beach. Summer visitors still flocked to the beach, but more and more people began traveling farther south.

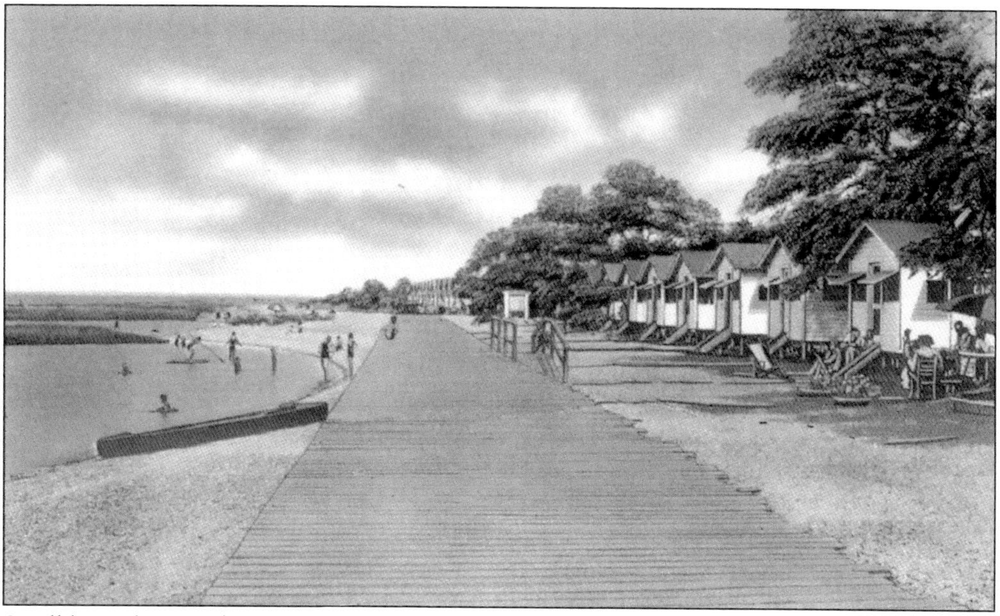

Small bungalows took over as the preferred vacation choice for many visitors. They were small but comfortable, and most had kitchen facilities that helped to spread vacation dollars. Visitors could rent them by the week, month, or season.

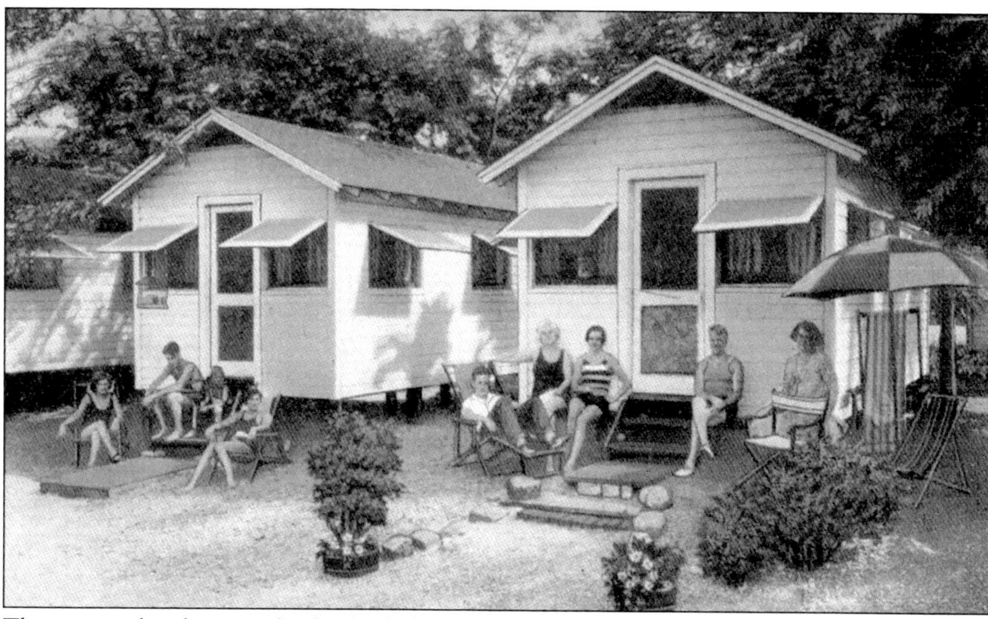

This postcard, exhorting the fun had along the Bay Shore, says it all: "Enjoying the proverbial life of Riley at Laurence Harbor, N.J., bungalow colony."

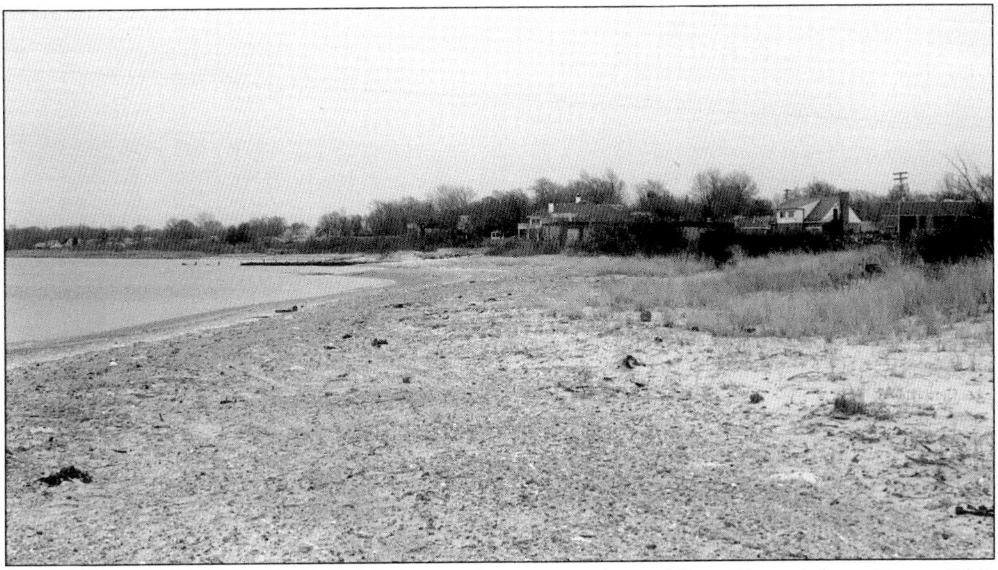

Today, Seidler's Beach is rarely visited, even by area residents. The old road from Route 35 is closed, and visiting from Laurence Harbor requires wading through or jumping over Margaret's Creek. Only a few foundations remain where a thriving vacation spot once stood. Compare this recent photograph to the one on page 104 to see the contrast. Old Bridge has plans to extend a walkway, already in place along Laurence Harbor's beach, through Seidler's Beach to Cliffwood Beach.

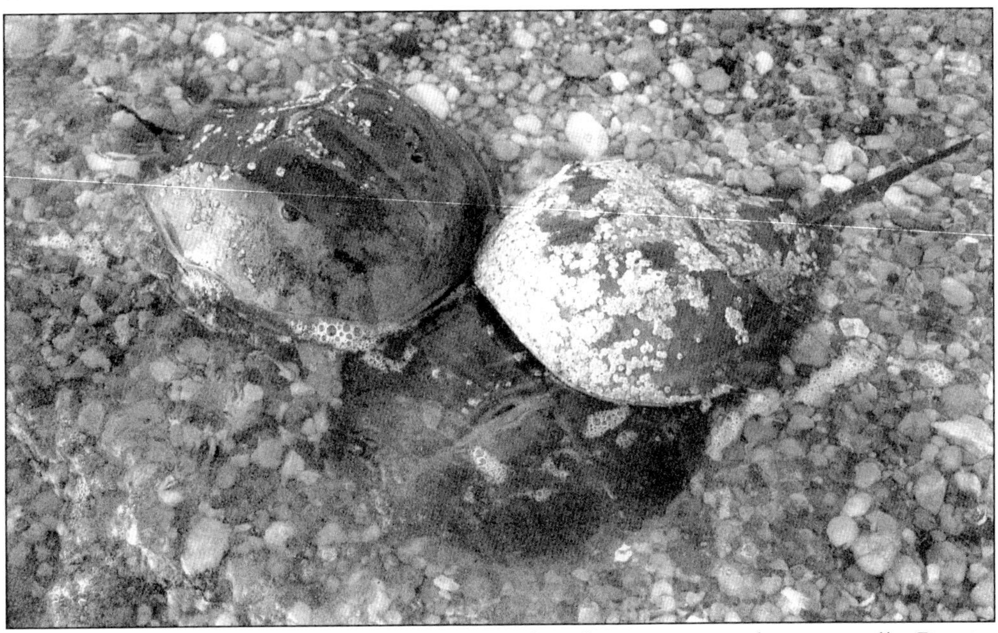

What may be the earliest visitor to Seidler's Beach still returns to its shore annually. Despite its fearsome appearance, the horseshoe crab (*Limulus polyphemus*) is harmless. It is considered a living fossil since it has not changed in 300 million years. It returns every year in the early summer during a full moon to spawn on the beach. One of the benefits of the lack of activity on Seidler's Beach is the preservation of this breeding ground. Fewer and fewer horseshoe crabs exist every year in the northeast, and they are becoming rarer and rarer.

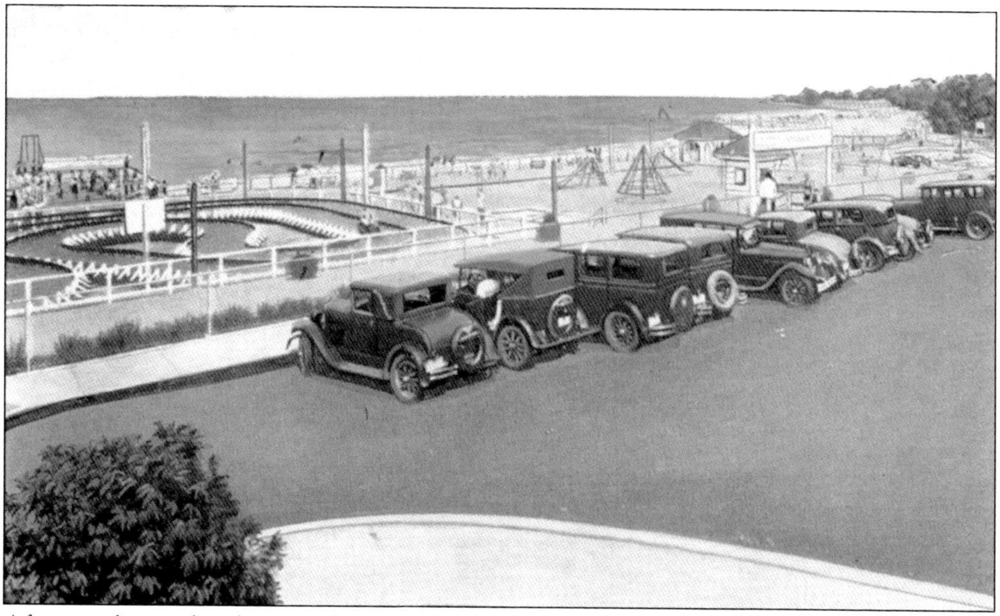

After a relaxing lunch at Burlew's Restaurant, you could let your children unwind at the playground and miniature golf course just a few yards away on the beach near the Laurence Harbor Circle. Old Bridge has recently built a new playground near this site. The bungalows at Seidler's Beach can be seen in the background on the right.

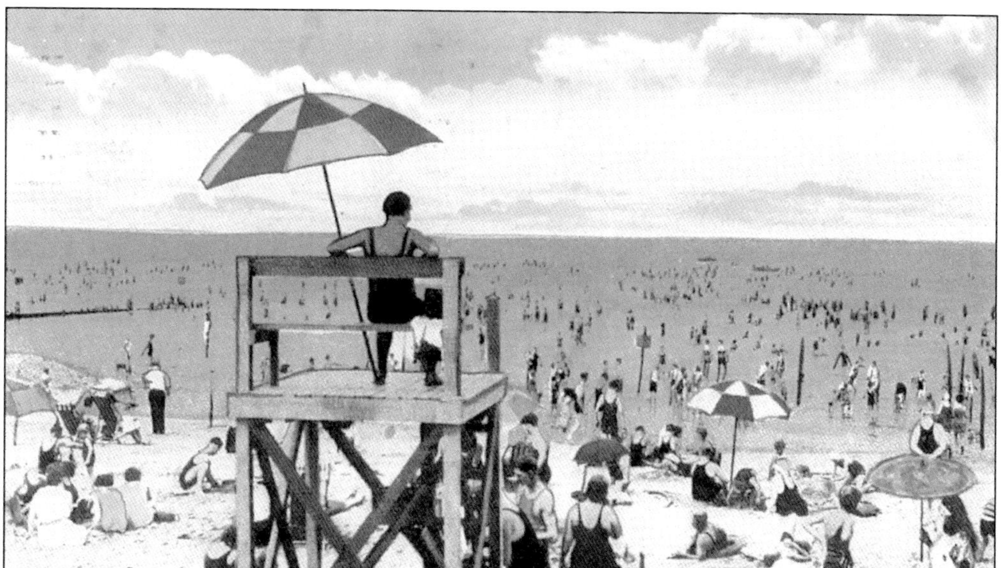

Cliffwood Beach, just south of Laurence Harbor and Seidler's Beach, on the Raritan Bay, straddles two municipalities and two counties. It is situated partially in Old Bridge and partially in Aberdeen Township in Monmouth County. This scene shows "thousands enjoying a cool refreshing swim." The back of this postcard also served as a complimentary ticket to the Cliffwood Beach Baths.

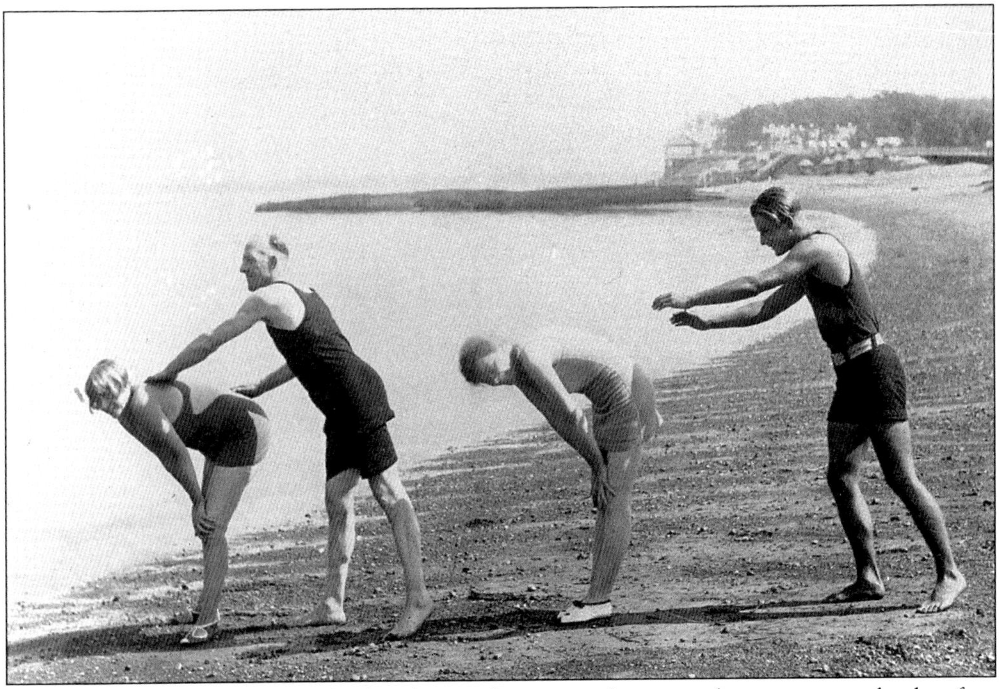

Showing us that frolicking on the beach is nothing new, these couples prepare to play leapfrog at Cliffwood Beach. The boardwalk can be seen in the upper right of the photograph.

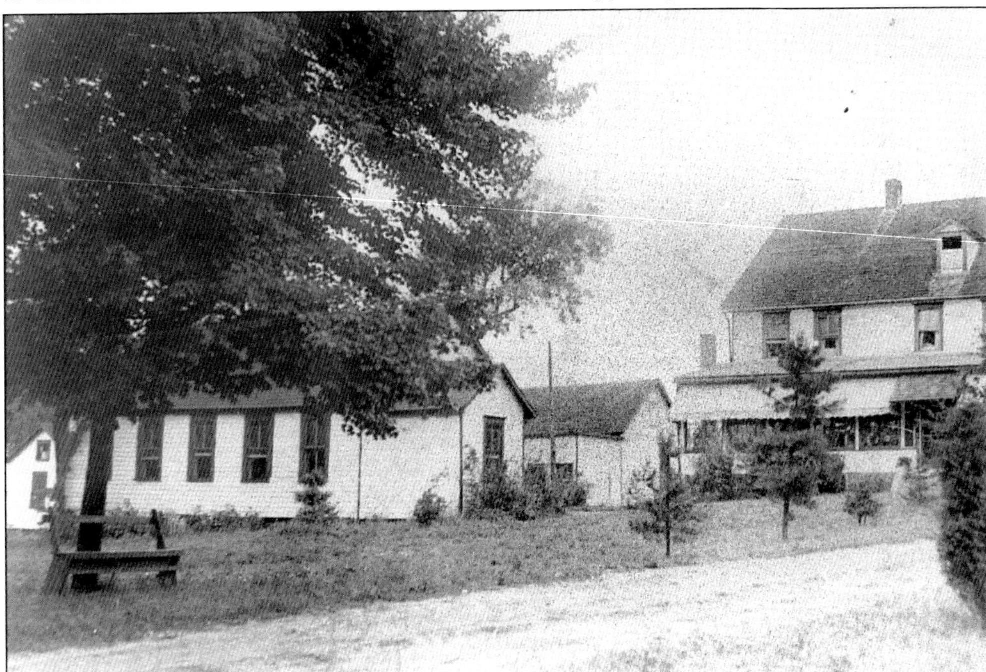

On the other side of town, on Texas Road, another vacation spot in Old Bridge was Serman Resort. Many urban visitors came here to enjoy the country life. Activities at the resort included horseback riding, swimming, hiking, sporting events, and everything else a city dweller needed to feel as one with the country.

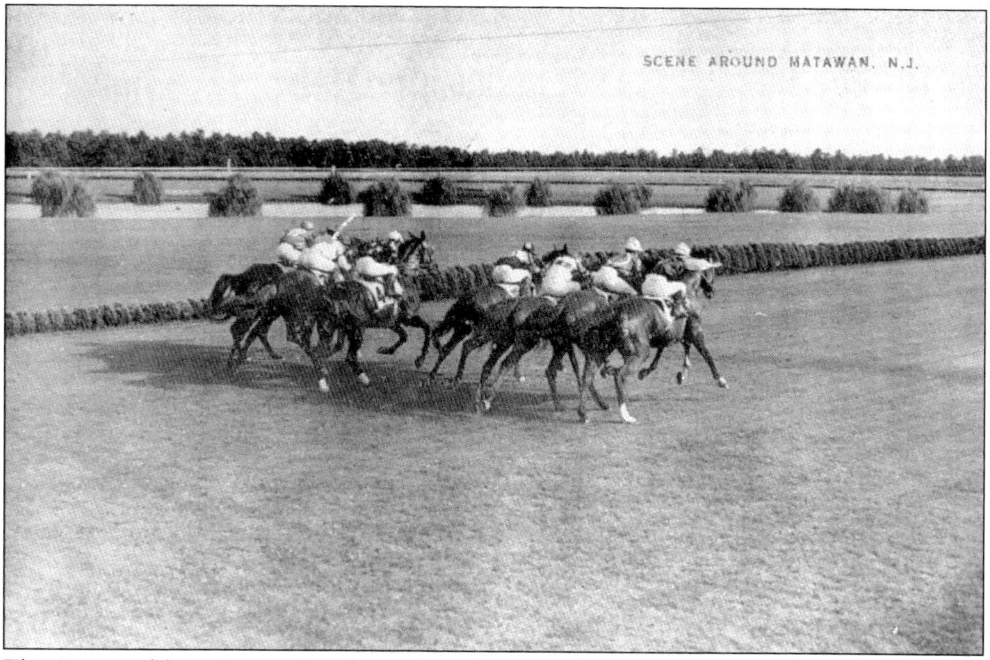

The "sport of kings" was also the sport of farmers and townspeople in Old Bridge. The Longstreet family operated a horse-racing track near Matawan border, off Route 516. There was another racetrack located off Route 9.

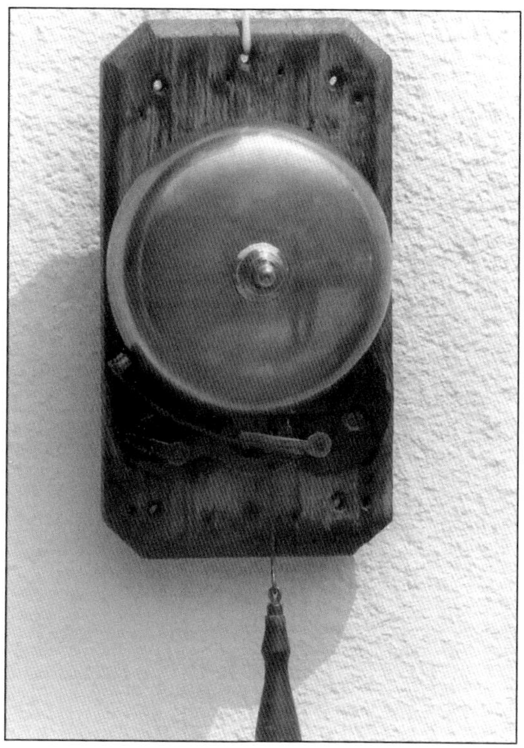

This starter's bell, in the possession of the Madison Township Historical Society, is all that remains of the Longstreet Racetrack. The site of the track is now occupied by the Lakeridge development.

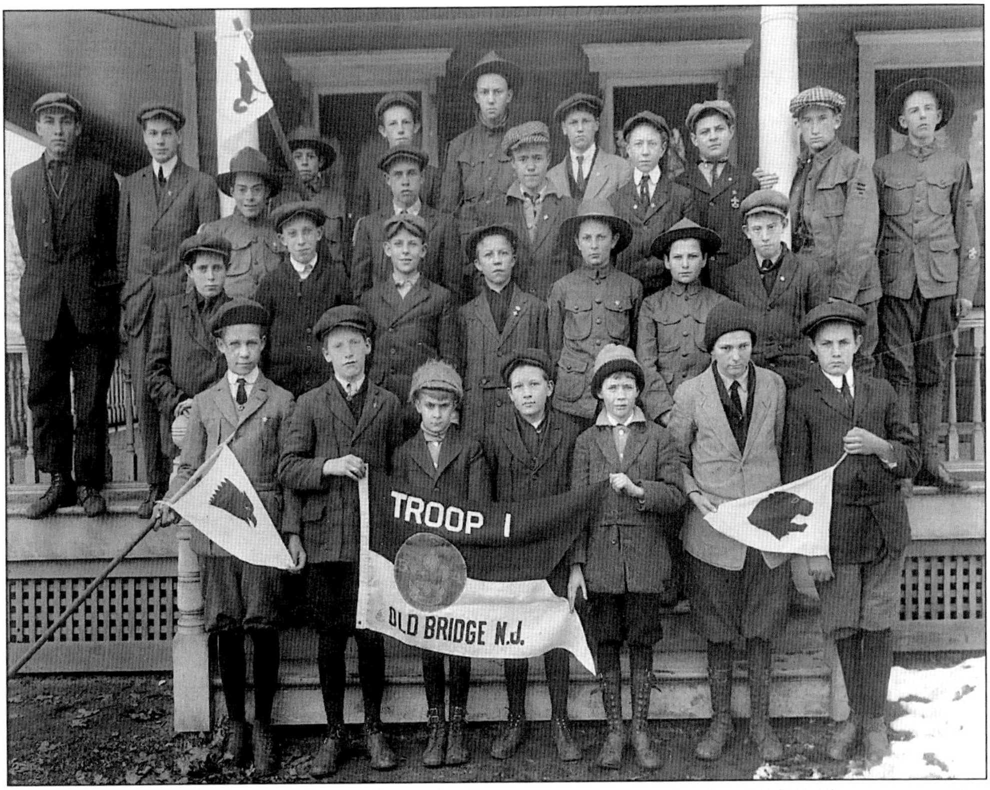

The Boy Scouts of America have always had a strong presence in the Old Bridge community. This early photograph shows Troop No. 1 of Old Bridge. Obviously, smiling is not part of the Boy Scout Oath. The troop was headquartered in the Historic Village of Old Bridge but drew many members from Old Bridge Township.

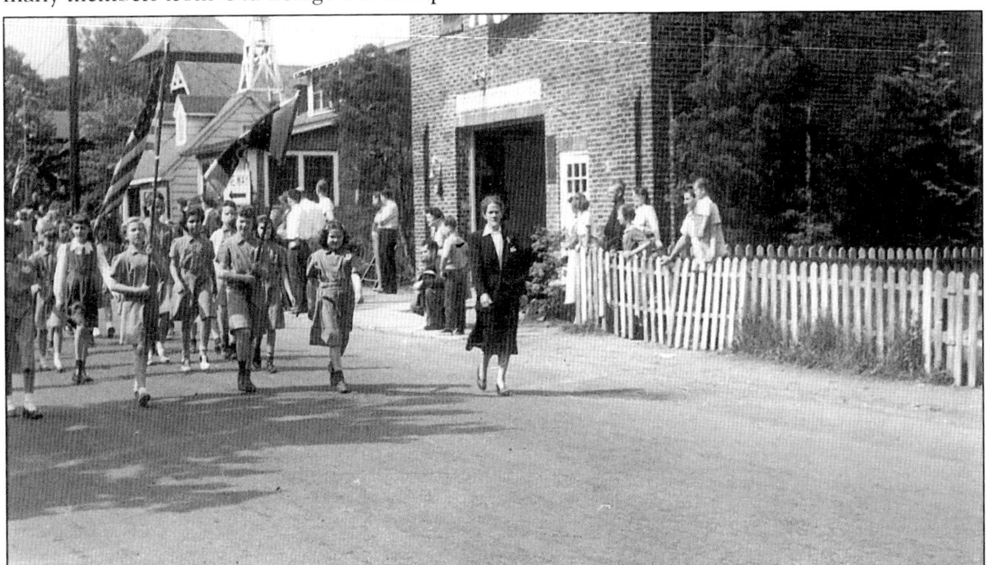

Alice Kerr leads a Girl Scouts of America troop in a parade in Laurence Parkway in Laurence Harbor. On the right are the Laurence Harbor Firehouse and the first-aid station.

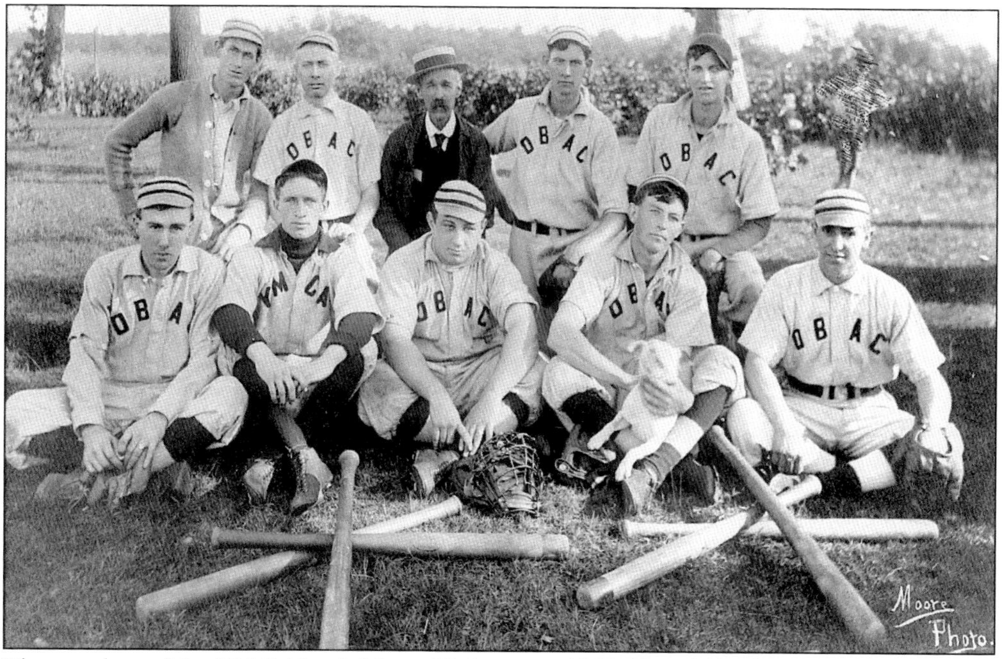

The members of the Old Bridge Athletic Club pose in 1909. Hopefully, they suffered no injuries, since there are only nine players. Note the team mascot being held by one of the players. Like the Boy Scout troop on the previous page, this group was based in the Historic Village of Old Bridge but drew many of its players from Old Bridge Township.

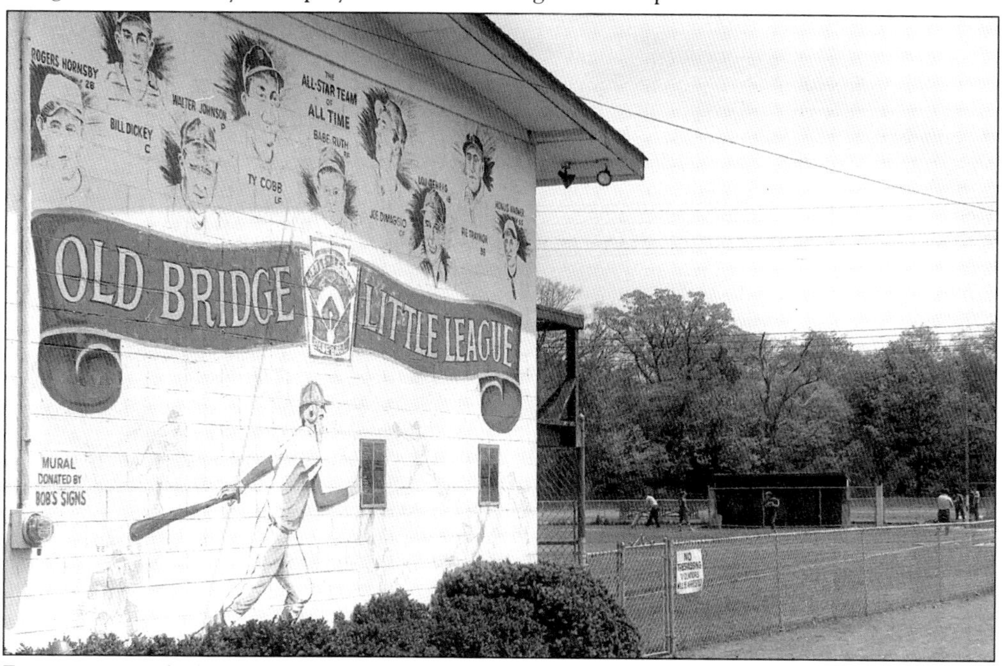

Every section of Old Bridge Township has its own Little League. Pictured here is the Old Bridge Little League clubhouse and fields located on Route 516. The clubhouse wall features portraits of the all-time all-star team as an inspiration to its young players. Other township Little Leagues are Laurence Harbor, Cheesequake, Madison Park, and Sayrewoods.

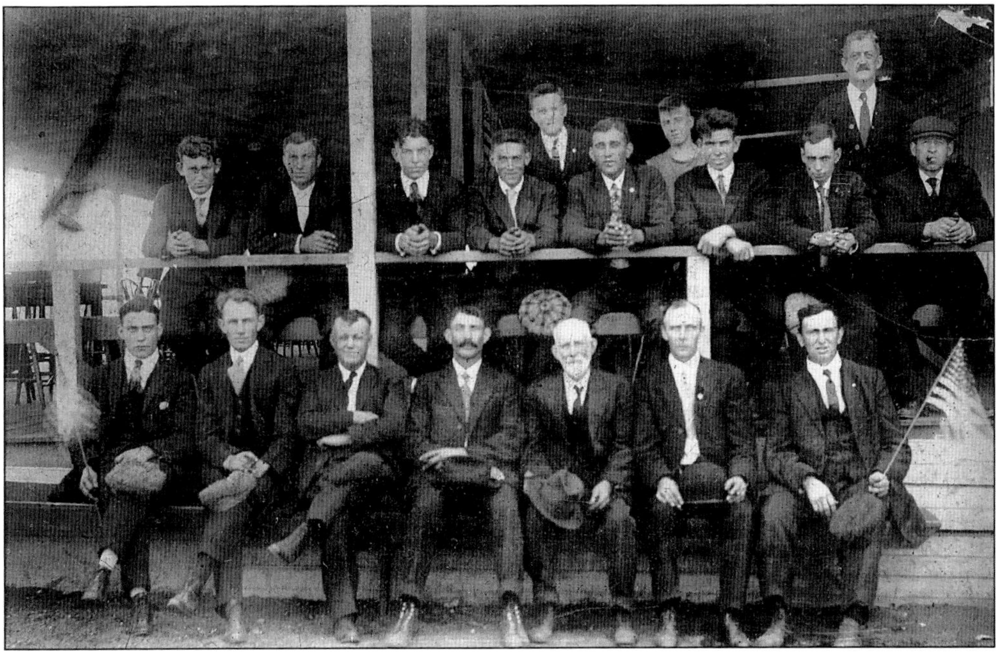

The Crescent Sporting Club was the first shooting club in Old Bridge Township. The members pose during a visit to Seidler's Beach. Despite increasing suburbanization, there are still a number of shooting clubs operating in the more rural areas of the township.

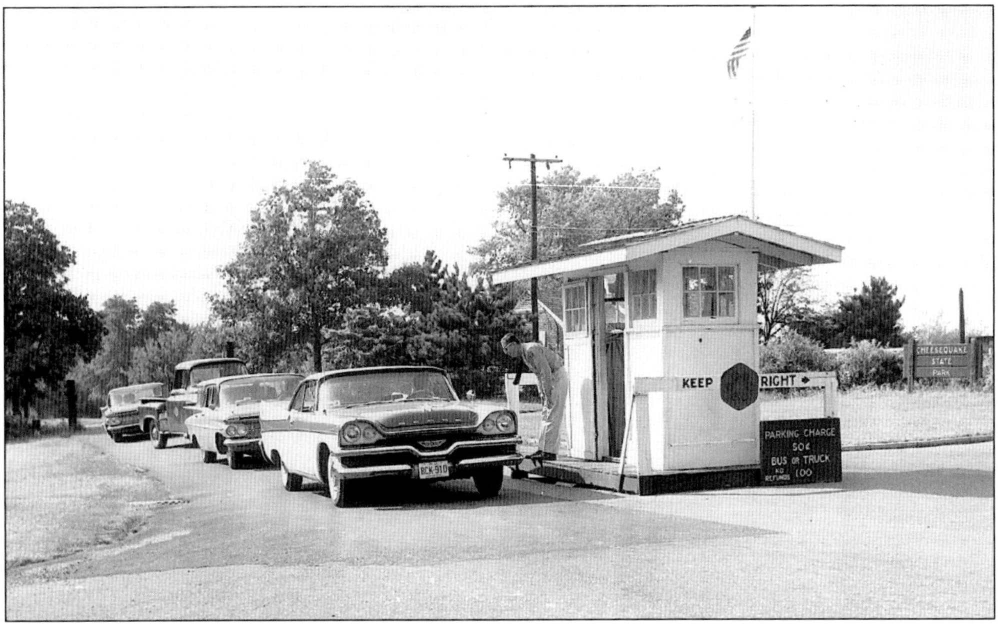

One of the oldest state parks in New Jersey is located in Old Bridge. Cheesequake State Park was created by the state legislature in 1932. Land acquisition began in 1938. Gradually, it grew to its present size of 1,250 acres of open land, woodland, and saltmarsh, with access to Cheesequake Creek. It was envisioned as a natural recreation area that was accessible to a large urban population. This photograph shows the entrance to the park in 1959. (Courtesy of Cheesequake State Park.)

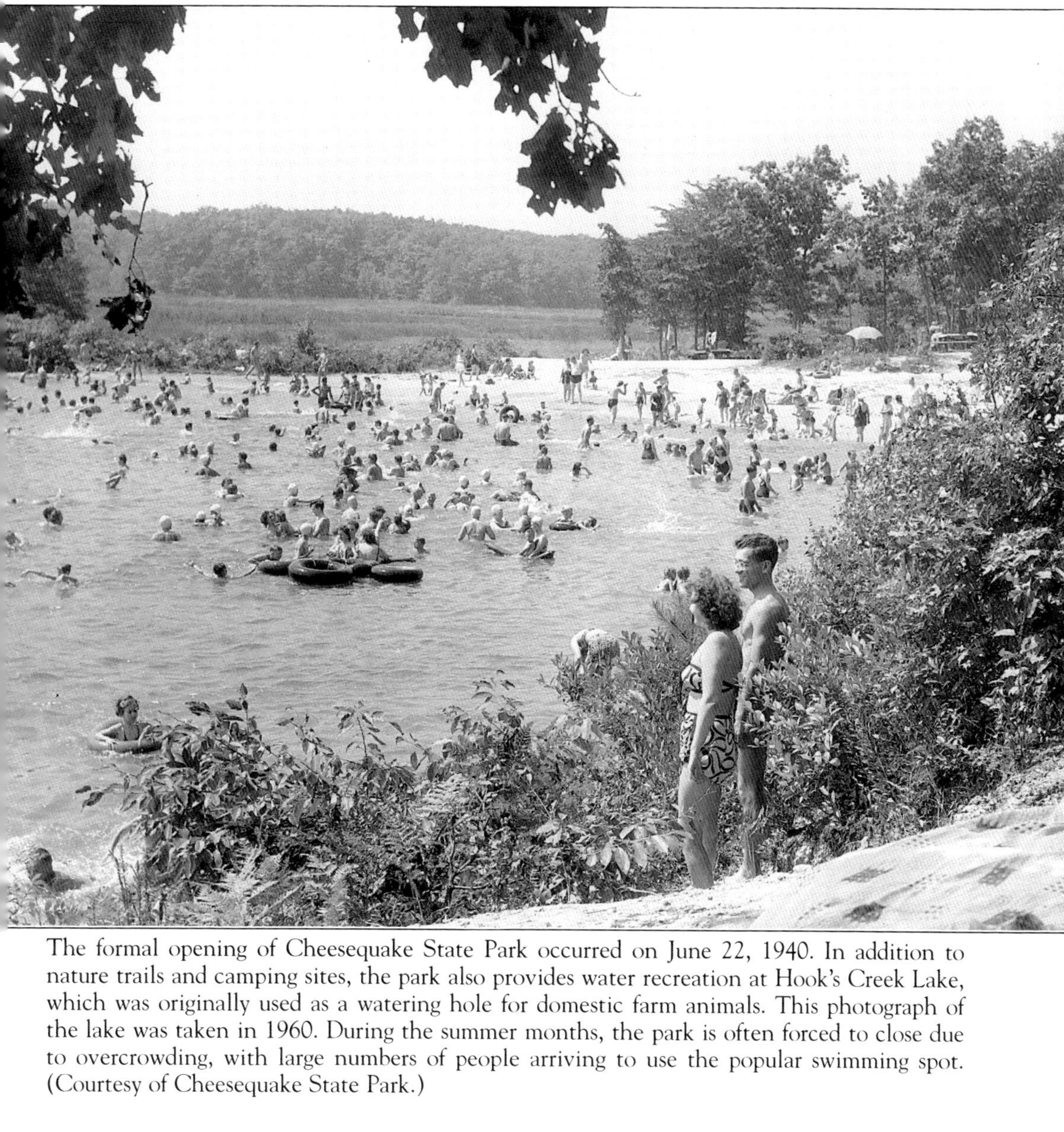

The formal opening of Cheesequake State Park occurred on June 22, 1940. In addition to nature trails and camping sites, the park also provides water recreation at Hook's Creek Lake, which was originally used as a watering hole for domestic farm animals. This photograph of the lake was taken in 1960. During the summer months, the park is often forced to close due to overcrowding, with large numbers of people arriving to use the popular swimming spot. (Courtesy of Cheesequake State Park.)

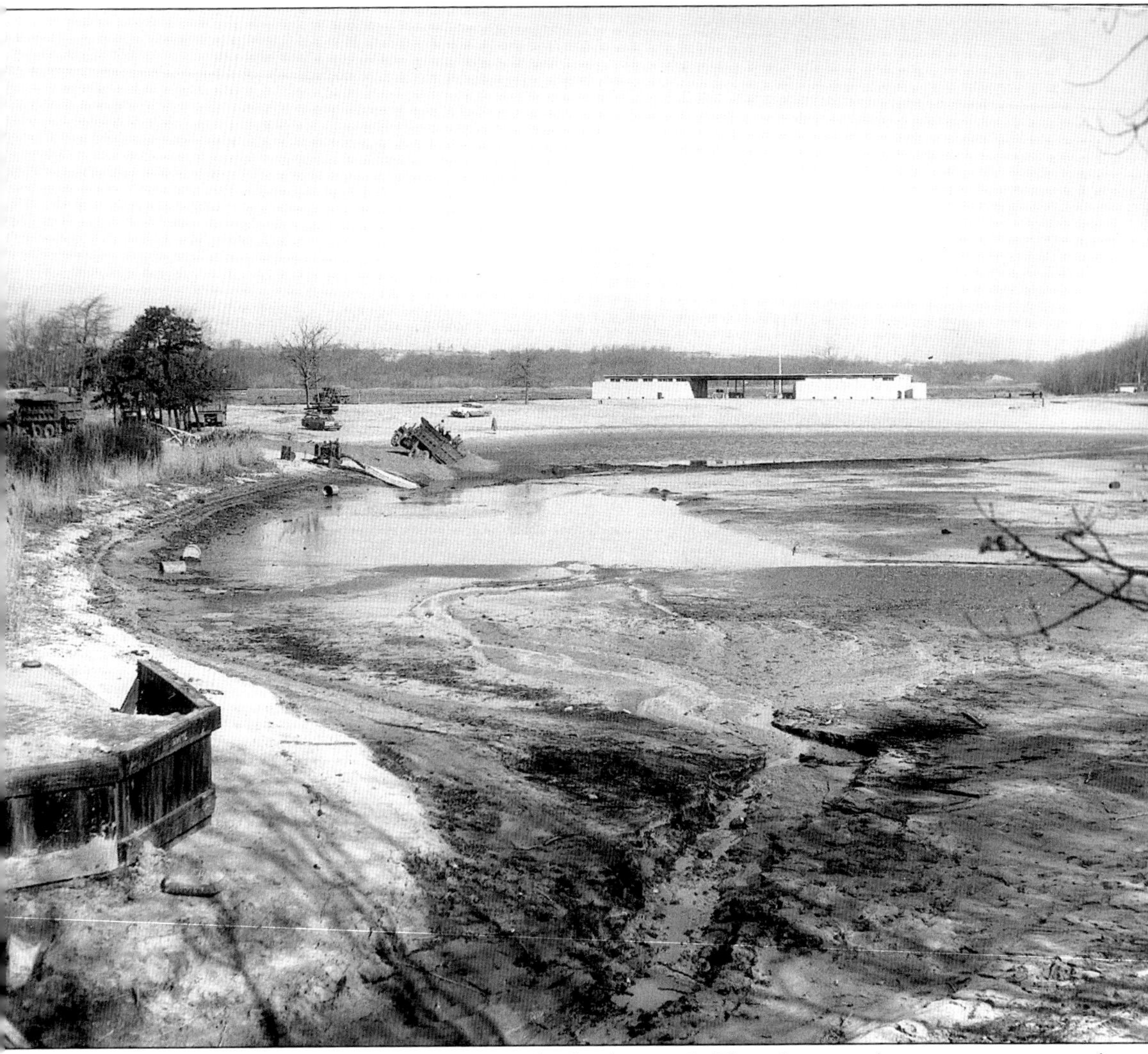

Do not be fooled by the 1950s car in the background. This photograph is more recent and shows Hook's Creek Lake in Cheesequake Park under renovation. Accidents happen, even to the most careful, as the driver of the dump truck that is stuck in the mud would surely attest. The lake was dredged and filled with a foot of sand. The state also built a bathhouse (shown in the background) and a clay dike to keep the marsh water out. (Courtesy of Cheesequake State Park.)

Six

ALL AROUND THE TOWN

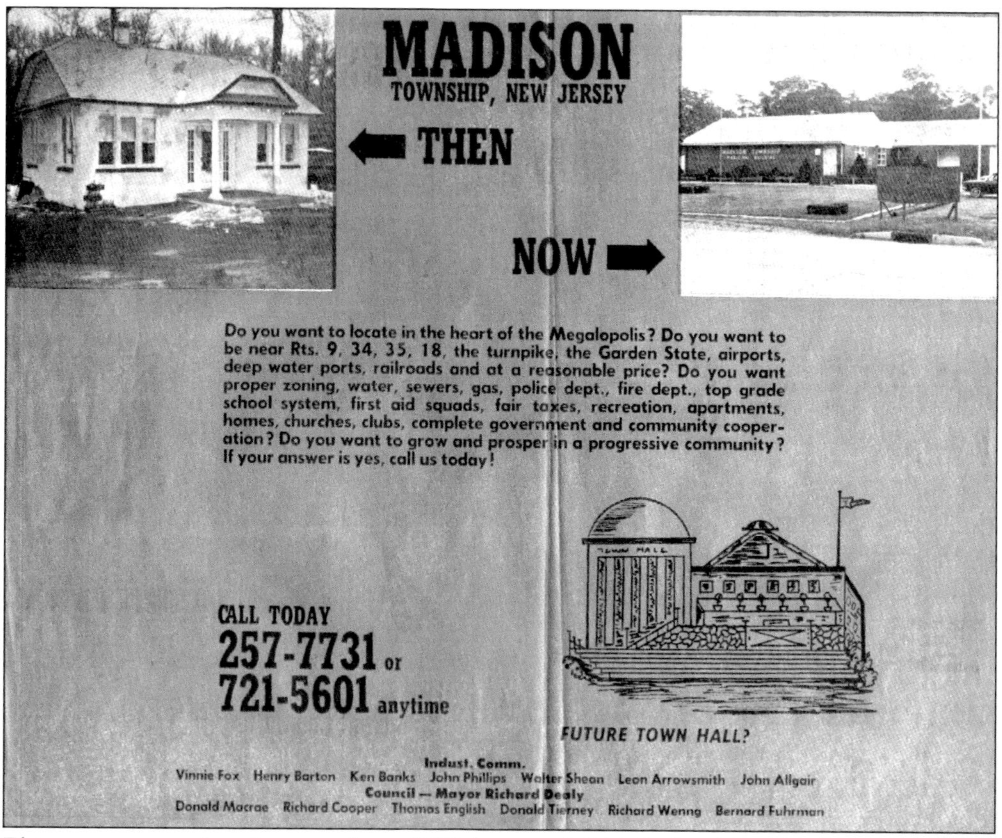

This newspaper advertisement from 1970 boasts of Old Bridge Township's amenities and location. It pictures the original town hall—its replacement, which was then in use, was located on Route 9—and a futuristic rendering of the new home of municipal government. Old Bridge did build a new municipal center in the 1980s, but it does not resemble the artist's vision.

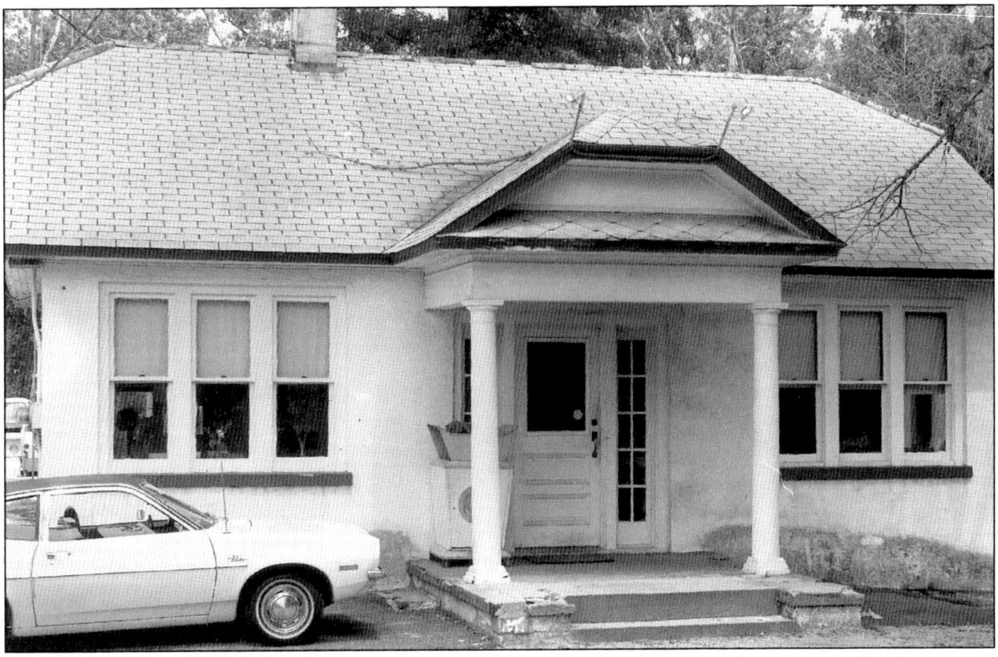

Old Bridge Township's first town hall, on Route 516, was abandoned in the 1960s for a new building located near the intersection of Route 9 and Route 34. The building next served as the road department's headquarters until the department moved into the new municipal center down the street, on Route 516 and Cottrell Road. The building still serves the township as a storage facility.

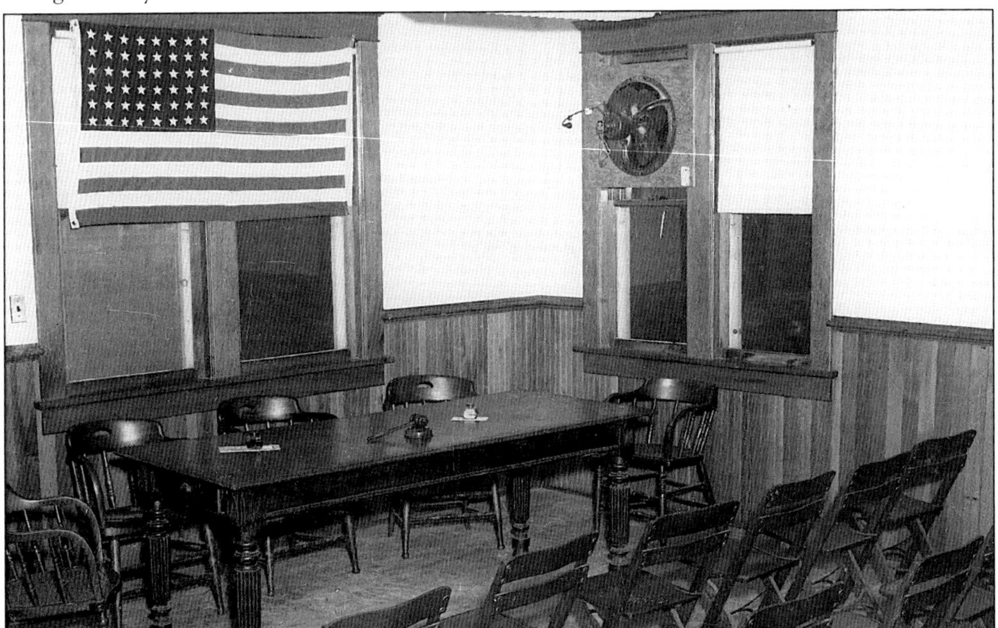

The original town hall was small and austere. This interior view shows the meeting room. The room was used for council meetings and other municipal and civic gatherings. It is a far cry from the more formal setting used for council meetings today.

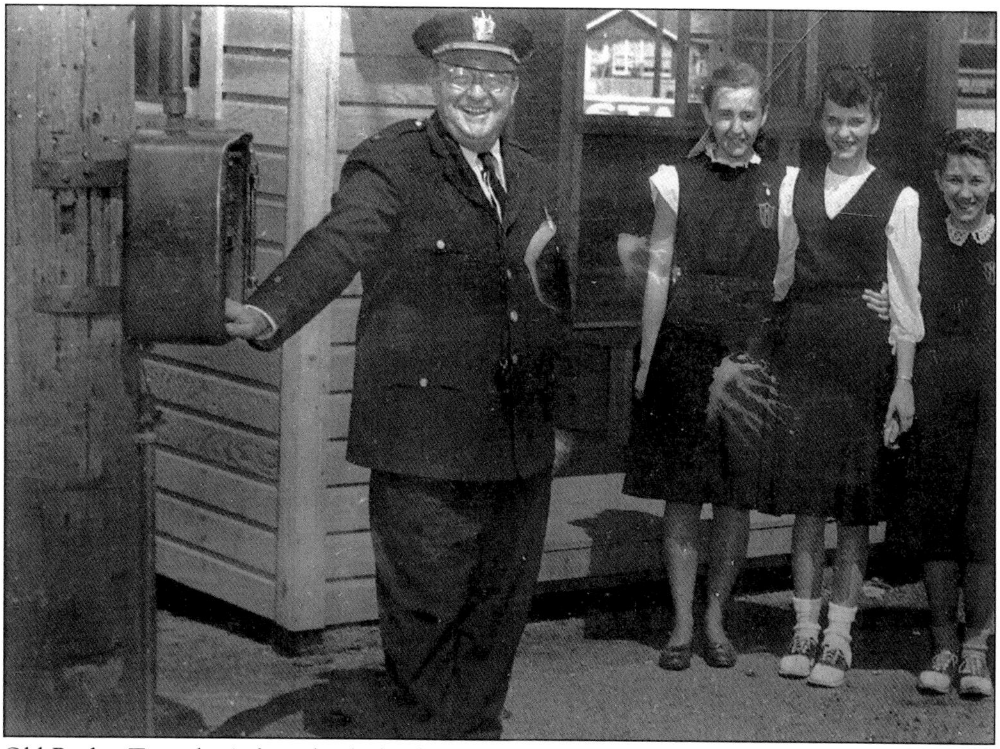

Old Bridge Township's first chief of police was Otto A. Kengetter. Here, he poses with three young ladies and a police call box. The photograph was probably taken in front of the old police headquarters in Laurence Harbor. The Laurence Harbor branch of the Old Bridge Public Library now occupies the building.

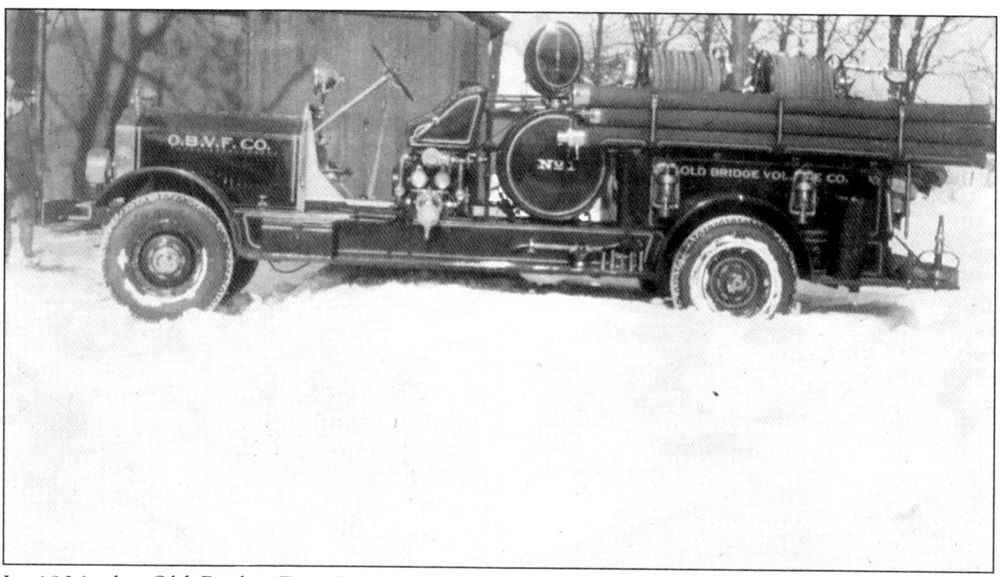

In 1906, the Old Bridge Fire Company was organized in what is today East Brunswick. Its first motorized fire truck is shown in 1926. The company served the Old Bridge section of the township until 1947, when the South Old Bridge Fire Company was organized.

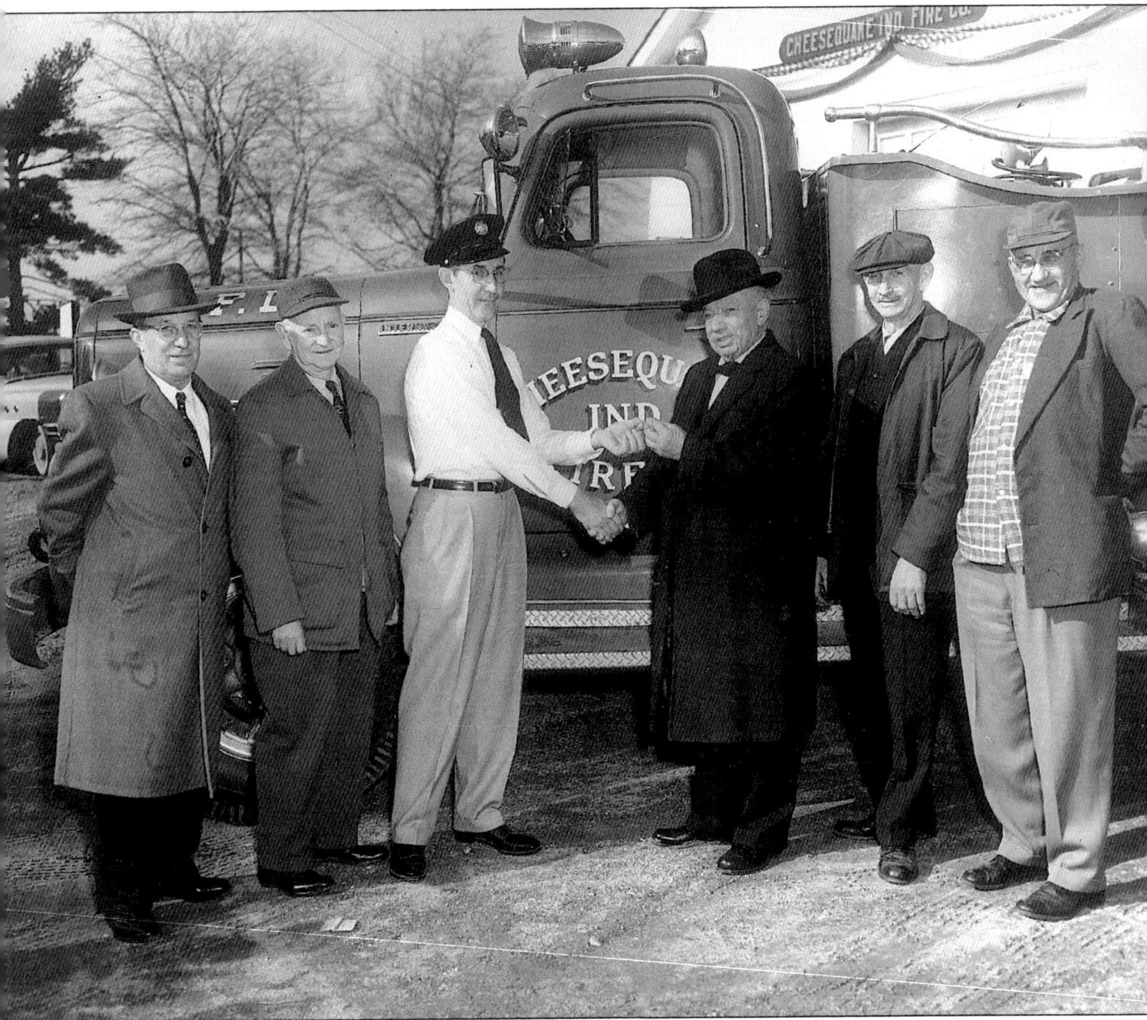

In 1960, the Cheesequake Independent Fire Company built a new firehouse. It was dedicated on May 7, 1960. The company still occupies the same building next door to the Cheesequake School on Route 34.

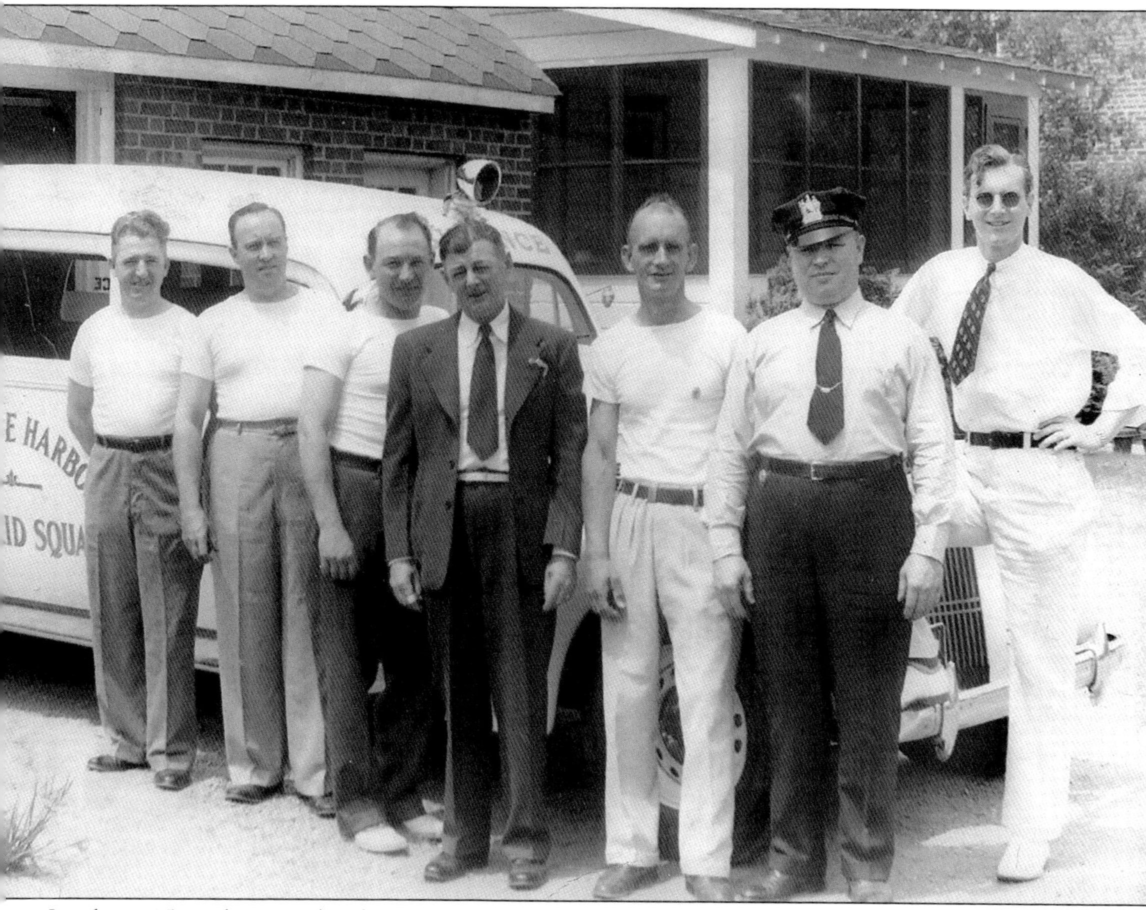

In this 1950s photograph, the members of the Laurence Harbor first-aid squad strike a more relaxed pose in front of their building on Laurence Parkway. They are, from left to right, William Kerr, Joseph Davies, Bill Towney, Thomas White, Hank Gall, Phil Parton, and George Muller.

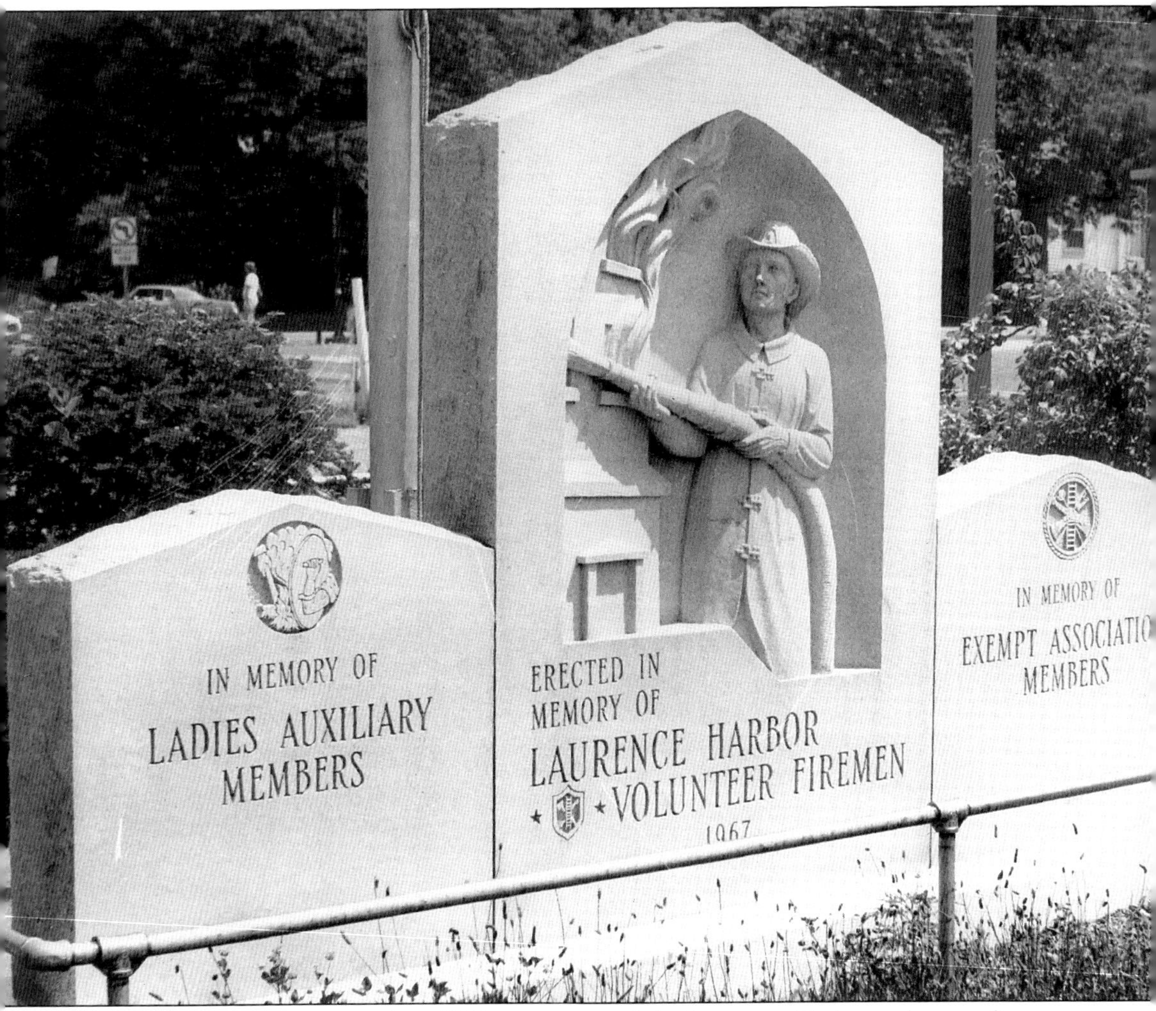

This memorial was erected in 1967 in memory of the Laurence Harbor volunteer firemen, as well as members of the Ladies Auxiliary and Exempt Association. It still stands in the center of Laurence Parkway opposite the firehouse and first-aid squad.

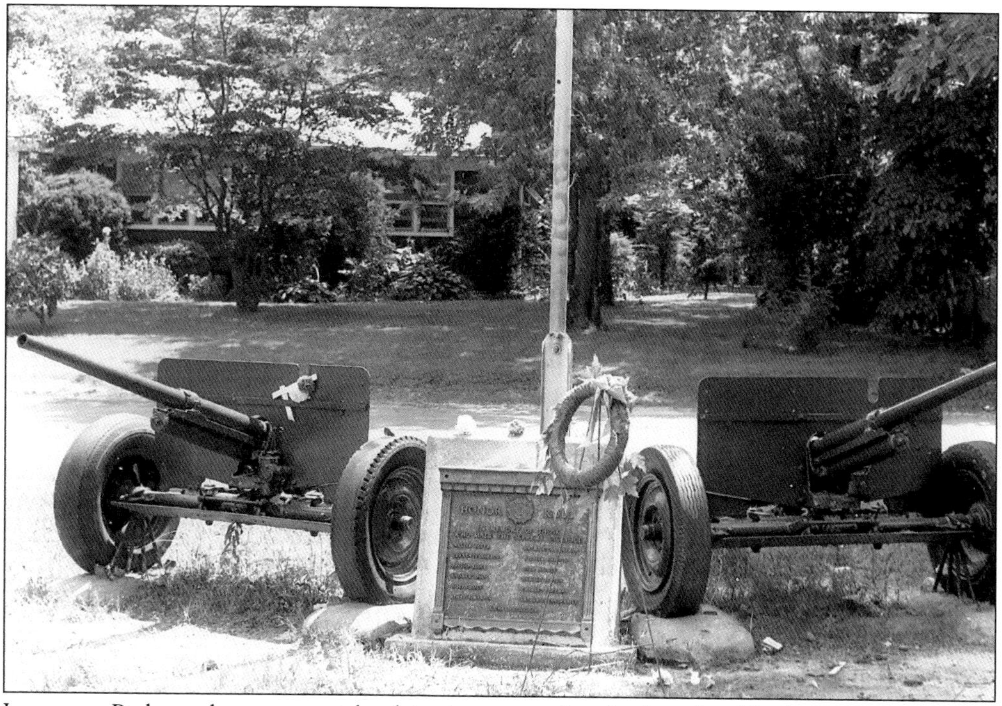

Laurence Parkway has a grass island in its center for the last few blocks before it reaches Route 35. It is known as "the Path" to locals and serves as a small park. This honor roll memorial is located there. It was dedicated "in memory of those who made the supreme sacrifice."

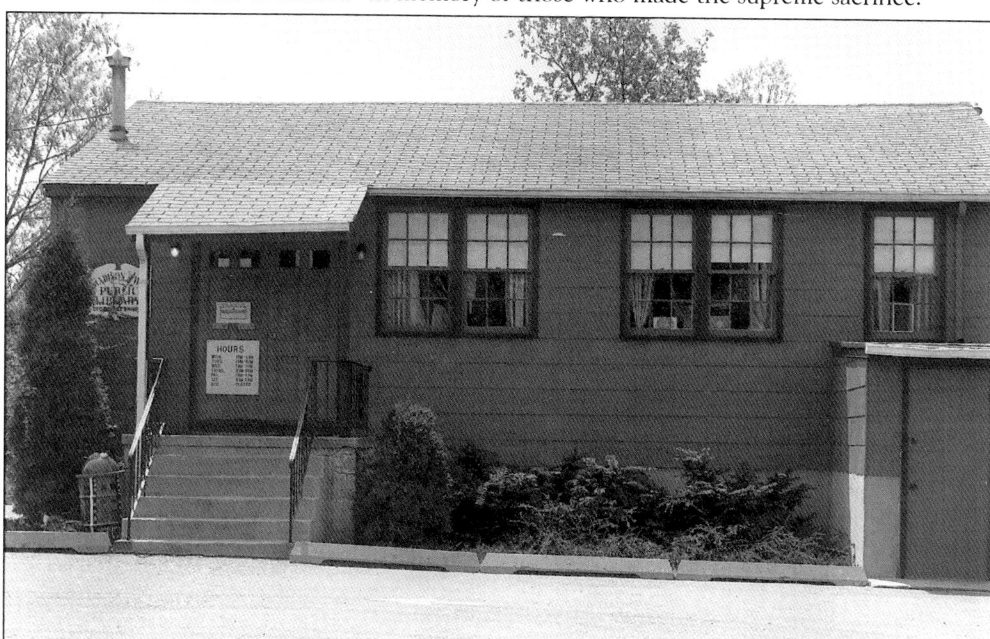

The Old Bridge Public Library was originally located on Route 516 in the Old Bridge section of the township. It began as a volunteer effort, but in 1970, the township assumed control after a voter referendum. The Laurence Harbor Volunteer Library was municipalized at the same time. The library moved to its current location in the municipal complex in the 1980s.

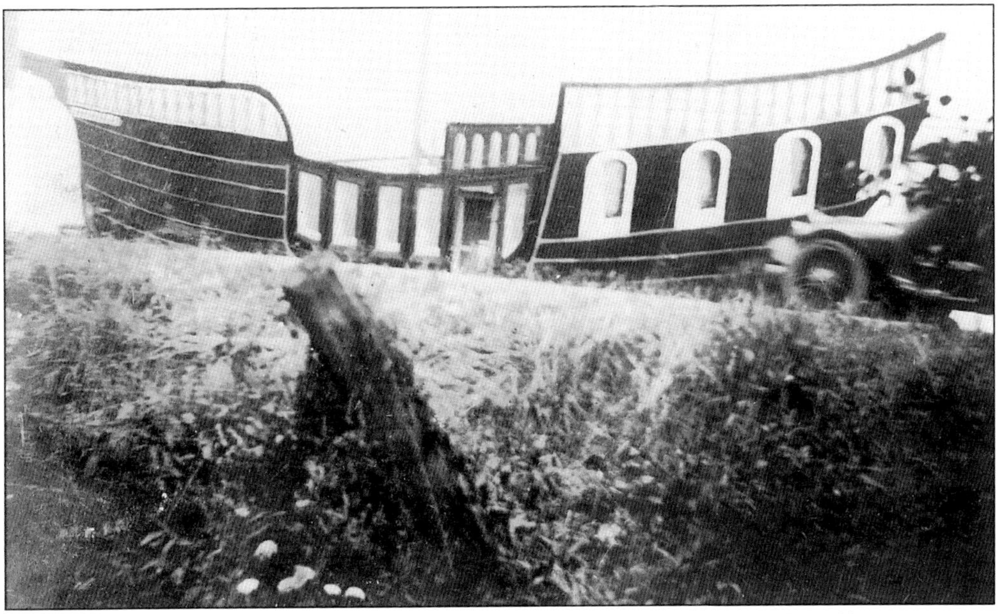

The Pirate Ship, located on Route 35, was the symbol of the Raritan Bay Shore to many visitors to the area. In 1921, it was built as the sales office for a new housing development. This 1924 photograph shows the Pirate Ship in its original location on the northbound side of the highway in Aberdeen Township. It was featured in a Laurel and Hardy film in the 1930s.

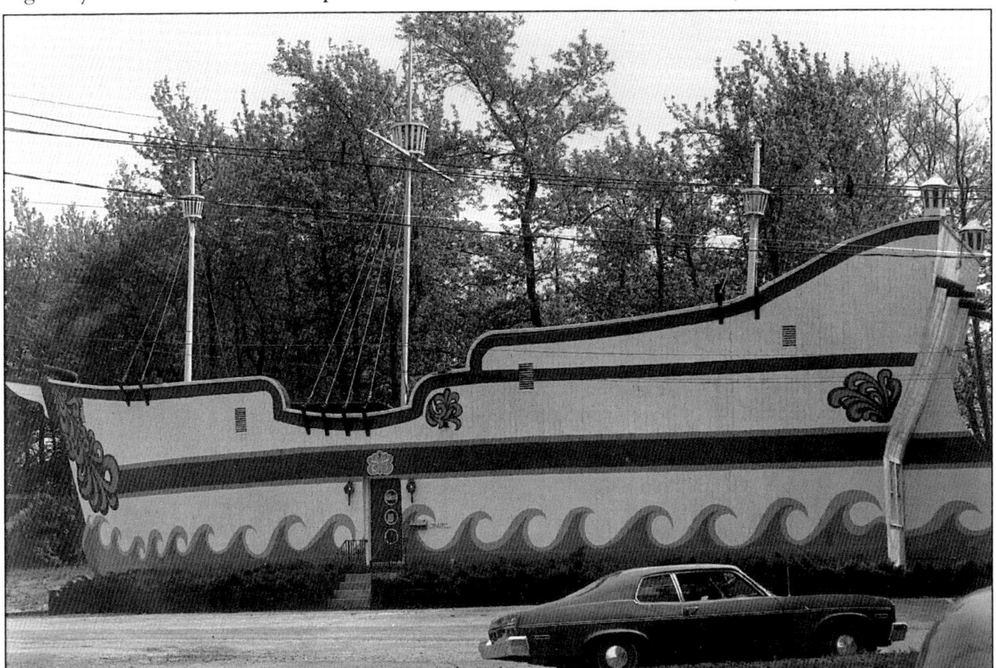

The Pirate Ship survived two moves. It was first transported north on Route 35 near Ocean Boulevard in Cliffwood Beach. In 1971, it sailed across the highway to its final destination, shown here, opposite the 7-11 convenience store. It was destroyed by an electrical fire on May 13, 1993. Although there were plans to rebuild it, the site still remains vacant.

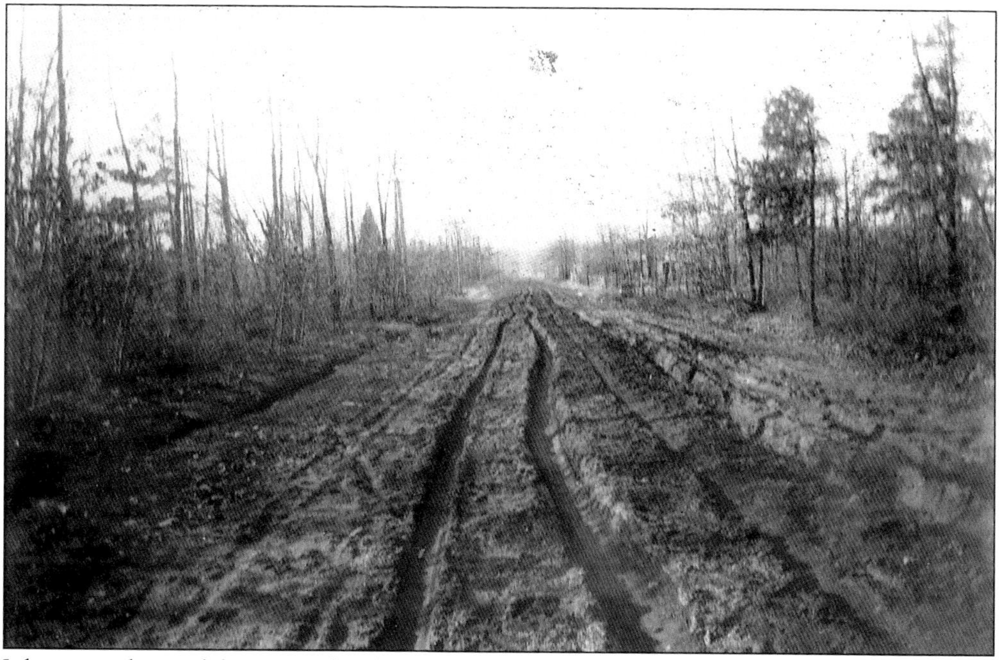

Like many thoroughfares in early Old Bridge, Englishtown Road was a dirt, or in this case mud, road when this photograph was taken. Although the road still retains some rural aspects today, more houses and businesses appear every year.

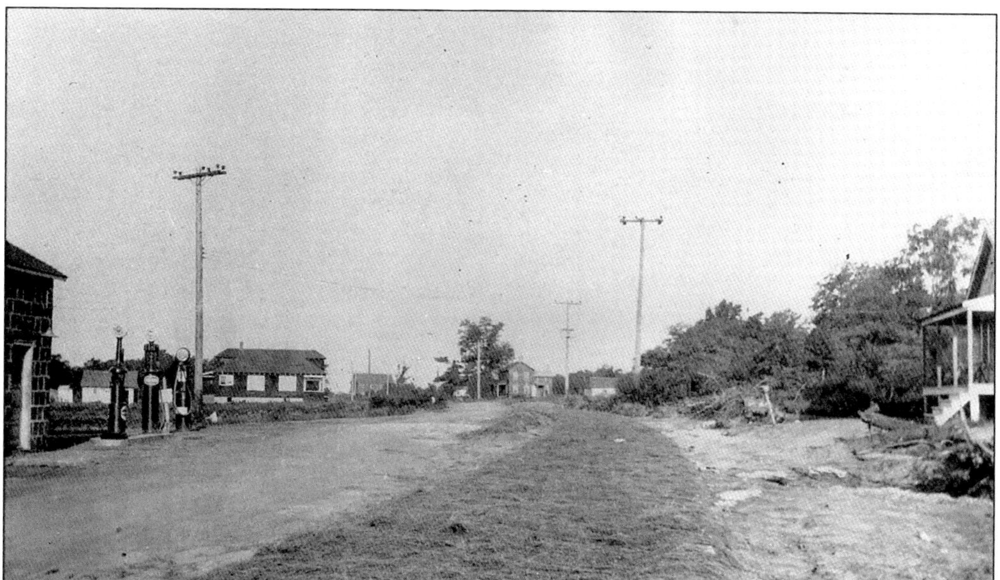

This 1928 photograph shows the construction of Route 34 at the intersection of Morristown Road and Old Amboy Road. Brown's Service Station can be seen on the far left, and Lester Drost's house is seen on the right.

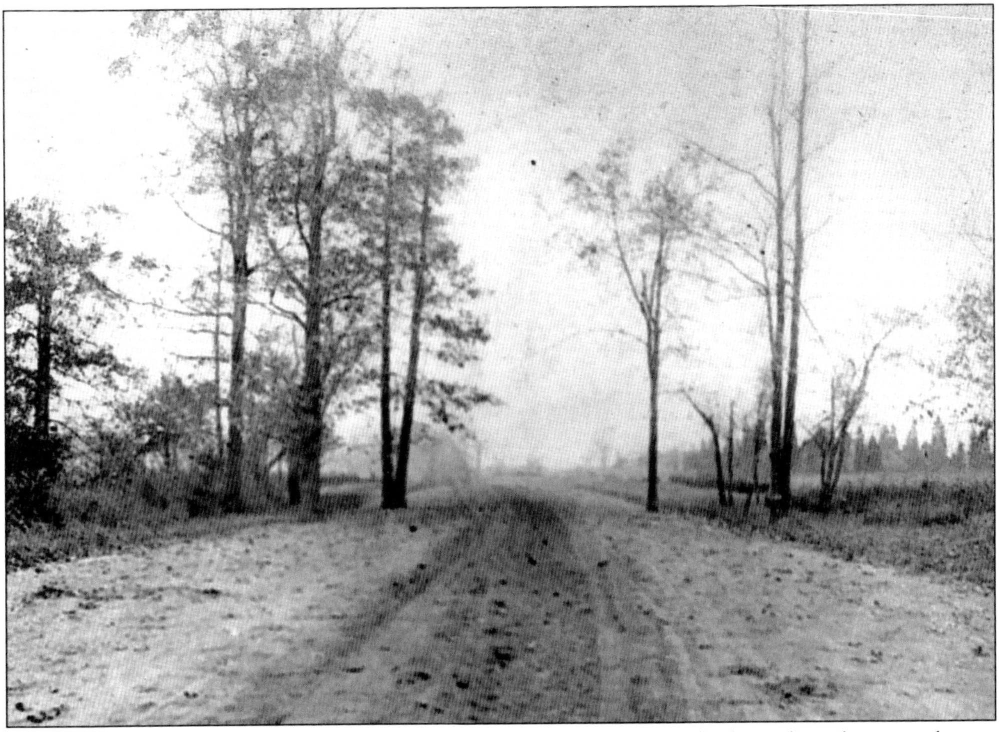

Laurence Parkway in Laurence Harbor was virtually uninhabited when this photograph was taken. The view is looking east toward Route 35 and the Raritan Bay.

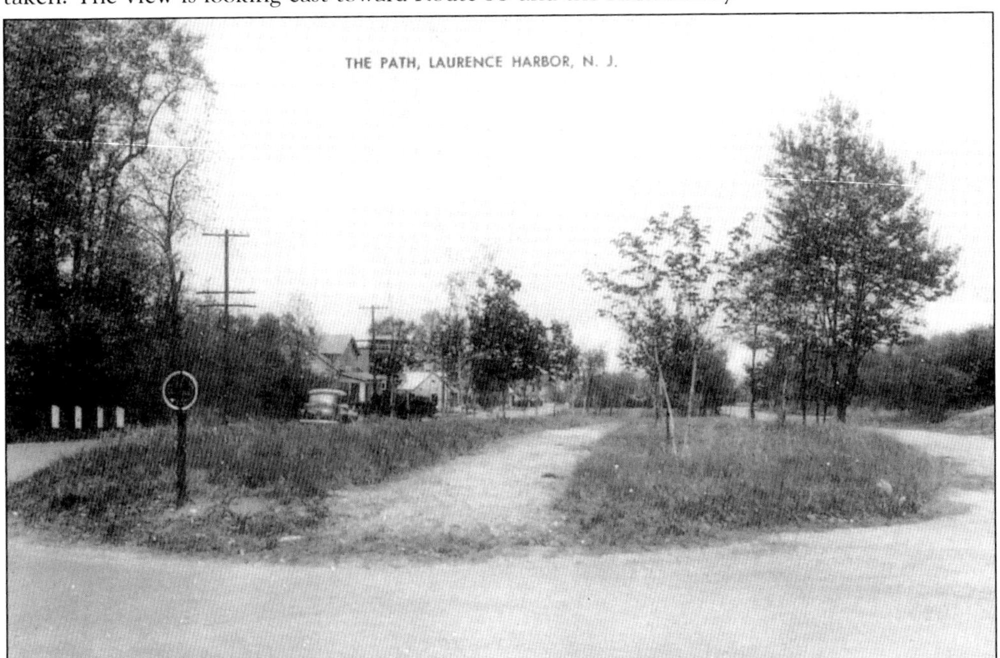

Here is the same view of Laurence Parkway, probably in the 1920s. You can see the Path in the center of the photograph. This island still exists and serves as a small park. There are now houses lining both sides of the road.

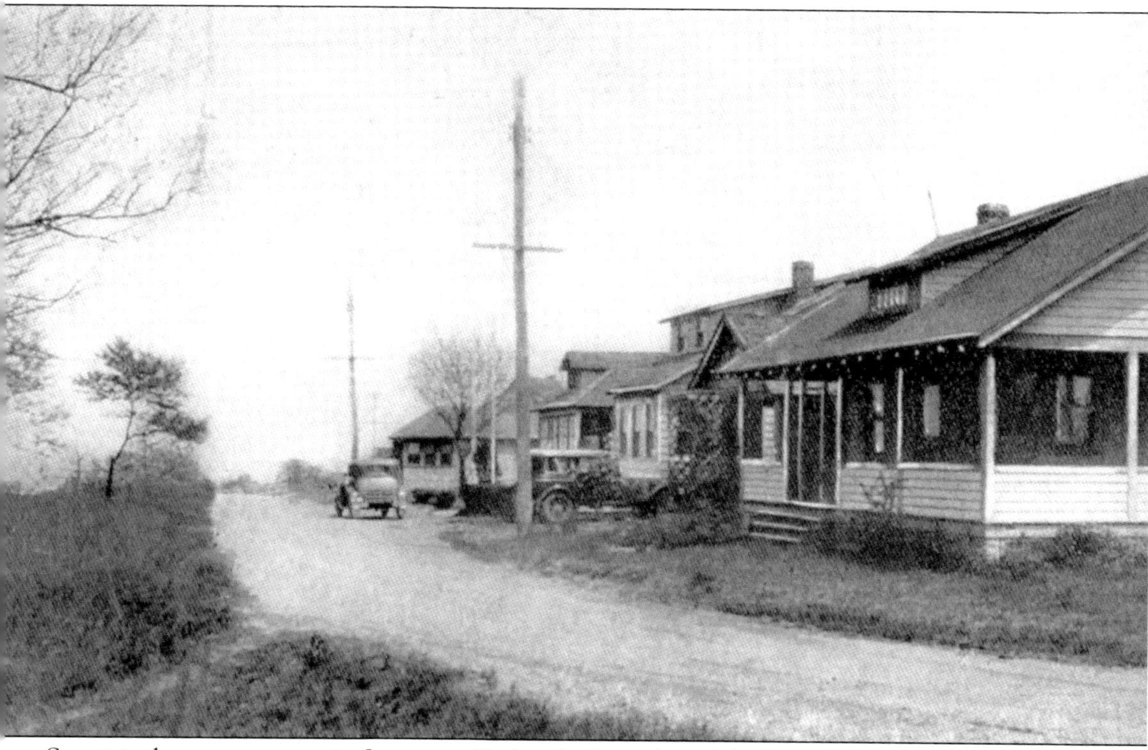

Surprisingly, many streets in Laurence Harbor look as they did when they were first built. This 1930s postcard of Shoreland Circle illustrates this. The road is now paved, and there is a guardrail along the left side, but otherwise little has changed. The Raritan Bay is just out of the picture to the left.

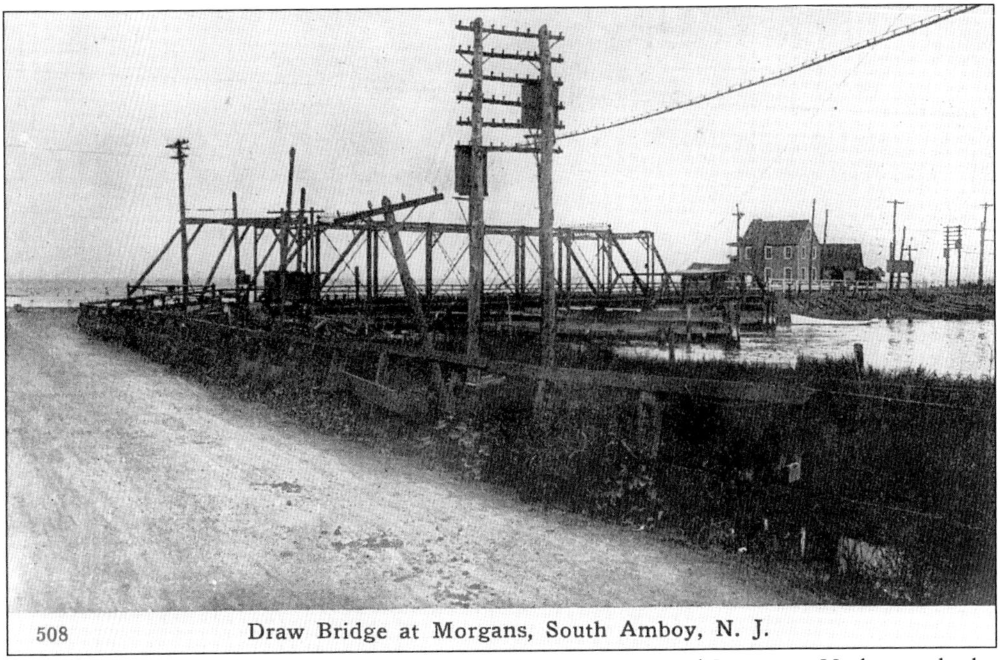

The original drawbridge over Cheesquake Creek that connected Laurence Harbor with the Morgan section of Sayreville crossed just downstream of where the current bridge stands. This view is looking from Sayreville at the foot of Old Spye Road. The sharp turn was sometimes referred to as "deadman's curve" and was the cause of many accidents.

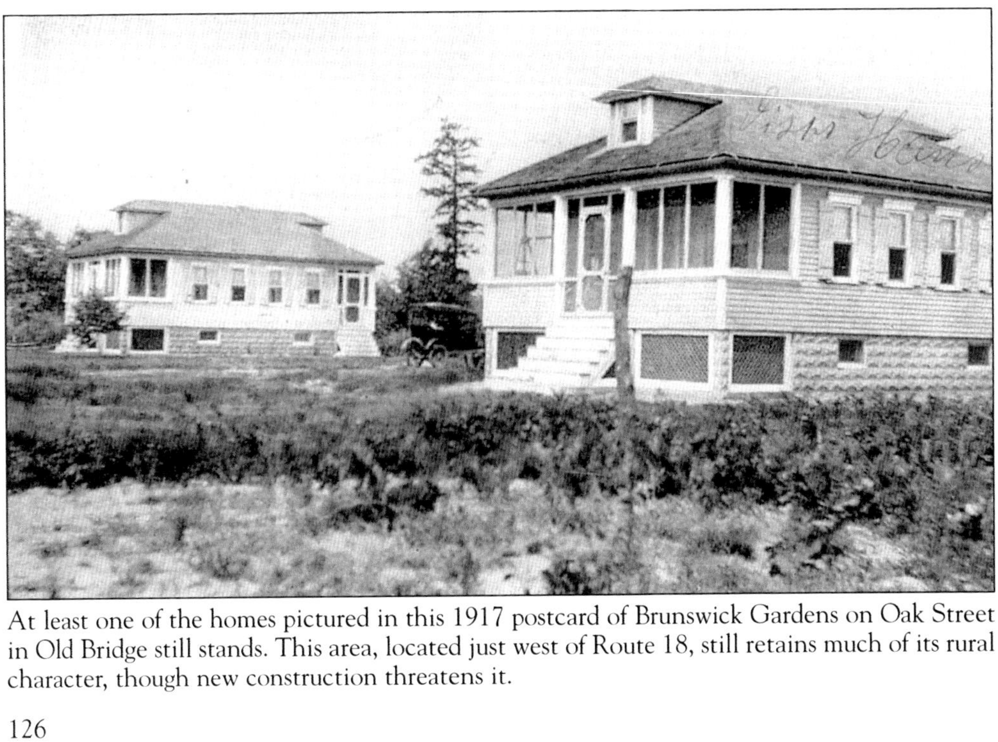

At least one of the homes pictured in this 1917 postcard of Brunswick Gardens on Oak Street in Old Bridge still stands. This area, located just west of Route 18, still retains much of its rural character, though new construction threatens it.

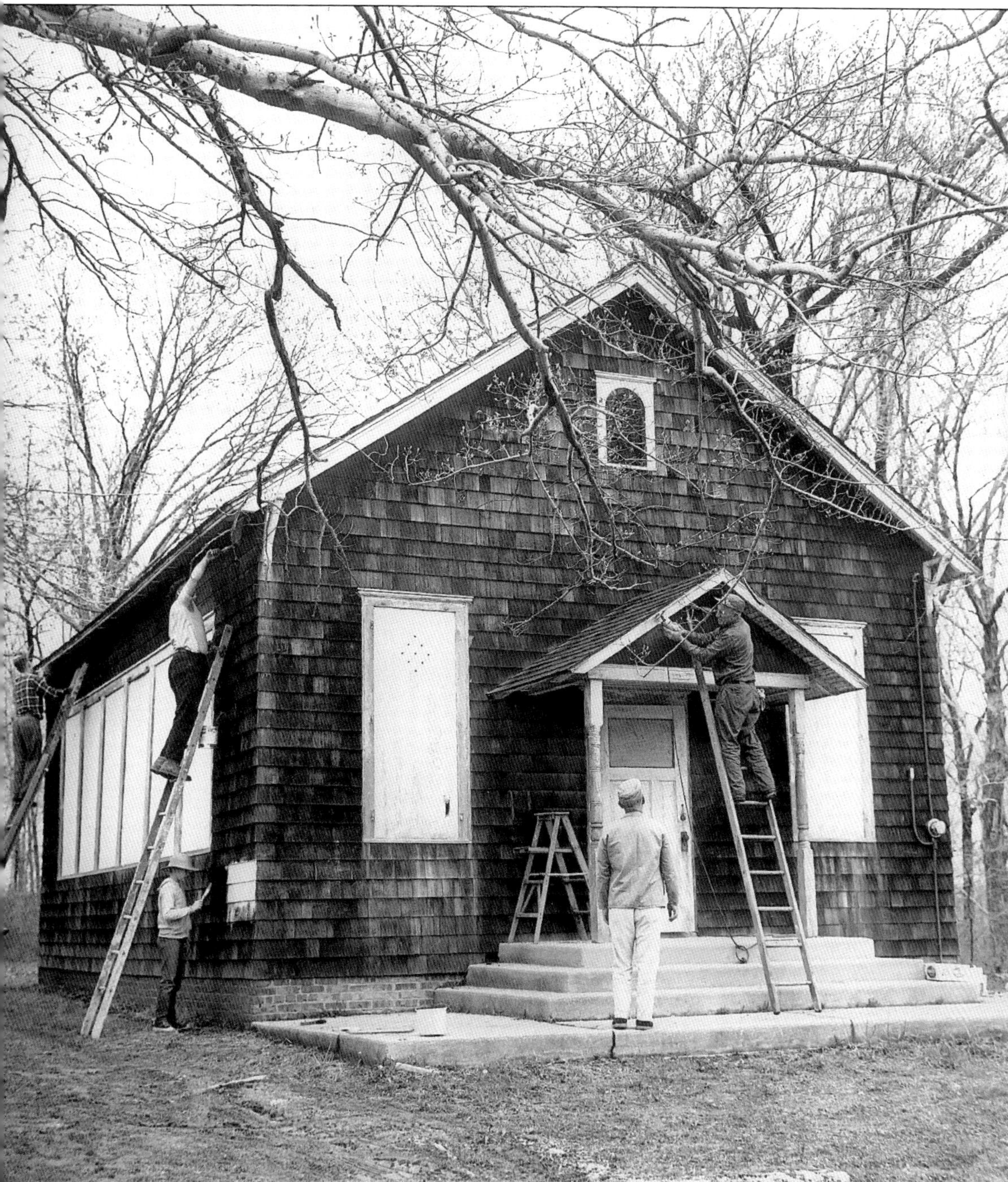

In 1964, the Madison Township Historical Society was organized to record and preserve the township's history. In that same year, it obtained a lease for the use of the Cedar Grove School as its headquarters. The society retained its name even after township was renamed Old Bridge. In 1969, the building was formally dedicated as the Thomas Warne Historical Museum and Library.

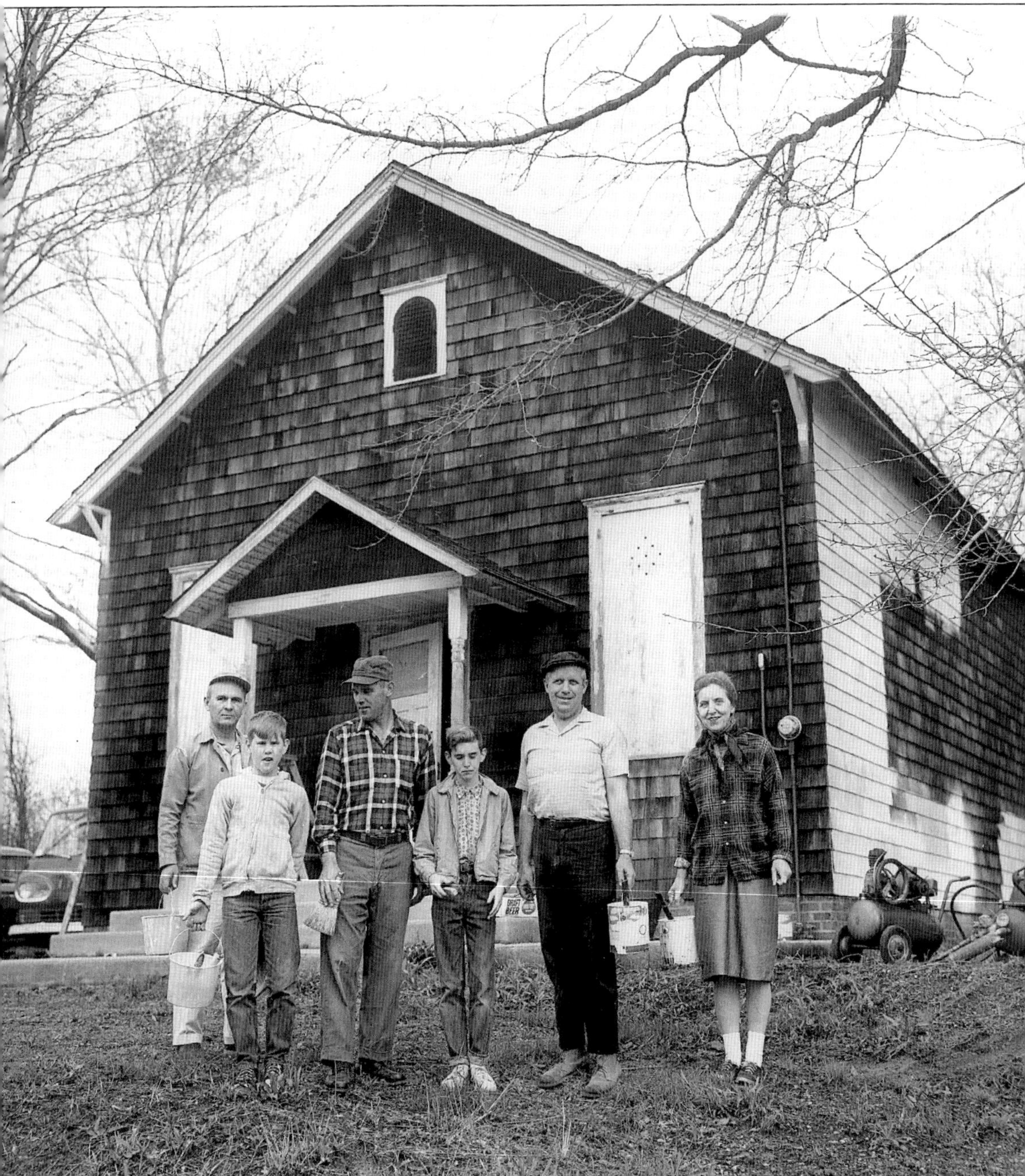

After extensive renovations and repairs, the museum was placed on the National Register of Historic Places in 1976. Pausing from their volunteer labor at the museum are, from left to right, Bill Griffiths, George Hauser, Clarence Hauser, John Hauser, John Partridge, and Susan Partridge. In 1998, an addition was constructed at the rear of the schoolhouse to provide additional gallery and office space.